Human Rights, or Citizenship?

While human rights have been enjoying unprecedented salience, the concept of the citizen has been significantly challenged. Rising ethical concerns, the calling into question of state sovereignty and the consolidation of the human rights regime have all contributed to a shift in focus: from an exclusionary, problematic citizenship to human rights. *Human Rights, or Citizenship?* examines this shift and explores its implications for democracy. In an accessible way, the book explores the arguments within contemporary democratic theory that privilege law and legally codified human rights over citizenship, questioning whether legalism alone could lead us to a better, more equitable politics. Does the prioritisation of law and legally codified human rights lead to depoliticisation? And do human rights always contest relations of power and subordination? Addressing these questions, *Human Rights, or Citizenship?* opens a debate about the role of citizenship and human rights in democracy. It will be invaluable reading for anyone interested in democratic politics today.

Paulina Tambakaki is a Senior Lecturer in Political Theory at the Centre for the Study of Democracy, University of Westminster. She has published articles in *Citizenship Studies*, *Critical Review of International Social and Political Philosophy* and *Parallax*.

Human Rights, or Citizenship?

Paulina Tambakaki

First published 2010
by Birkbeck Law Press
2 Park Square, Milton Park, Abingdon, Oxon OX14 4RN

Simultaneously published in the USA and Canada
by Birkbeck Law Press
270 Madison Avenue, New York, NY 10016

*Birkbeck Law Press is an imprint of the Taylor & Francis Group,
an informa business*

© 2010 Paulina Tambakaki

Reprinted 2010

Typeset in Times and Gill Sans by
RefineCatch Limited, Bungay, Suffolk
Printed and bound in Great Britain by
CPI Antony Rowe, Chippenham, Wiltshire

British Library Cataloguing in Publication Data
A catalogue record for this book is available from the British Library

Library of Congress Cataloging-in-Publication Data
Tambakaki, Paulina.
   Human rights, or citizenship? / Paulina Tambakaki.
      p. cm.
   1. Human rights.   2. Citizenship.   3. Political ethics.   4. Social
ethics.   I. Title.
JC571.T1448 2010
323—dc22   2009045007

ISBN10: 0-415-48163-5 (hbk)
ISBN10: 0-203-88077-3 (ebk)

ISBN13: 978–0-415-48163-2 (hbk)
ISBN13: 978–0-203-88077-7 (ebk)

Contents

Acknowledgements

The ideas and arguments for this book have developed out of my PhD dissertation, and various teachers, friends and colleagues have helped me to articulate them in the process. I am especially thankful to Chantal Mouffe for her guidance, assistance and support throughout the years. Chantal has been a constant source of inspiration for me and I have learned a lot from working with her. I am deeply grateful. I would also like to thank Yannis Stavrakakis for the insights he gave me into my work, and Andrew Schaap for inviting me to the Exeter workshop on law and agonism. The exchanges and papers, presented at the workshop were especially useful and beneficial. Thanks are also due to David Chandler for reading the first chapter of the book, and to the two anonymous referees from Routledge for their interesting suggestions and comments. I would also like to thank Mary Ikoniadou for putting up with me during the last stages of this project and to all those friends and colleagues who, at various stages and in different ways, were particularly encouraging: Lila Kotsi, Christina Christoforou, Melita Skamnaki, Yannis Thomatos, Liza Griffin, Aidan Hehir and Tom Moore. My warmest thanks go to Martyn Oliver for the many discussions we have had on my work, for his technical assistance and for his support. I must not forget to thank the staff from Routledge, especially Holly Davis and Colin Perrin; also to Christopher Long and Melvyn Dyer. Finally, I cannot find enough words to express how grateful I am to my parents for their unconditional help and support. Without them, this project would not have been possible. I dedicate the book to them.

Paulina Tambakaki
December 2009

Introduction

Of the principles that define modern democratic politics, citizenship and human rights transpire certainly as the most salient, indispensable and talked-about principles. Protective and empowering at the same time, they serve as the primary means for political subjectification and the anchoring point for securing democratic aspirations. For is there a twentieth-century struggle that has not been fought in the name of citizenship, if not human rights? And is there a political achievement that has not been celebrated in retrospect as a victory of citizenries and their basic rights? Although in determining whether it is citizenship or human rights that frame democratic struggles much depends on the historical period and particular circumstances we focus on, it is not an exaggeration to assume that, when it comes to consolidating democratic idea(l)s, both principles are central to their promotion and pursuit.

But the case is not simply that citizenship and human rights constitute the vehicle for practising democratic politics, it is also that they comprise the very horizon that at a given time shapes and defines what we understand by and expect of democratic politics. In this second respect, far from transpiring as principles with fixed meaning, citizenship and human rights emerge as signifiers overflown with meaning, the subject of continuous debate and philosophical interpretation, democratic contention and transformation. This openness at the heart of all analyses invoking citizenship and human rights justifies partly why the two principles are rarely treated together as the subject of a single enquiry.

But there are other curiously interesting reasons for this gap in the literature. While citizenship is considered one of the privileged subject matters of political and democratic theory, linked with explorations of nations and states, human rights are the focus of legal theory, one of the principal normative vocabularies expounded by lawyers and critical legal theorists. Given thus the disciplinary divide between the two giants of the social sciences, the norm has been encouraged to pursue separate rather than single investigations into the two ideas. In addition, another divide, forceful for the most part of the twentieth century, has further consolidated this same norm.

The domestic/international divide, which the Cold War rivalry helped to sustain, both posed a challenge to efforts that sought to bring together the two principles and, notably, contributed to the marginalisation of the human rights discourse. One reason for this is that by being precariously situated between the domestic and the international, the realm of superpower competition, human rights introduced as a notion further complexity to theorisations that put them on a par with citizenship, the bastion of sovereign politics. More importantly, by being distinguished into different types of rights and thus being subject to ideological division and rivalry, human rights were seen to be one more tool to superpower struggle and hypocrisy. In effect, they were pushed to the margins of political analysis and debate. It is worth noticing that theorisations of citizenship, although by no means free of ideological disagreements, gained unprecedented momentum during this same period, precisely because citizenship, was seen to buttress rather than subvert nation state politics. Moreover, if we add to these explanations the notional ambiguity permeating both terms, the tensions, contradictions and paradoxes underpinning their philosophical presuppositions, then it comes as little surprise why a single enquiry has often been considered a daunting task to undertake.

Still, might it not be the case that there is simply not much of interest in the way in which citizenship and human rights relate to one another? On one level, it could certainly be argued that although central to democratic imaginaries in their own right, the relation between the two principles is not intricate enough to instigate further exploration. Being a citizen of a liberal democracy, so the argument goes, presupposes access to and respect of certain basic legal rights, and basic legal rights in turn inform and deepen the practice of citizenship. Viewed thus from the angle of liberal democracy, the relation between the two principles appears interdependent and for that reason unproblematic. When demands for more rights are growing, or struggles for securing already entrenched rights are intensifying, it is the given take on either citizenship or human rights that therefore takes centre stage inviting revision – not the relation between the two. On a different level, it could also be argued that although potentially interesting from a historical perspective that traces its emergence in the democratic revolutions of the eighteenth century, the relation between citizenship and human rights is rather too evident to capture our imagination. Since we still live in a world of nation states, so the argument goes, it is always state citizenries that frame and define the content of human rights, not the other way round. With states thus being the primary units determining access to human rights, it is the body politic that appears to influence the shape of human rights concerns. Hannah Arendt, one of the few theorists to draw our attention to the relation between the two principles, confirmed the priority that the world of nation states has accorded to citizenship.

Writing in the aftermath of the Second World War, which confronted the nation state system with stateless people who had lost everything apart from their humanity, Arendt argued that 'the very conception of human rights broke down' (1968: 299). Human rights were proved to be unenforceable, and Man in his nakedness, as a mere human being, was shown to be a nonentity. For Arendt, this was partly because of the perplexities inherent in the notion of human rights inaugurated by the French Declaration of 1789. The abstract human to whom they referred did not appear to exist anywhere at the time of her writing. More than that, the institutions were not in place to secure and protect the mere human. And it was unclear what the loss of human rights exactly entailed. 'Man could lose all so called Rights of Man without losing his essential quality as man, his human dignity', upon which human rights are supposed to be premised (1968: 297). But, closely related, it is also because human rights were, from their inception, based paradoxically on the rights of the citizen. Membership in a political community granted through citizenship, according to Arendt, alone seemed to guarantee protection. By thus challenging the promise of security offered by human rights, statelessness both exposed the paradox at the root of the *adaequatio* between citizenship and human rights, and made apparent the primacy of political belonging, of a right to have rights. Arendt is emphatic on this point: 'Only the loss of a polity itself expels Man from humanity' – nothing else (1968: 297).

Of course, much has changed since Arendt was writing. Not only have human rights been extensively codified in international law, and international institutions are now supposed to observe and secure them – thus it is no longer solely up to the body politic to institute laws that respect human rights principles – but also the individual, next to the national citizen, has been identified as the subject of human rights, the entity whom human rights are called on to protect. Although, to be sure, some of the definitional ambiguities of human rights still remain, and there are still weaknesses of enforcement and implementation, it is possible to speak of the consolidation of a consensus around human rights principles. Given impetus by the much-talked-about triumph of liberal democracy, the intensification of the processes of globalisation and the revival of cosmopolitanism, this consensus around human rights only confirms their ever-growing salience and centrality. What does this change then mean for our understanding of citizenship and human rights?

In charting this change, this book aims to open the debate about citizenship and human rights, their relation, and their role within the democratic imaginary. By asking *Human Rights or Citizenship?* it alludes, ironically, to the idea that, by virtue of their increasing salience and codification in international law, human rights are now argued to be more relevant and forceful political means than citizenship. Far from posing therefore an either/or case, the book captures with its title the ever stronger support given to the idea that by privileging legally codified human rights over citizenship, we reinvigorate democratic politics in the face of the challenges posed – challenges that issue from the intensification of processes of globalisation, and the emergence of a deterritorialised and postnational politics. The book argues that the move to privilege human rights over citizenship, law over politics, carries important implications for democratic politics. Not only does it risk weakening and impoverishing democratic politics by reducing it to one principle, but it also potentially depoliticises. Of course, central to this argument, suggests the book, is what one understands by democratic politics. If one follows a proceduralist and rationalist understanding of democracy, which reconciles law with politics, then the option of privileging human rights is available. If by contrast one understands democracy in agonistic terms, as a way of living where strife and contestation play a central role, then privileging human rights is not an option. Speaking thus from an agonistic perspective on democratic politics, the book rejects the turn to law to address political problems, and suggests instead that we rethink and reassert citizenship in agonistic terms.

This argument unfolds along five chapters. In the first chapter, which serves mainly as an introduction, setting up the debate for the rest of the book, we argue for a constitutive tension between citizenship and human rights that manifests itself at different contexts and levels of analysis. Why does this tension go often unrecognised in the literature? And what role does it play for democratic politics? In addressing these questions, the chapter discusses, first, the part played by certain changes in the way in which we perceive citizenship and human rights in disguising their tension and affirming the position of those theorists who already underplay it; second, the chapter introduces the deliberative and agonistic perspectives on democratic politics with the aim of showing how the way in which these two perspectives approach the relation between citizenship and human rights ultimately determines the suggestions one makes when reconsidering democratic practice. Thus, in a nutshell, the aim of this first chapter is to introduce the broader landscape surrounding debates about citizenship and human rights, to explore the changes encouraging the case for privileging human rights and to identify the two approaches to democratic politics that frame the investigation of the book.

The second chapter concentrates on and explores the argument that privileges human rights. It engages with the writings of Held, Bohman and Benhabib who claim to reinvigorate citizenship while recasting democracy in global or transnational terms. The chapter distinguishes their approach as 'democratic' and 'deliberative', and explicates the ways in which this influences their conception of citizenship, leading them to identify it with human rights. It argues that despite resisting the idea of universal inclusion and retaining the term 'citizenship' in their writings, Held, Bohman and Benhabib end up revising citizenship in unavoidably human rights terms. But do human rights actually take us out of the problems confronting citizenship?

The third chapter addresses this question by undertaking a theoretical investigation into the idea of human rights. It focuses on the writings of Lacan and shows that there are inherent limitations in the notion. The limitations pertain specifically to the type of subject that human rights presuppose, a subject that Lacan exposes as unavailable. But the limitations pertain also to the idea of legally codified rights itself. Douzinas' Lacanian argument, which the chapter examines in its last section, exposes the fantasy scenario that legally codified rights bring into play. A shift to law can thus have negative implications for democracy, suggests the chapter.

The fourth chapter explores these implications. It argues that, from the perspective of a conflictual understanding of politics, the argument that privileges human rights is seen to be anti-political. The chapter concludes by introducing Mouffe's agonistic conception of democracy. Within the context of an agonistic pluralism, it suggests, human rights cannot be prioritised over citizenship; rather, it is citizenship that is being rethought in the face of the problems confronting it.

Finally, the last chapter focuses on the reconceptualisation of citizenship. It explores the agonistic conception of citizenship, which it recovers from Mouffe's writings in the early 1990s, and argues that this is a conception that both overcomes the limitations of the liberal and civic republican accounts of citizenship, and addresses the problems confronting the concept in the light of global and postnational developments. The book concludes with some reflections on the role of human rights within the imaginary of an agonistic democracy.

Chapter 1

Citizenship and human rights in tension

Changes, issues and approaches

A single enquiry into citizenship and human rights immediately stumbles over the question of how exactly the two principles relate to one another. Are they equivalent or antithetical? The case for their antithesis proceeds from their distinct logics. While citizenship rests on dynamics of both inclusion and exclusion, human rights presuppose only inclusion. The idea of common humanity on which they are based transcends national and territorial borders. By contrast, the case for their equivalence convincingly proceeds from their common function. Since citizenship and human rights are both means for challenging relations of power and subordination, the case might be that they are not two opposed principles, but rather one dual principle constitutive, in its duality, of political empowerment. This book starts from the first assumption, but in a slightly modified form. It argues that although citizenship and human rights are not outrightly antithetical, they are certainly in tension. This tension manifests itself at different levels of analysis and consists of several facets.

To explore those facets, our first task is to disentangle the contexts within which a discussion about citizenship and human rights develops. This enables us to show, first, how the terms of the debate change, depending on the context, and second, how the tension remains, despite different focuses coming into play. In addition, a probe into the various manifestations of the tension puts us in a better position to introduce the broader landscape and to identify the specific angle from which the argument of this book proceeds. What then are the contexts within which discussions about citizenship and human rights develop?

The first is that of the French Declaration of the Rights of Man and the Citizen, one of the first documents that constitutes a close relation between citizenship and human rights.[1] Against the backdrop of the Declaration and the democratic order it initiated, analyses of citizenship and human rights concentrate on two entwined aspects of their founding, which confirm that the two principles have been in tense relation from their very inception. The first aspect involves their opposing foundations. While citizenship rights emerge with the formation of political communities and are invested in the nation, human rights, which pertain to all men equally, are seen to be founded outside the remit of political associations and theoretically challenge these. This is the 'real turning point in the theory and practice of politics', argues Norberto Bobbio (1996: 101). By positing the rights of the individual – conceived in a state of nature in which there is no external authority – next to the contractual rights of the body politic, the French Declaration paved the way for the individualistic conception of society on which modern (liberal) democracy rests (Bobbio 1996: 105).[2] Thus what we encounter in the case of the Declaration and its legacy is the shaping of two political principles explicitly entangled and implicitly in tension. Entangled, in that they together subvert the *ancien régime* and constitute the new imaginary that comes to replace it; in tension, in that they are founded on presuppositions that do not immediately converge. One is founded on the nation and its political expression in the state; the other is founded on natural law and theories of natural rights that challenge, supposedly, the state. Later in the chapter, we will see how the focus on natural rights has been substituted today by a focus on humanity and international law.

Of course, it could be objected that the embroilment of the two principles in the new imaginary that replaced the *ancien régime* confirms not their tension, but their equivalence. This is the reading of Etienne Balibar in his essay '"Rights of Man" and "Rights of the Citizen": The Modern Dialectic of Equality and Freedom'. There, Balibar argues that it is precisely in the identification of the rights of man with the rights of the citizen that the radical import of the Declaration lies.[3] To understand Balibar's point, we need to stress that the tension that surfaces against the background of the French Declaration is consequential upon the democratic order that emerges in its wake – that is, that we speak of a founding tension only *after* we recognise that the body politic, as a dual body of men and citizens, is now in a position to exercise power (rather than the king). This novelty, which Balibar describes as the development of an 'egalitarian sovereignty', leads him to valorise the duality of the people and immediately to dismiss the possibility of a tension between the rights of a body politic founded on a social contract and the rights of man justified by the natural law tradition. He rejects that there is continuity with the natural law tradition. And he rejects the idea that the Declaration deals with a question of founding. As he puts it:

> The Declaration does not posit any 'human nature' as an underlying foundation or exterior guarantee. Instead, it integrally identifies the rights of man with political rights and, by an approach that short-circuits theories of human nature as well as those of theological supernature, identifies man, whether individual or collective, with the member of political society.
>
> (1994: 45)

Reflect further on the idea that violations and restrictions of rights always affect men *and* citizens as members of political society rather than as two separate entities, and then it becomes apparent why the two principles could be seen as identical. Is Balibar thus correct to suggest that there is no tension between citizenship and human rights?

On the one hand, Balibar's argument is quite convincing. If we view the two types of right against the wider context of the democratic revolution of the eighteenth century, as Balibar does, then what appears to be central is that they in tandem establish a break with the monarchical order, not how they are founded or how they differ. Moreover, if we consider that citizenship and human rights together promote democratic politics, then again we find some resonance in his position. On the other hand, however, we could argue that there is something problematic in Balibar's argument that surfaces once we start looking where the tension is situated, because Balibar does see a tension emerging, but he locates this externally, at the level of practice, rather than theory. When we make politics, he says, when we challenge established powers and struggle for rights, there is a permanent tension between what is considered universal and what is particular, between the universality of the right to politics as enunciated by the Declaration (man equals citizen) and its always necessary (re)inscription in particular conditions and institutions. Yet if this tension arises, as Balibar says, only in practice, when there is a particular politics (say of a nation or of a state), then why should not we assume that it is the citizenry, as separate from humanity, which ultimately makes this particular politics – thus reinstating in practice the tension that already exists in theory?

The second aspect of the tension that surfaces against the backdrop of the Declaration seems to confirm this point. For the friction between the universal and the particular is precisely what we come up against when we shift the terms of the debate and enquiry into the type of rights to which the Declaration gave rise. Bound inextricably with the nation, citizenship rights transpire as particular. In contrast, human rights, which embrace everyone, are understood to be universal. From this angle, which brings into focus the different traits of the two types of right, the tension emerges once we move slightly forward and insist on who founds what. In so doing, we confront two options. Either universal rights guarantee and reinforce the particular rights of citizenries – as Bobbio earlier implied and Balibar altogether rejected – or the reverse is the case, the particular founds the universal. Article 2 of the Declaration states: 'The aim of all political association is the preservation of the natural and imprescriptible rights of man. These rights are liberty, property, security, and resistance to oppression.' Thus what we notice here is that while the Declaration bound the two principles together, it ambiguously leaned towards prioritising the particular – by investing the sovereign nation with the 'preservation' of those universal rights that in principle transcend it.

Still with us today, this second facet of the tension reappears behind two questions: first, in the question of who has access to human rights; second, in the question of whether human rights are in fact universal. More specifically, and in the light of growing numbers of non-citizens residing within state territory, be they illegal immigrants, asylum seekers or resident aliens, two parallel developments are taking place. On one side, state policies are increasingly influenced by moral concerns and human rights considerations enjoy unprecedented salience. On the other side, however, there is growing pressure and uneasiness about the entry, residence and political activity of foreigners – an uneasiness manifested in ever more restrictive citizenship policies, border controls, and arranged deportations both in Europe and in the USA. To be sure, since we still live in a world of nation states, such policies could be viewed as the by-product of a territorial politics reinforced by economic concerns and fears over security in the light of the terrorist threat. Yet might it not also be the case that such policies simply confirm that it is state citizenries who ultimately determine the rights, if any, of those who are only human?[4] Just consider how prominently immigration policy figures in electoral campaigns, or how the rise and popularity of the extreme right thrives often on its anti-immigration stance. Or even how different countries within Europe differ with respect to the rights they accord to those residing within their territory – so that, in the city of Amsterdam, a non-European permanent resident has the right to vote in local elections and to form political parties at the local level, yet this is not the case, for example, in the city of Berlin.[5] What such variations therefore demonstrate is that *pace* Balibar, the tension between the particular and the universal does not just arise in practice, but is already inscribed in theory, in what is invested in citizenship and human rights, and how the two principles are seen to shape one another. The second question that arises follows from this observation and the question is this: if we assume that citizenries potentially define human rights, do we also assume that human rights are not universal? In the absence of political rights for the mere human as well as growing disagreements about what are seen to be Western, rather than universal, human rights, we have enough reason to anticipate deeper tensions over the universality of human rights.[6] No matter, therefore, the angle from which we view the road opened by the French Declaration, it becomes apparent that far from asserting one dual right to politics, a universal right to a paradoxically territorial politics, it has left us with a legacy of an inescapable tension between citizenship and human rights.

This inescapability becomes more astute when we examine analyses of the two principles against the backdrop of discussions about state sovereignty. Within this context, we notice that although the tension remains, still triggered by the root difference between a particular citizenship and universal human rights, there is a subtle change in the terms of the debate. At issue is no longer the (founding) presuppositions underpinning the two principles, but rather their emancipatory potential. While human rights are seen to be the emancipatory means *par excellence* because they are not associated with the state, citizenship that is necessarily bound to the state is doubted as a means to emancipation. Viewed as a formal right to participate in elections, citizenship wanes in this context and the language of political empowerment draws chiefly on the vocabulary of human rights. Of course, the justification for this argument depends largely on the part of the world on which we focus. However, it could be argued that the tension that comes into play when we delve into the emancipatory potential of the two principles remains visible even within mature liberal democracies. An example from the UK illustrates this point. On the eve of the G20 summit in London in March 2009, it was revealed in the press that the UK police force holds, in the name of security, an ever-expanding database with the names and pictures of people who (regularly) attend demonstrations, including journalists who cover these public protests. What is relevant and of interest for us in this case is that although the right to protest and to cover protests in the press is deeply ingrained in citizenship practice, traced back to the fundamental democratic principle of casting light on power, the debate that issued in the UK was construed not in terms of citizenship, but of human rights. Seen as a breach of privacy under Article 8 of the Human Rights Act 1998,[7] the surveillance tactics of the UK police force were problematised as a challenge to the human rights culture. They were not problematised as a challenge to the democratic framework in place – perhaps because, *in* this framework, waving human rights is deemed to be more empowering than simply waving citizenship rights. Does this then reveal something about the role of human rights in a democracy? This question brings us to the third context within which analyses of citizenship and human rights develop.

In *The Political Forms of Modern Society*, Claude Lefort argues that what characterises modern democracy is division and indeterminacy, a dissolution of all markers of certainty as to basis of law, power and knowledge, and a process of constant questioning. No longer residing in the body of the king, law and knowledge become disentangled, he says, and the locus of power is empty. In Lefort's words:

> The political originality of democracy . . . is signalled by a double phenomenon: a power which is henceforth involved in a constant search for a basis because law and knowledge are no longer embodied in the person or persons who exercise it, and a society which accepts conflicting opinions and debates over rights because the markers which once allowed people to situate themselves in relation to one another in a determinate manner have disappeared.
>
> (1988: 34)

If we thus follow Lefort and assume that the distinguishing marker and merit of the democratic framework lie precisely in the vacuum of power it instantiates, then it appears that human rights, which incessantly interrogate embodiments of power, play a crucially symbolic role within that framework. The question of their universality, therefore, gripping us in discussions about state sovereignty, appears irrelevant against the backdrop of modern democracy. Instead, what is relevant is that the act of mobilising human rights against forms of state power carries with it an enormously symbolic force that not only defines but also ensures that there is a democratic politics. Lefort insists on this point:

> Only by recognising in the institution of human rights signs of the emergence of a new type of legitimacy and of a public space, only by recognising that individuals are both the products and the instigators of that space, and only by recognising that it cannot be swallowed up by the state without a violent mutation giving birth to a new form of society, can we possibly hope to evaluate the development of democracy and the likely fate of freedom.
>
> (1988: 30)

However, it could be argued that at precisely the moment at which we evaluate the role of human rights in modern democracy, the tension with citizenship reappears. And the tension is the following: while human rights owe their force to their symbolism, citizenship rights owe their force to their exercise. Thus what we encounter here is the distance between one principle operating at the level of the symbolic and another principle operating at the level of exercise, or better, *praxis* – which indicates that, far from being simply antithetical, citizenship and human rights are in tension because they intermesh with and shape one another despite operating at different levels.[8]

Another way to conceptualise this distance, which anticipates a later focus in the chapter, is to follow Bobbio and suggest that liberty and equality, which citizenship and human rights exemplify, cannot be fully realised together except at the expense of one another (1990: 32). Traced back to two distinct traditions, the liberal and the democratic, liberty and equality are antithetical values. Liberty, inscribed in human rights, is individual and ever-expansive, ascribed to all on an equal basis and subject only to judicial limitations – which indicates that pure liberty threatens egalitarianism. Democratic equality, inscribed in citizenship, is collective and exclusive because the *demos* as a collective body of equals excludes those not part of it – which in turn indicates that totalising equality potentially threatens liberty. What we therefore notice in moving into the context of liberal democracy is that, by being rooted in different traditions,[9] citizenship and human rights reinstate in a way the tension that already exists between these two traditions: maximum individual liberty as promised by human rights weakens the unity and cohesion of the body politic, while strong unity as required by citizenship constrains individual liberty. Of course, it is important here to emphasise that this facet of the tension that reappears against the backdrop of liberal democracy does not simply lie on their antithesis. The assumption of antithesis would lead us not only to view citizenship and human rights as incompatible, which is certainly not the case, but also to underplay their necessary interdependence. Bobbio explains this interdependence well when he says that although in liberal democracies:

> ... the best available remedy against all possible forms of abuse of power is the direct or indirect participation of citizens, and of the greatest possible number of citizens, in the formation of the laws ... It is only if the citizen who places his or her paper in the ballot box enjoys liberty of opinion, a free press, rights of free assembly and association, and all those liberties which are the essence of the liberal state ... that democracy functions well.
>
> (1990: 38–39)

By thus viewing the relation between citizenship and human rights in terms of a tension, rather than antithesis, we are in a position to capture both this connection that Bobbio brings to the fore *and* their difference, which always questions their interdependence.

The liberal democratic framework, therefore, which establishes an intrinsic relation between citizenship and human rights, provides the specific context within which the argument of this book develops. This is important to isolate and explain at this stage for three reasons. First, it draws attention to the idea that we cannot evoke citizenship and human rights together unless we already operate within the framework of liberal democracy – that is, that by inimitably synthesising liberalism with democracy, liberty with equality and human rights with citizenship, liberal democracy is that *necessary* context which informs and shapes the theme of the book. This recognition, far from yielding to a defence of liberal democracy, puts us in a better position to reflect on the limitations of its different interpretations, and their implications for democratic life today. Second, since a concern with democracy today is precisely what drives the focus of this book, it is important to explain that specific questions which concern human rights, such as, for example, the universalism/relativism debate, are not here addressed. Instead, what is addressed is the question of how to revitalise citizenship, and in effect democracy, without downplaying the challenges confronting it, including among these the increasing salience of the human rights discourse. Third, and closely related, by recognising the centrality of liberal democracy for an enquiry into citizenship and human rights, we further justify why the book does not make an either/or case – either citizenship or human rights – but rather a case for problematising the priority accorded today to human rights as legally codified rights.

Approaching thereby human rights as legal rather than moral rights implicates us inevitably in discussions about the relation between law and politics. This is the last context within which the tension between citizenship and human rights manifests itself. Codified extensively in statutes, conventions and treaties, human rights are the cornerstone of the legal system in a double sense: as entitlements that the law identifies and bestows; and as protections that the legal system observes and enforces. Although, as legal privileges and protections, human rights certainly play a political role, empowering the individual and limiting the power of the sovereign, they are foremost a rights discourse rooted in the legal tradition. Citizenship, by contrast, which instantiates popular sovereignty, is deeply ingrained in the political and democratic tradition. Notwithstanding the liberal interpretation that takes it as a status bestowing upon the individual an array of rights, it is precisely the idea of exercise or practice in the affairs of government that singles out citizenship as the political principle *par excellence*. Of course, this is not to say that while citizenship is political, human rights are not; rather, it is to recognise that, by virtue of their different origins, the two principles bring into democratic politics different dynamics at play. In the light therefore of these dynamics, the question that arises is this: does the tension between citizenship and human rights reappear in the wider categories of law and politics that the two principles embody and represent?

In reflecting on the relation between law and politics, Bonnie Honig (2007) identifies three paradoxes: the paradox of politics, the paradox of democratic legitimation and the paradox of constitutional democracy. Conceptualised first by Rousseau, the paradox of politics revolves around the origins of law and points to its paradoxical co-implication with popular sovereignty. To understand the paradox, we only have to consider where good law comes from. While the sovereign people are seen to decide the law, it is paradoxically the law that defines and delimits the sovereign people. Or as Honig explains the paradox:

> In order for there to be a people well formed enough for good law making, there must be good law for how else will the people be well formed? The problem is: where would that good law come from absent an already well formed, virtuous people?

(2007: 3)

Thus the paradox that we here encounter is close to the tension that we earlier identified between the particular and the universal, only that it is here formulated along the broader lines of law and politics (is it the law that shapes political wills, or political wills that shape the law?). Although, strictly speaking, this is a paradox of founding and Honig certainly recognises it as such, she convincingly argues that it is recurrently relived:

Every day, after all, new citizens are born, and still others immigrate into established regimes. Every day, already socialised citizens mistake, depart from or simply differ about the commitments of democratic citizenship. Every day, democracies re-socialise, recapture or reinterpellate citizens into their political institutions and culture in ways those citizens do not freely will, nor could they. [Thus] the problem that Rousseau seems to cast as a problem of founding recurs daily.

(2007: 3)

Indeed, if only we reflect on ever-growing (re)definitions of legally codified rights, we realise that this co-implication between law and politics, human rights and citizenries, is in fact a central and ever-present feature of democratic practice – not a straightforward affair, but a paradox, pointing to the need to recurrently negotiate both the law (what is codified as such) and the citizenries (who comprises the body politic).

A similar conclusion issues from the second paradox that Honig identifies. In the paradox of democratic legitimation, at issue is no longer the origins of law and popular will, as was the case with the paradox of politics, but rather the legitimating source of the law's constraining powers. In order for the law to be legitimate, the will of the people must coincide with the general will. Given, however, that in a democracy there are always tensions and frictions between the collective and the individual, the general and the particular, then it appears that the law never fully captures this general will, the people as a unified whole. The point therefore relevant for us here is that although the legal system (legally entrenched rights) draws its force and legitimacy from the general and the universal and even paves the way for these, the general and the universal that law supposedly instantiates escape it and remain undecidable. This undecidability of the people, as Honig hints, is a further necessary feature of democratic practice. Not only does it enliven it, calling attention to the ever-pressing need in a democracy to recurrently motivate and channel 'the energies of the people assumed to be independent of law rather than partly its products', but also, ultimately, it leaves the space open for the people to decide (Honig 2007: 8). However, it is precisely this moment of decision, a necessary and inevitable moment in democratic politics, that seems to slide away when we look at the third paradox that Honig identifies, the paradox of constitutional democracy.

At issue here is the alienating force of the law crystallised in a constitution. While past generations willed and decided this constitution, present and future generations experience its force as a constraint. A gap therefore opens between the sovereign people, who are supposedly the ultimate decision takers in a democracy, and the constitution, which, in being shaped in the past, limits and restraints them. Honig explains:

Recasting the conflict in this way divides the ruled (the people) and ruler (law, the founders, or the constitution) and restages the paradox of politics as a generational divide . . . Thus, the paradox of constitutional democracy externalises the conflict that the paradox of democratic legitimation subtly put at democracy's heart. The unwilled, constraining element of rule is now identified not with democracy per se, but with the constitution which may be right or necessary, and the paradox is now not internal to democracy (which seeks impossibly to combine will of all and general will, rule and freedom); rather, it is a feature of one kind of democracy, *constitutional* democracy, which impossibly but necessarily combines written constraint with free popular sovereignty and then derives its legitimation from that impossible, tense combination.

(2007: 9)

It proceeds that what is of interest for us in this paradox is the idea that constitutionalism and popular sovereignty, legal rights and citizenship, although necessarily co-implicated in liberal democracy, also appear to be at odds with one another. Popular sovereignty, which freely decides on its affairs, is constrained by the constitution and the necessary limits that the constitution places on popular sovereignty, if they are to be legitimate, must be based on popular justifications.

By thus broadening our discussion to encompass the categories of law and politics that citizenship and human rights represent, what we notice is that we return full circle to the very idea of a necessary tension between the two principles. The interesting question that therefore arises at this point is why is it that this tension is rarely recognised? It could be argued that the reason the tension goes often unrecognised is because it is either dismissed or underplayed within the relevant literature. It is dismissed when the success of liberal democracy as a form of government constitutes the starting point in discussions among democratic theorists. Seen as the best possible regime, liberal democracy is celebrated on this perspective for what it promotes in tandem: liberal attitudes *and* democratic equality; the rule of law *and* popular sovereignty; citizenship *and* human rights. It is not valorised as the best regime by virtue of the tension it implants at the core of democratic practice, not only because tensions point disturbingly to precariousness and instability and they need to be addressed, but also because tensions from within the liberal democratic framework appear secondary and meaningless once it is the success of this framework that (uncritically) enjoys priority. By thus silencing or undertheorising that which remains underneath and hidden *within* liberal democracy, one is ultimately led to dismiss the tension between citizenship and human rights. But there is another explanation to the same effect – only that this proceeds from the opposite end of the spectrum. No longer prioritising the binary successes of liberal democracy but rather their separateness (not necessarily their antithesis), the case is often made, especially in the human rights literature, that although intimately related within the context of liberal democracy, when liberal democracy is not immediately into focus, the two principles are conveniently separate. One is bounded with the state and is thus dismissed as stale (citizenship); the other is bounded with international law and ever-evolving moral standards, and is thus celebrated as liberating (human rights). Failing thereby to recognise the connection between advances in human rights culture and citizenship practice, it is external justifications – legal or moral – that are often seen to drive and inspire struggles for rights. Hence the tension between citizenship and human rights disappears on this perspective, because to have a tension, you need to establish first a relation, and the relation is here either undermined or simply effaced.

Further, it could be argued that when the tension between the two principles is recognised, yet seen as resolvable or dissolvable, then it is certainly underplayed. Jürgen Habermas's later work mostly exemplifies this position, since Habermas is one of the most influential theorists who expounds the case for co-originality between citizenship and human rights.[10] Without wishing to probe here deep into his position, which we will explore in more detail later in the chapter, it is essential to indicate that at issue in this case is what one understands by 'democracy'. As Bobbio notes, if by 'democracy' one understands a body of rules, then historically democracy is linked with the liberal state and its emphasis on individual rights and the rule of law. If, by contrast, one emphasises 'the ideal of democratic equality on which democratic government must find its inspiration', then the relation between democracy and liberalism, citizenship and human rights, appears to be more complex (Bobbio 1990: 31–32) – if not tense, we might add.

This tension and complexity, however, is precisely what developments unleashed in the second half of the twentieth century challenge and diminish. As the next section therefore demonstrates, there has been a change in what we understand and expect of citizenship and human rights, and this change gives great impetus to the position of those who either dismiss or underplay the idea of a tension between the two principles.

A changed setting

To explain those developments and changes that confirm rather than abate the case for one rather than two principles in tension, the section distinguishes between changes that specifically affect citizenship and changes that specifically concern human rights. Although therefore closely related and unfolding in tandem, these changes are, for purposes of clarity, viewed here separately. By exploring them, the section has a twofold aim: first, to show how they conceal and promise in the first instance to dissolve the tension between citizenship and human rights; second, to demonstrate how they lead one who already underplays this tension to privilege human rights. What then are these changes that today give momentum to human rights – often at the expense of citizenship?

In looking into the human rights culture that has come into being since the end of the Second World War, we notice two interrelated changes: a change of subject, in that common humanity has now replaced human nature and theories of natural rights as the anchoring subject of human rights; and a change in international law, the consolidation of an international human rights regime that increasingly monitors, exposes and limits state actions in breach of human rights principles. Douzinas comments:

> If the first proclamation of rights was a reaction against monarchic absolutism, the international law of human rights was a response to Hitler and Stalin, to the atrocities and barbarities of the War and the Holocaust. In this latest mutation of naturalism, humanity or civilisation was substituted for human nature ... international institutions and law makers replaced the divine legislator or the social contract and international conventions and treaties became the Constitution above constitutions and the Law behind laws. An endless process of international and humanitarian law making has thus been put into operation, aimed at protecting people from the putative assertions of their sovereignty. To paraphrase Nietzsche, if God, the source of natural law, is dead, he has been replaced by international law. [And] the higher status of human rights is seen as the result of their legal universalisation, of the triumph of the universality of humanity.
>
> (2000: 116)

Indeed, tangible and intangible at one and the same time, common humanity is a powerful concept. As something we immediately identify and empathise with in situations in which there is unfreedom, pain or persecution, common humanity draws its force ironically from its absence rather than presence. Proofs of its leverage therefore are always negative: only when it is denied, is common humanity a forceful concept to invoke; when affirmed, it appears devoid of meaning. Aligned then closely with the mobilisation of empathy and sentiment, common humanity entwines with and opens the way for the pursuit of the moral and the prudential. In contrast with human nature, a thoroughly philosophical term subject to much theorising and disagreement, common humanity is a simple and straightforward concept (at least in the first instance) strong enough to rally to its support anyone, from politicians to media consumers and NGO activists.[11] Therein, in common humanity, human rights owe today their salience. Although it could be argued that, by virtue of its magnitude, humanity is not a concept that can be easily pinned down, the normative and the moral to which it points chimes well with that which the law encapsulates and promotes – especially if the law is seen as the local application of universally valid normative moral standards.[12]

Indeed, the growing codification of normative standards in international law, coupled with the consolidation of the human rights regime, further attest

to the weight given today to the human rights culture. Here two interconnected developments are of particular interest to us. The first concerns
what has been identified in the relevant literature as a human rights regime.
Benhabib explains: '. . . by an international human rights regime, I understand
a set of interrelated and overlapping global and regional regimes that
encompass human rights treaties as well as customary international law or
international "soft" law' (2004: 7). With examples of the human rights regime
ranging from the Convention Against Torture and Other Cruel, Inhuman or
Degrading Treatment or Punishment to the European Convention for the
Protection of Human Rights and Fundamental Freedoms, Benhabib singles
out three particular areas in which there have been considerable advances in
human rights legislation. These are war crimes, transnational migration and
humanitarian intervention. More specifically, and in the light of the creation
of a permanent war crimes tribunal[13] capable of prosecuting individuals as
perpetrators of crimes against humanity, as well as further specifications of
norms regarding individual conduct in (civil) wars, it appears that human
rights legalism increasingly influences even cases of outright hostility. At the
same time, a growth in legislation protecting freedom of movement both in
Europe and at the global level, especially Articles 13–15 of the Universal
Declaration of Human Rights, including the creation of the United Nations
High Commissioner on Refugees, indicate that it is not only states that
protect their individual citizens, but also international institutions that, in
keeping an eye on human rights treaties, ensure that there is respect for human
rights principles. Finally, a rise in humanitarian interventions following the
will not of states but of the international community further confirms the
ever-growing attention given to human rights.

As a result therefore of this expansion of international law, state sovereignty is not as unlimited as it used to be. Although limitations derive partly
from the codification of such normative concerns as human rights, they also
derive from the multiplication of actors monitoring and/or contesting state
actions. This is the second development of special interest to us. In particular,
the stable proliferation of non-state actors monitoring and contesting state
sovereignty, ranging from voluntary associations to social movements and
transnational NGOs, points increasingly to the emergence of an additional
layer of governance, of a global civil society capable of holding governments
accountable when they breach human rights principles.[14] Through the use
of new communications media, civil society makes its actions known and
poses its demands on a global scale generating mass support that potentially
challenges state actions. Goodhart explains:

> transnational networks usually target specific global issues . . . Their
> influence derives from their efficacy in shaping the international agenda,
> in negotiating with various international forums, in strengthening and
> supporting local organisations and networks, and in using their moral

authority to pressure officials and raise consciousness. Such networks frequently draw on already established norms of democracy and human rights to construct frames for collective action and opposition to oppressive regimes. Global civil society can claim some success in influencing states and international regimes: the expanding role of NGOs and other organisations in global summits and conferences, and even in some formal regimes, further encourages the hope that they might play an important role [in remoulding the international system].

(2005: 99)

What civil society activism thus demonstrates next to the growth of human rights legalism is that the authority of the state to rule over a bounded territory, including its ability to determine domestic policy, is significantly curtailed. Not only do states today have to abide by the rules of regulation regimes and international institutions to which they are signatories, but they also have to consent to external interference in their affairs if and when they breach international standards of action. Given, moreover, that human rights are at the centre of these changes, in that they are the one area in which challenges to state sovereignty are salient and observable, then it comes as little surprise that a change has also been brought about in the way in which we perceive human rights.

To grasp this change, we need first to distinguish between what the human rights culture delivers and what it promises. Although there are certainly weaknesses of enforcement and implementation, both domestically and internationally, and indeed much more needs to be done if we are to secure respect for human rights, there is at the same time an inescapable and all-the-more-encouraging promise in the consolidation of the human rights culture. And the promise is this: human rights that are today central enough to merit extensive codification could be the most effective means to political empowerment. By virtue of the attention they command in public opinion and the clout given in international law, human rights can be *successfully* augmented, not just protected. Notice here that the change does not just lie in the abstract idea that human rights are more emancipatory than citizenship, a theoretical idea that we have already examined in the course of this chapter; rather, the change consists precisely in that human rights are now seen, first, as dynamic rather than purely protective rights, and second, as more dynamic than citizenship. Of course, the key here is the word 'dynamic'. Given that one of the most elementary differences between citizenship and human rights concerns their different functions, in that citizenship is dynamic because it is exercised, while human rights are passive because they protect, it is exactly the reversal of this understanding that we today witness. The rationale behind this reversal is straightforward: since international law often challenges and limits the state, human rights that are codified in international law and transcend the state could be used to the same effect – namely, to challenge and override state actions. Thus from the Turkish Parents Association in Berlin, which in the name of human rights demanded school instructions to be conducted in their mother tongue, to the headscarf affair in France, what we see is that calls for rights and equality are increasingly being posed in terms of human rights, not citizenship.

Encouraged by this shift, Soysal goes so far as to suggest that a notion of universal personhood has come to replace nation state citizenship as the organising mechanism for allocating rights and obligations within nation states. By drawing her case from the patterns of incorporation of guest workers in Europe, Soysal argues that political membership is more and more conditioned by the global discourse of human rights. Not only because human rights are used as justification for rights claims, but also because they bring about such inclusive patterns of incorporation that the rights and privileges that guest workers have come to enjoy in Europe no longer differ significantly from those of citizens. For example, guest workers have access to educational, welfare, economic and civil rights that have been originally reserved for the citizens of the national polity. And they have access to these rights, according to Soysal, because they are dignified human beings. From these observations, Soysal thus concludes:

> . . . universal personhood replaces nationhood; and universal human rights replace national rights. The justification for the state's obligations to foreign populations goes beyond the nation state itself. The rights and claims of individuals are legitimated by ideologies grounded in a transnational community, through international codes, conventions and laws on human rights independent of their citizenship in a nation state. Hence the individual transcends the citizen.
>
> (1994: 142)[15]

Although we do not need to go as far as Soysal does in order to affirm the growing salience of human rights, there is something valid in her observations that merits further attention. This is the idea that while human rights are growing in forcefulness, nation state citizenship appears to be increasingly problematic. There are three reasons why citizenship appears problematic. The first concerns its boundedness with the national and territorial state. Given that the role and functions of the state are changing as a result of the intensification of processes of globalisation, citizenship still remains tied to it. It is granted by territorial states – even though states are not as central as they used to be. It is exclusively exercised within states' delimited territories – even though politics increasingly takes place at the global level (in intergovernmental institutions, in which citizens do not currently participate).[16] And citizenship is still accorded to the members of the nation, despite large numbers of aliens residing within state territory. Growing apprehension towards the nation, moreover, all the more prevalent in the face of transnational migration and a multicultural politics, raises serious questions about the exclusionary dynamics of the nationally bound citizenship – about the idea that only nationals access immediately the rights and privileges of membership. And this is precisely where, in a nutshell, the problem with citizenship lies. Within the context of a postnational and deterritorialised politics, where calls for all-inclusion abound, citizenship transpires as too particular, too exclusive and too divisive. In contrast, human rights are universal, they are not particular – the law is general and neutral. Human rights are not exclusive – since the law derives from the will of all and applies to all. And human rights *pace* citizenship are not divisive – because the law addresses disagreements and promotes a more equitable order.

Could it then be that, by virtue of the solution they offer to the challenges confronting citizenship, human rights are now a more relevant political means? Brysk and Shafir comment that 'human rights promise more than nation state citizenship. Implicitly, and sometimes explicitly, they suggest not only the possibility of an international order, which a well ordered state sovereignty system also promises, but a global community' (2004: 4–5). Indeed, if we consider that the world today is increasingly depicted as a global community, then it becomes apparent why human rights could now be more relevant than citizenship.

But the case is not simply that human rights surface as most relevant political means, there is also significant disaffection with citizenship as a political institution. This is the second reason why it appears problematic. In particular, growing disenchantment with parliamentary politics, manifest in low voter turnouts and lack of engagement with formal political institutions, such as political parties, indicate that citizenship as an institution means less and less to the citizens, save a right to participate in elections in which choice is curtailed.[17] Although for some theorists – as, for example, Mark Warren – this disenchantment is an indication of citizens' changing expectations from their state, of their growing criticism rather than mere indifference, we also have to recognise that it is citizenship as a formal state institution that transpires as weak in this context. Warren notes:

> Increasing disaffection from formal political institutions seems to be paralleled by increasing attention toward other ways and means of getting collective things done. Certainly, part of the reason that individuals are 'apathetic' about politics is that they conceive 'politics' as equivalent to the state. If the state becomes less significant as a site of collective action, then individuals . . . are likely to be organised around work, family and friends, schools, clubs, recreation, and other kinds of associations.
> (2002: 682)

Far from signalling therefore the end of political activism, current disenchantment with formal channels of participation opens the way for local initiatives and DIY politics – *not* a citizenship politics. At the same time, a lack of identification with citizenship in the face of its link with nationality explains further why political disengagement prevails at the state rather than local level – especially within multicultural societies. Finally, a widespread sense that citizenship is not as effective a means for promoting democratic struggles confirms further why its practice appears today discredited.

The third reason why citizenship seems problematic has to do with its value and exclusivity. To understand this problem we need to reflect on the varying statuses of political membership created in European counties. For example, there are citizens of member states of the European Union who enjoy a privileged set of rights except the national vote (denizens[18]), dual citizens who hold a double allegiance to different nation states,[19] citizens of Commonwealth countries (in Britain) who can also vote in national elections, and permanent as well as temporary third-country residents who enjoy an array of civil and social rights. What these varying statuses of political membership thus demonstrate is, first, that the rights and privileges accompanying access to citizenship are no longer dependent upon its conferment, and second, that the centrality and exclusivity of citizenship as an institution is weakened and challenged. Benhabib offers an additional insight into these developments. She notes:

> In the process of rearticulation of rights through different regimes of residency and membership, citizenship rights are transformed . . . While admittance policies into EU member countries get stricter, for those foreigners who are already in the EU, the progress of Union citizenship has given rise to discrepancies between those who are foreigners and third country nationals [enjoying various social and civil rights], and those who are foreign nationals but EU members [and have the right to vote in local elections and elections of the European Parliament] . . . The consequence of these developments [is that] a situation has emerged in which divergent normative principles are at work in different contexts. I would like to name this process the disaggregation of citizenship rights. While civil rights are increasingly universalised . . . political and social rights show great variation across national boundaries.
>
> (2005: 14)

By thus astutely capturing the emergent situation in terms of a 'disaggregation of citizenship rights', Benhabib points to the increasing importance attached to the status of residence, since it is residence rather than citizenship that appears to condition full or partial access to the rights and privileges of citizenship. Jacobson also confirms this shift when he says that 'social, economic and even political rights have come to be predicated on residency. Citizenship, consequently, has been devalued in host countries' (1997: 9). Of course, the reason why citizenship appears devalued is now clear: it is no longer that excusive institution conferring rights on the members of the nation.

It follows that the challenges facing citizenship today, next to the growing impetus given to human rights, serve to conceal in the first instance the tension between the two principles. Present developments conceal their tension by confronting us with a situation of disarticulation rather than articulation: on one side, they point to a problematic citizenship in urgent need of recasting – if it is to address the challenges posed to it by diminishing state sovereignty, disenchantment with the state, and disaggregation of its rights; on the other side, they confirm that human rights that have grown in centrality do not only tally well with the emergence of deterritorialised politics, but also appear to be more forceful than citizenship. A gap therefore opens between citizenship and human rights, and this gap drives their tension out of sight. For what tension can there be between two principles that follow their separate ways, one attesting to the changes brought about by globalisation and the other challenged by these changes? Alternatively, it could be argued that the gap separating citizenship from human rights serves precisely to consolidate the position of those who already suggest that the tension between the two principles could be resolved. Conceived as a gap in democratic practice specifically, since it is citizenship that appears problematic, it points to the idea that by privileging the rights of humanity, which are co-original with citizenship, we could in fact reinvigorate democratic practice. In the name of democracy therefore, of recasting democratic practice so to meet the demands of a changed setting, various arguments have emerged that suggest that human rights could be perhaps the answer to a problematic citizenship.[20] But there is a caveat here: suggesting that human rights could substitute for the political function of citizenship is an option available only to those theorists who understand democracy in proceduralist terms, as a set of processes that reconcile political participation with legally codified rights. This is not an option for theorists who view democracy in agonistic terms. For agonistic theorists, not only is the tension between citizenship and human rights impossible to resolve and productive for democracy, but also it is citizenship that needs to be reasserted in the face of the problems confronting it – not human rights privileged.

In returning therefore to the terrain of democratic politics within which the argument of this book develops and suggesting that present developments challenge this politics, we notice that we encounter two options: either to argue that human rights could take on the political role of citizenship or to reassert citizenship (given that it is citizenship that appears problematic). Because the option we choose largely depends on what we understand by 'democratic practice', a debate can be delineated between theorists with different starting points and thus different suggestions regarding the future of democratic life. This is the citizenship human rights debate that this book addresses. To introduce this debate, the next section takes a first step by exploring the deliberative and agonistic accounts of democratic politics.

Deliberative and agonistic accounts of democratic politics

In looking into the deliberative and agonistic perspectives on democratic politics, this section has three aims. The first is to bring into focus the idea that there is an intimate connection between a deliberative understanding of democratic politics and arguments that privilege human rights. Although it is not until the next chapter that we will look at such arguments in more detail, it is important to sketch here in broad terms the perspective from which these arguments proceed. The second aim is to examine the ways in which the agonistic and deliberative perspectives approach the relation between citizenship and human rights, and to show how this determines the suggestions one makes when reconsidering democratic practice. The third aim of the section is to introduce broadly the agonistic perspective that informs the argument of this book – leading us in Chapter 5 to reassert citizenship. The deliberative perspective comes first.

In elucidating the deliberative approach to democratic politics, the section draws on the work of Jürgen Habermas, whose writings have been immensely influential for those theorists who, as we will later see, privilege human rights. Habermas notes: '. . . the model of democracy which I would like to propose relies on those conditions of communication under which the political process can be presumed to produce rational results because it operates deliberatively at all levels' (1999: 346). From this quote, we can derive two ideas specific to the Habermasian approach to democracy: first, a focus on discursive processes of participation – in which democracy consists; second, an emphasis on rational results – issuing from democratic processes so conceived. In particular, communication or discourse, a universal medium in which all citizens share, is the means that both enables and facilitates democratic deliberations about the terms of common coexistence. At the same time, by becoming institutionalised in law, discursive processes of deliberation lead to rational agreements on the rules that secure the fair and equal participation of all in the affairs of the polity.

> Discourse theory invests the democratic process with normative connotations stronger than those found in the liberal model but weaker than those found in the republican model. In agreement with republicanism, it gives centre stage to the process of political opinion and will-formation, but without understanding the constitution as something secondary; rather, it conceives constitutional principles as a consistent answer to the question of how the demanding communicative forms of democratic opinion-and-will-formation can be institutionalised. According to discourse theory, the success of deliberative politics depends not on a collectively acting citizenry, but on the institutionalisation of the corresponding procedures and conditions of communication.
>
> (Habermas 1996: 298)

Approached, therefore, as an institutionalised process of rational deliberation, democracy denotes a set of procedures on this perspective. So long as these procedures are fair, impartial and legitimate, they are democratic.[21] And such democratic reason-giving procedures hold open the possibility for a consensual coexistence – precisely because reason promises to address, if not resolve, disagreements.

Thus rationality, together with discourse, plays a catalytic role in Habermas's perspective: first, it warrants legitimacy and impartiality; second, it provides a basis for the formation of a democratic 'we consciousness'; third, it secures consensus. Let us briefly examine these presuppositions in turn. Starting from the assumption that cooperation among citizens of diverse ethnic backgrounds is unviable in a democracy unless there is some sort of prior agreement about the institutions in place, Habermas emphasises the role that reason plays in furthering such democratic cooperation. With a validity claim that transcends cultural attachments, reason heightens precisely the need and necessity of constructing a procedural framework that is in the equal interest of all. By therefore pointing to what is in the equal interest of all – namely, procedures that do not discriminate against any one conception of the good – reason sanctions impartiality. Notice here how the link that Habermas draws between reason and impartiality adds another layer to his case for communicative rationality as the basis of democratic politics. Rationality does not just define democratic deliberations through the Habermasian lens, but also drives them: it buttresses the idea that only processes that are in the equal interest of all secure democratic cooperation. Benhabib explains further why impartiality, warranted by reason, furnishes democratic processes with legitimacy. She notes:

> The basis of legitimacy in democratic institutions is to be traced back to the presumption that the instances which claim obligatory power for themselves do so because their decisions represent an impartial standpoint said to be in the equal interests of all. This presumption can be fulfilled only if such decisions are in principle open to appropriate public processes of deliberation by free and equal citizens.
>
> (1993: 69)

Hence in the absence of impartiality, democratic legitimacy weakens in this perspective.

But the case is not only that rationality opens the way for legitimacy and impartiality, it also serves as a minimum basis for the formation of a democratic 'we consciousness'. To understand this point, we need to counterpoise Habermas's focus on rational deliberations with the alternative, communitarian focus on the ethnos – that is, the idea that democratic cooperation is possible only so long as citizens share in some common ethnic substance. *Pace* this much-rehearsed idea, Habermas argues that civic solidarity, necessary in a democracy, need not be tied with ethnic homogeneity. Instead, participation in public and institutionalised exercises of reason could enable citizens with different conceptions of the good to bond around the shape, rather than substance, of the terms of their coexistence. By thus creating and agreeing on the rules of the democratic game, citizens partake in the formation of a minimal 'we consciousness' that is not nationally bound. Of course, interesting here is the idea that via deliberations citizens both bond and agree about the rules governing their coexistence. What then does the deliberative perspective suggest when it anticipates the conclusion of impartial agreements on democratic coexistence?

Waldron comments:

> Deliberation offers not just impartiality but consensus. Inasmuch as we are each oriented toward an impartial solution, we are each oriented toward the same solution; and this sense of common orientation guides us in our deliberation with one another. Or to put it the other way round: any lingering plurality of views, any lingering dissensus, is a sure sign that some partial interests have not yet been transformed into impartial ones.
>
> (1999: 211)

This presupposition that 'deliberation offers consensus', as Waldron puts it, reveals a particular, consensual, approach to the political. On one side, deliberative politics, if rationally and impartially conducted, addresses, if not resolves, disagreements. On the other side, there is a necessary prior agreement on the advantages of such politics: precisely because it addresses disagreements, deliberative politics leads to cooperation. A double consensus therefore underpins this conception: consensus of origin as the political process emerges because of a prior agreement, but also consensus of results as a net agreement on the terms of common coexistence, a resolution of all disagreements is considered both feasible and desirable. It follows that the procedural approach to democracy has a point of contact with this understanding of the political. A consensual or harmonious being together is that which democratic processes ensure and facilitate by reinforcing the rights of deliberating subjects, and by setting up and enhancing the constitution and the institutional forums of deliberation. However, a clarification is important here. Suggesting that the deliberative approach envisages a consensual coexistence does not mean that disagreements are simply dismissed on this perspective. To be sure, conflicts and disagreements do enter the procedural schema. Instead, the case is that the deliberative approach, by virtue of the emphasis it places on the force of intersubjective reason, holds out the promise that disagreements are essentially resolvable. This promise becomes more evident once we consider the role that the Habermasian approach reserves for the constitution.

As we have already mentioned in passing, the constitution is what fastens

the institutionalisation of deliberative procedures – precisely because institutionalisation, according to Habermas, is necessary for the smooth operation of democratic deliberations. On a different level, however, we could
also argue that the constitution is the end product that finalises a rational
consensus on coexistence, not only because it entrenches the rules on which
citizens have procedurally agreed, but also because it embodies an
impartial means of justice licensed to address those disagreements that arise
in practice. If we consider moreover that the constitution is in itself a
rational and impartial construction according to Habermas, arrived at
through rational deliberations, then it becomes apparent that, alongside their
obvious impartiality, democracy and constitutionalism share some significant, albeit familiar, common ground: consensus and rationality. While
consensus (or at least the prospect of consensus) is that at which democracy
and constitutionalism aim, reason is the means that bridges the distance between the two, making them appear reconciled. Saturating constitutionalism and informing democratic deliberations, reason both ensures the
democratic character of the constitution and furthers its operational-
isation – because, once crystallised, the constitution safeguards the rules
rationally decided on. The relevant question that therefore arises at this
point is this: if democracy and constitutionalism are thus entwined through
the Habermasian lens, what is the precise relation between citizenship and
human rights, the two principles that, as we have seen, exemplify the legal
and democratic traditions?

Habermas views citizenship and human rights as co-original. The core
idea behind the co-originality thesis is straightforward and directly follows
from the above observations. Whereas the practice of citizenship gives birth
to those basic legal rights that every rational participant in deliberative
procedures accepts, basic legal rights in turn entrench and safeguard the
practice of citizenship. Habermas explains:

> The internal relation between human rights and popular sovereignty
> consists in the fact that the requirement of legally institutionalising
> self-legislation can be fulfilled only with the help of a code that simul-
> taneously implies the guarantee of actionable individual liberties. By
> the same token, the equal distribution of those liberties can in turn be
> satisfied by a democratic procedure that grounds the supposition that the
> outcomes of political opinion-and-will-formation are reasonable . . . If
> one introduces the system of rights in this way, then one can understand
> how popular sovereignty and human rights go hand in hand and hence
> grasp the co-originality of civic and private autonomy.
>
> (1996: 455, 127)

What Habermas thus tells us is that, by participating in public exchanges
of reason, individuals both construct their basic rights and institutionalise

the procedures that bring about such rights – hence a circular process. Of course, the clear implication of this process is that it resolves all tension between citizenship and human rights since what we are now dealing with is not two opposing principles that push and pull in different directions (one towards inclusion, the other towards exclusion), but rather two equivalent principles that unite and combine around reason, the rational exchanges which effect their reconciliation.[22] It proceeds that, in so reconciling citizenship with human rights, the Habermasian perspective ultimately prepares the way for those arguments that suggest that by privileging human rights we could today reinvigorate democratic practice.

To see the affinity between the case for prioritising human rights and the deliberative account, we need to return to the idea that citizenship today appears problematic because it is devalued, underrated and anachronistic, by virtue of its link with the nation state. From this idea it follows that human rights that co-found the democratic order could, if privileged, reinvigorate it. For there is nothing in the deliberative account that theoretically stops this progression in argumentation. As rights codified in law, human rights do not only exemplify the rationality and consensus that define deliberative democratic practices, but also, much like citizenship, human rights can be exercised. At the same time, human rights, which override national and territorial boundedness, can promote the minimal democratic 'we consciousness' that citizenship promotes. And human rights guarantee, indeed, impartiality. Precisely because they include everyone and draw on what people share in common, they can be rationally approached as impartial means for practising democratic politics. More importantly, by virtue of their all-inclusivity, human rights both theoretically agree with and further the consensual coexistence that the Habermasian perspective valorises. Not only do they potentially override conflicts and disagreements rooted often in different conceptions of the good, and supposedly tame and address these, but they also reinforce the prospects for securing minimal, rationally informed agreements on the rules of democratic coexistence – since they draw on basic humanity. Although, in the next chapter, we will further justify this suggestion by looking at the particular arguments of Held, Bohman and Benhabib, here it suffices to notice that the deliberative conception of politics that resolves the tension between citizenship and human rights serves as a credible anchoring point for recasting democratic practice in all-inclusive terms – an option that is not available for agonistic theorists. The agonistic perspective therefore comes next.

In examining the agonistic perspective on democratic politics, the first point to note is that agonism does not denote a unified position, rather, theorists who identify as agonists, such as Connolly, Honig and Mouffe, to name a few, are variously indebted to different lines of thought, ranging from Nietzsche to Arendt and Schmitt, place divergent emphases in their writings and often embrace different normative vocabularies. Despite their issuing differences and disagreements, however, we could identify four assumptions as central to their perspective. The first assumption is that democratic life presupposes incompletion, uncertainty and openness – neither consensus nor a harmonious coexistence. This is because the pluralism of value systems and conceptions of the good that is constitutive of democratic politics, according to agonistic theorists, always involves frontiers between 'us' and 'them', relations of identity/difference that cannot be resolved through appeals to common reason, and which effectively prevent finality and the completion of the democratic ideal. As Kalyvas puts it:

> A key innovation of [the agonistic account] is to have brought into attention the relevance of identity and difference to politics. The main problem agonal democracy addresses is how can a free political order emerge without generating sameness and an oppressive consensus, that is, without eradicating plurality and difference in the name of an over-assertive and dominant identity that claims to represent the universal, the rational, the right and the normal.
>
> (2009: 21)

Although this is not to suggest that the emphasis that the deliberative perspective places on consensus effaces plurality, it is to reflect on a potential implication of this perspective: the consensual democratic coexistence it envisions might be an oppressive coexistence, in which a singular rationality has prevailed over many often irreconcilable rationalities. But it is not only that consensus might be dangerous and oppressive through the agonistic lens, it is also impossible to secure permanently. A conflictual plurality of worldviews, next to ever-present frontiers, shows that consensus, if attained, is only partial and precarious, not permanent. This is one of the most fundamental differences between deliberative and agonistic theorists. Whereas the former suggest that an intersubjective reason and the force of the better argument bridge frontiers and reconcile differences, the latter argue that differences and frontiers are ever-present and, notably, constitutive of democratic life.

With the aim therefore of encouraging the expression of differences and consolidating plurality, agonistic theorists place emphasis on contestation. This is the second assumption central to their perspective. Contestations channelled through democratic institutions expose and challenge relations of power and subordination for agonistic theorists, and ensure that democratic politics remains dynamic and alert at instances of closure. In Honig's words, contestatory practices 'challenge existing distributions of power, disrupt the hegemonic social, and proliferate political spaces when they interrupt the routine, predictability, and repetition on which . . . dominant patterns of private realm identity depend' (1993: 532). Contestations play therefore a dual role in the agonistic perspective: first, they channel conflicts and constitutive differences; second, they challenge given distributions and constellations of power. Tully explains further that, in agonic games, what happens precisely is that 'the contestants seek to modify and often reverse the rules of recognition of the game, not once and for all, but as their identities and diverse ways of being themselves change over time and generations' (1999: 175). Indeed, the agonic contestations that are part and parcel of democratic politics, according to agonistic theorists, are neither predetermined nor given – nor is, for that matter, the identity of the subjects who initiate such contestations. Rather, as Tully's observation alludes to, political subjects become (re)constituted the moment they engage in such contestations. In contrast therefore with the deliberative perspective, which places emphasis on deliberations, the agonistic perspective places emphasis on contestations. While deliberations entwine with a discursive reason and aim at addressing conflicts and disagreements, contestations entwine with affective identifications and aim at challenging, and even overturning, relations of power and subordination.

This last comment leads us to the third assumption underpinning the agonistic perspective: namely, that democratic contestations presuppose the construction of common projects and positions, and the cultivation of an affective identification with those projects and positions. For what democratic politics seeks to establish, according to Honig, 'is to multiply the sites of affect, coordination, and organisation that move people into (and sometimes out of) politics on their own behalves and on behalf of others' (2001: 40). This is a further core difference between the deliberative and agonistic perspectives. While affective identifications with common projects and discourses motivate political mobilisations for agonistic theorists, and are therefore necessary for practising democratic politics, affects and emotive attachments are arbitrary and obstructive for deliberative theorists. Not only do they hinder democratic deliberations and are thus extraneous to processes shaping the rules, rather than substance, of coexistence, but they also dissipate in the face of the force of an intersubjective reason. Besides, recall here how minimal is the 'we consciousness' that Habermas envisages for contemporary democracies: except for an attachment to procedural rules and rational deliberations, it appears that there is little else to which this 'we consciousness' lays claim.

Finally, and as it might have already surfaced from the above exposition, democracy through the agonistic lens is not something that is imposed so to ensure a transparent coexistence, but it is an ethos (of disturbance), a way of living, which needs to be developed and nourished. As Connolly explains, democracy is:

> . . . an ethos through which newly emerging constellations might reconstitute identities previously impressed upon them, thereby disturbing the established priorities of identity/difference through which social relations are organised . . . it is a political culture in which a variety of constituencies responds affirmatively to uncertainties, diversities, heterogeneities,

and paradoxes of late modern life by participating in the construction and reconstruction of their own identities.

(1995: 154)

In contrast therefore with the procedural understanding of democracy, here we confront an altogether different conception that does not reduce democracy either to a body of rules or a form of government; rather, democracy denotes on this account a way of living in which strife and affective mobilisations play a central role. They elicit plural interpretations of political ideals and entice continuous redescriptions of the democratic imaginary, attesting thereby to its constitutive openness and pluralism.

In a respect, we could argue that, given the emphasis that the agonistic perspective places on frontiers and democratic contestations, it tallies well with the idea of reasserting citizenship in view of the problems confronting it – instead of privileging human rights. On one level, this is self-evident. While human rights efface frontiers, citizenship, which rests on dynamics of inclusion and exclusion, democratises these frontiers by providing an outlet and a means for the political expression of differences. Moreover, since it is the citizens who practise and contest democratic politics, they are clearly the agents who mobilise and promote the democratic ethos of disturbance that agonistic theorists valorise. On another level, however, assuming a necessary affinity between citizenship and theories that approach democracy as an ethos of disturbance not only appears intricate, but also hasty. This is partly because a problematic citizenship must be redefined if it is to address the challenges confronting it in the face of an increasingly deterritorialised and postnational politics. But it is also because there is a plethora of terms, such as 'political agency', 'democratic subjectivity' or 'passionate subjectivity', which Norval (2009) talks about that could convincingly follow from an agonistic understanding of democracy, without stumbling over the problems confronting citizenship discourse. Why citizenship then? Because *pace* such terms, citizenship is not only political through and through, if by 'politics' we understand frontiers and democratic engagements, but also carries connotations of responsibility and commitment, democratic unity and, indeed, affective identification – the stuff of an agonistic approach, in other words. But there is another reason why an agonistic perspective on democracy could serve as anchoring point for arguments that recast democratic practice by reasserting citizenship rather than privileging human rights. This has to do with the way in which agonistic theorists view the relation between citizenship and human rights. The argument of Chantal Mouffe in *The Democratic Paradox* is relevant to explore in this regard.

In particular, Mouffe argues that there is a manifest, necessary and productive tension between citizenship and human rights, liberalism and democracy. They are not co-original as they are for Habermas. The tension is manifest because citizenship and human rights represent two distinct

traditions with incompatible logics according to Mouffe. While the democratic tradition (which citizenship represents) presupposes frontiers because
of its focus on equality, the liberal tradition (which human rights represent)
negates frontiers because of its focus on liberty, the rule of law and individual
rights. Although the incompatibility between the liberal and democratic
logics could warrant that liberal democracy is an unviable regime,[23] this is far
from the case for Mouffe. Instead, what she argues is that the tension between
liberalism and democracy makes modern liberal democracy a paradoxical
regime. Grasping the democratic paradox enables us to see why the tension
between citizenship and human rights is necessary through Mouffe's lens.
The paradox is the following: while it is the citizenry that defines all rights
and liberties in a democracy, the exercise of popular sovereignty is always
informed and limited by the rule of law and human rights that the liberal
logic promotes. Whereas therefore the *demos* defines liberty, it is in the name
of liberty that the actions of the *demos* are limited. Mouffe explains at length:

> Democratic logics always entail drawing a frontier between 'us' and
> 'them', those who belong to the *demos* and those who are outside it. This
> is the condition for the very exercise of democratic rights. It necessarily
> creates a tension with the liberal emphasis on respect of 'human rights',
> since there is no guarantee that a decision made through democratic
> procedures will not jeopardise some existing rights. In a liberal democracy
> limits are always put on the exercise of the sovereignty of the people.
> Those limits are usually presented as providing the very framework for
> the respect of human rights and being non-negotiable. In fact, since they
> depend on the way 'human rights' are defined and interpreted at a given
> moment, they are the expression of the prevailing hegemony and thereby
> contestable. What cannot be contestable in a liberal democracy is the
> idea that it is legitimate to establish limits to popular sovereignty in
> the name of liberty. Hence its paradoxical nature.
>
> (2000: 4)

Thus what we notice here is that the tension between citizenship and human
rights plays a necessary role in democratic politics: first, it ensures that there
is democratic practice (a *demos*) *and* necessary limits to that practice (issuing
from human rights); second, the limits placed on democratic practice
are always contestable, and thus subject to reassessment and revision. Rather
than viewing therefore the tension between citizenship and human rights as a
problem that needs to be addressed, Mouffe brings into focus its centrality
in the democratic imaginary. She emphasises, in other words, the productive
effect of this tension: it secures that democratic politics remains alert at challenging established hegemonies and given constellations of power. This is the
real strength of liberal democracy, according to Mouffe.

In conclusion therefore to this chapter, we see that there is a slight shift in our enquiry into the citizenship/human rights debate. From the assumption of a tension apparent in different contexts and levels of analysis, to an examination of the changes disguising this tension and their implications for different conceptions of democratic politics, we have now moved our enquiry into the role that the tension between citizenship and human rights plays for democratic politics. Could it be that, by privileging human rights in the belief that they are co-original with citizenship, we end up impoverishing democratic politics by reducing it to one principle? While the remainder of the book endeavours to develop an answer to this question, the next chapter closely examines the deliberative case for privileging human rights.

Chapter 2

Privileging human rights[1]

The aim of this chapter is to examine the argument that privileges human rights. This argument comes as part of a wider case in the literature to rethink the nature and dynamics of democratic politics in the face of the challenges posed to it by the intensification of processes of globalisation, the rise of transnational migration and the salience of the human rights discourse. Underpinning this argument is the twofold idea that democracy is too limited and too exclusive in the context of an interconnected world in which calls for political, legal and ethnic inclusion abound. To bring democracy thus into line with current developments, it is argued that we need to dissociate it from dynamics of national and territorial exclusion. For such dynamics no longer resonate in a setting different to the one within which democracy was originally advanced. In this setting, it is the prospect of universal democracy, global or transnational, which appears relevant and compelling.

The case for universal democratisation addresses two main challenges confronting democratic politics at the turn of the century: the first revolves around the *topos* of politics. By reformulating democracy across state borders, its proponents show us that diminishing state sovereignty does not irreversibly weaken democracy; rather, defining democratic markers such as transparency and accountability could be secured at the global layer of governance. The second challenge revolves around political *logos* or participation. By invoking the cross-border activism of a nascent civil society, democratic theorists show us that political action could develop out of global concerns. And by valorising the potential of institutionalised deliberation to empower and emancipate individuals qua human beings, they identify a way in which political agency could be actualised both within and beyond nation state borders. Yet what the proponents of universal democratisation appear to pay less attention to is the implications of their thesis for citizenship. For political agency does not always concur with citizenship.

While political agency, understood as deliberation about political affairs, presupposes neither a fixed setting nor a common bond – since a variety of concerns could instigate political involvement in the temporal dimension – citizenship as a concept, in both its liberal and civic republican formulations, rests, as we will shortly see, on something more than temporary political engagement. As a status that, once acquired, bestows upon the individual an array of rights, citizenship clearly distinguishes between the members of the *demos* who exercise the full array of rights and the non-members. And as a participatory activity, which is how civic republicans conceive of citizenship, it presupposes not only common mores and a civic bond among the citizenry, but also constitutes communities that are bounded and thus exclusive. Precisely, therefore, because citizenship is premised on difference, on the clear distinction between those who are included *and* excluded from the *demos*, it activates a bond that is collective and egalitarian, and an identification with the good that is common to all. Would this still be possible if citizenship, much like democracy, were to become reformulated in universal terms? Or does the prospect of universal democracy necessarily imply the end of citizenship as a concept?

This chapter argues that an implication of the case for universal democracy is that it undermines citizenship while it privileges human rights. To justify this argument, the chapter engages with the writings of Held, Bohman and Benhabib, who suggest that, by reformulating democracy in global or transnational terms, we take a step towards strengthening and reinvigorating democratic practice. What brings together these three authors is, first, their profound concern with democratic practice and their openness to recasting it in universal terms, and second, and more importantly, their resistance to universal inclusion – that is, although Held, Bohman and Benhabib defend the prospect of universal democratisation, they recognise in their own ways that democracy presupposes relations of both inclusion and exclusion. This recognition not only leads them to resist the idea of substituting the political function of citizenship with human rights, but also emphatically to retain the term 'citizenship' in their writings – yet reformulate it in universal terms. Hence Held, Bohman and Benhabib unite here in their insistence that they recast citizenship, not privileging human rights. Third, all three authors share in a deliberative understanding of democracy. By distinguishing therefore their approach as 'democratic' and 'deliberative',[2] the chapter explicates its influence on their conception of citizenship. In effect, what we notice here is that the case for privileging human rights is not a straightforward one; rather, it is precisely the aim of the chapter to show and justify how a deliberative understanding of democracy leads one to prioritise human rights while undermining citizenship – when ironically it is in the name of citizenship that democratic practice becomes recast in universal terms.

The structure of the chapter goes as follows. The first and second sections explore those developments that trigger the argument that privileges human rights. While the first section elucidates the two dominant accounts of citizenship that inform the arguments of Held, Bohman and Benhabib, the second section examines the challenges posed to these accounts. Although, in the previous chapter, we mentioned in passing some of the problems confronting citizenship today, the focus of this second section of the chapter is somewhat narrower and different from that to which we have so far given attention. By distinguishing between challenges to democratic unity and challenges to democratic legitimacy, the section shows where exactly the problem with the liberal and civic republican accounts of citizenship lies. At the same time, by approaching the challenges posed to citizenship in terms of unity and legitimacy, the section prepares the ground for the arguments of Held, Bohman and Benhabib – who suggest that their proposals meet calls for both civic solidarity (weak in contemporary democracies) and/or legitimacy (which has waned in the face of institutions of global governance). Subsequently, the third section of the chapter moves to examine the different ideas that Held, Bohman and Benhabib put forward in the attempt to reformulate citizenship. Finally, the chapter concludes by arguing that their conception of citizenship is so minimal that, in the process of resolving the problems confronting it, they inevitably collapse it into human rights.

Liberal and civic republican conceptions of citizenship

A close look at the dominant accounts of citizenship is a good starting point for shedding light on the argument that privileges human rights. This is partly because the idea of a problematic citizenship is precisely what drives some political theorists to rethink it in human rights terms. But it is also because citizenship is one of those concepts that, although simple to grasp and identify, is difficult to pin down and define. Indeed, citizenship is a contested concept. And as Judith Squires notes:

> There is a long standing debate about how best to define citizenship arising from whether one understands membership of a community as a status or an activity: whether one possesses citizenship rights (the liberal perspective) or participates in citizenship responsibilities (the civic republican perspective).
>
> (2000: 1)

A probe, therefore, into the liberal and civic republican understandings of citizenship serves two particular purposes: first, it enables us to introduce the two distinct theoretical approaches that, as we will later see, Held, Bohman and Benhabib reconcile – while Mouffe, as we will explain in Chapter 5, selectively combines; second, it puts us in a position to show that the problem with citizenship does not simply arise in practice, as we discussed in the previous chapter, but is rather already inscribed in theory, in what is understood by citizenship – an objective that the next section explores in more detail. The liberal account of citizenship comes first.

Liberal citizenship is conceived as a status that, once acquired, bestows upon the individual citizen an array of rights. A classic formulation of liberal citizenship is to be found in the writings of T. H. Marshall. Specifically, Marshall, interested primarily in the relationship between citizenship and social inequalities in post-war Britain, divided citizenship into three sets of rights – civil, political and social – each unfolding linearly in the course of the eighteenth (civil rights), nineteenth (political rights) and twentieth (social rights) centuries. These rights, Marshall argued, were to be equally enjoyed by all individuals by virtue of their membership in a common civilisation. Accordingly, he defined citizenship as 'a status bestowed on those who are full members of a community. All who possess the status', he contended, 'are equal with respect to the rights and duties with which the status is endowed' (1992: 18). An idea therefore of social justice undercuts the liberal conception of citizenship. As a status, bestowing upon all those who possess it equal civil, political and social rights, citizenship mitigates against social inequalities: it provides those people partaking in the 'common civilisation' of a political community with an equal and socially homogeneous identity that transcends their (social) particularity. Or as Squires puts it:

> Everyone has a common set of political entitlements whatever their social, cultural and economic status ... The primary focus of concern here tends to be the relation between citizenship and economic inequality, requiring a minimum level of redistribution to overcome the pressures of social exclusion. Citizenship is conceived as a political identity working to mitigate other (primarily economic) identities.
>
> (2000: 1)

Moreover, it is not only that citizenship is an equal identity according to the liberal perspective, it is also an individual and public identity.

The individual and his/her rights comprise a fundamental tenet of the liberal vocabulary. Considered as an autonomous entity with the right to determine and pursue his/her own conception of the good, the right to be free from external constraints, the individual is all that matters for liberal theorists. This focus on the individual reflects, of course, on the liberal conception of citizenship. First, the acquisition of citizen status does not affect the individual pursuit of self-interest – a point to be further clarified when we compare this conception of the citizen with the civic republican one. Rather, as one identity among others, citizenship reinforces the capacity of individuals to 'form, revise and rationally pursue their own conceptions of the good (Rawls 1996: xlvi). Second, liberal citizenship, a formal status of rights, requires minimum state interference. Given that liberals place paramount importance on respect for individual rights, the less the state intervenes in individuals' affairs, the better protected they are as citizens to pursue their own conceptions of the good. The rights of the individual therefore take precedence over their conceptions of the good through the liberal lens. This is an important point to grasp because it points to a basic difference from the civic republican conception. Although civic republicans, as we will shortly see, approach political participation in constitutive terms, for liberals who prioritise individual rights, 'participation is required only insofar as it is necessary to protect people's basic rights and liberties' (Miller 1995: 437).

At the same time, a further feature of liberal citizenship is that it is a public identity. To explain this feature, we need to recall that, in the light of class inequalities in post-war Britain, citizenship was for Marshall an egalitarian (i.e. equal rights for all), homogeneous (i.e. share in the common civilisation) and universal status (i.e. transcendental of particularities). By virtue of its egalitarianism, homogeneity and universality, it mitigated against social inequalities. For present-day liberal theorists, such as Rawls for example, it is in the light of cultural pluralism that citizenship transpires as egalitarian, homogeneous and universal. This is because present-day liberals place emphasis on the plurality of conceptions of the good, which individuals should be free to define and pursue as they see fit. However, individuals can only do so in their private lives. As citizens, they are required to set their private identities aside and reach an agreement on the institutional framework that best protects their rights as individuals and enables them to pursue unhindered their self-interest – so long, of course, as its pursuit does not infringe the rights of others. Citizenship, therefore, is a public identity on the liberal perspective, transcendental of cultural particularities and conceptions of the good. Its members have equal rights in determining the procedures necessary for coexistence. As Derek Heater comments, in the liberal understanding of citizenship:

> The individual remains an individual. The acquisition of citizenly status does not necessitate abandonment of the pursuit of self-interest. Public and private spheres are kept distinct, and citizens are under no obligation to participate in the public arena if they have no inclination to do so. Nor have citizens any defined responsibilities *vis-à-vis* their fellow citizens. All are equal, autonomous beings, so that there is no sense that the state has any organic existence, bonding the citizens to it and to each other ... Citizenship largely means the pursuit of one's private life and interests more comfortably because the private life is insured by state-protected rights.
>
> (1999: 6–7)

This liberal understanding of citizenship clearly contrasts with the civic republican one.

Kymlicka and Norman explain that what 'distinguishes civic republicans ... is their emphasis on the intrinsic value of political participation for the participants themselves' (1994: 362). Whereas therefore liberal theorists view citizenship as a status, civic republicans view citizenship as a participatory activity, which constitutes both subjects as citizens and communities. Individuals are considered as autonomous entities with a positive liberty (freedom to say, constitute and express themselves through their participation in the communal affairs). Moreover, according to civic republicans, individuals are socially embedded. Oldfield emphasises that:

> Central to civic republicanism is a conception of individuals rather different from that of liberal individualism. First of all, individuals are not thought of as being logically prior to society. They receive their very names in a social context ... Secondly, and consequently, individuals have no sovereign or overriding moral priority. Claims may legitimately be made on their time, their resources, and sometimes even on their lives. These claims are duties associated with their very identification of themselves as citizens; not to fulfil them is to cease to be a citizen.
>
> (1990: 181)

From this, it follows that an emphasis on responsibilities, such as the civic duty to participate in the political process, lies at the core of the civic republican conception of citizenship. Through their political participation, individuals constitute themselves as citizens and pay their duties as members of a political community. At the same time, it is through their participation that citizens define their common good. This is not expressive of a mere agreement in formal procedures, as in liberalism; rather, it is something that becomes constructed through citizen deliberation. Civic bonds are thus necessary so as to identify and construct the good shared by all of the participants in the process of deliberation. Civic virtue and mores are also necessary. The citizen needs to exhibit a specific character and this can be taught through the relevant education. Of course, the emphasis that civic republicans place on participation, and the virtues and mores necessary for its promotion, does not mean that they dismiss the significance of individual rights. Rather, as Miller clarifies:

> The contrast between republicanism and liberalism is not that the liberal recognises the value of entrenched rights whereas the republican does not, but that the liberal recognises these rights as having a pre-political justification while the republican grounds them in public discussion. One institutional corollary is that liberals will seek to make the judiciary the supreme arbiters of constitutional rights – in effect the interpretation of liberal citizenship is entrusted to them – while the republican gives this role to the citizen body as a whole. Thus the constitution will have a different status in a republican regime. It will constrain everyday politics, but will itself be open to amendment if the rights and liberties it protects

are judged, following public discussion in which all have opportunities to participate, to stand in need of revision.

(1995: 449)

What we therefore notice at this stage is that in contrast with the liberal conception of citizenship, which transcends individuals' particular identities, the civic republican conception suppresses them since citizenship is, through the civic republican lens, an overriding political identity. At the same time, however, the civic republican conception of citizenship, much like the liberal one, promotes both egalitarianism and homogeneity – because all members of the *demos* have equal rights to participate in the political process and to partake in the democratic 'we consciousness'. Both conceptions, moreover, 'assume citizenship to exist within a territorially bounded nation state and both aspire to a form of universalism within its boundaries' (Squires 2000: 2). On one side, liberal citizenship is understood as that status confirming membership to the national state. The array of rights, accompanying the status of citizenship, is confined within the remit of territorial states. On the other side, civic republican citizenship stresses the national embeddedness of the citizenry. The latter is depicted as participant in the affairs of territorially delimited and sovereign states. Advanced at the time of homogeneous, autonomous and sovereign nation states, citizenship now appears, in both its liberal and civic republican conceptualisations, to be challenged by multiculturalism and the intensification of processes of globalisation. The next section explores these transformations and challenges posed to the two dominant accounts of citizenship.

Challenges confronting the liberal and civic republican accounts of citizenship

Both the liberal and the civic republican accounts of citizenship, we have argued, are bound with notions of nationality and territoriality. As a status or an activity that national citizenries attain or practise within state territories, citizenship today appears to be a problematic notion. At issue is whether a nationally and territorially bound citizenship can meet the demands of a different kind of setting to the one within which it was originally advanced. Can it address global issues, survive the development of potentially postnational polities such as the European Union, and meet the issues and demands raised by ethnically diverse societies? Given, in other words, that the homogeneity, sovereignty and autonomy of the nation state itself have been put into question, is nation state citizenship still an adequate notion? To address this question, the section distinguishes between two types of challenge posed to a bounded citizenship. The first challenge concerns democratic unity, and arises specifically within the context of multiculturalism and growing apprehension towards the nation. The challenge is the following: if the nation, one source for engendering civic solidarity, no longer holds the privileged position it used to within democratic imaginaries, can a national citizenship still inscribe and promote the necessary democratic unity in constitutively plural settings? With suggestions thus ranging in the literature from rethinking citizenship as friendship (Kahane 1999) to constitutional patriotism (Habermas 1996, 2001) and liberal reinterpretations of national principles (Miller 1995), the question lingering is how (and whether) a national citizenship can be so reconceptualised that, while it respects pluralism, it fosters democratic unity. The second challenge posed to a bounded citizenship concerns legitimacy and arises specifically in the face of institutions of global governance. The challenge is the following: if political decisions are increasingly being taken at the global and regional layers of governance, within which state citizenries do not participate, then how can democratic legitimacy and accountability still be promoted and secured in these settings? The remainder of the section explores these two challenges in turn.

Balibar notes:

> By definition, citizenship can exist only where we understand a notion of city to exist – where fellow citizens and foreigners are clearly distinguished in terms of rights and obligations in a given space. This formal distinction is in no way threatened by the existence of intermediary categories such as *metoikoi* (foreigners living permanent in Athens and enjoying special rights) and residents, provided that those who belong to these sub-categories do not enjoy these rights of sovereignty reserved for full citizens. In this respect, the modern nation is still – and must still consider itself – a city.
>
> (2002: 108)

As 'an international filing system' (Brubaker 1992: 31), a mechanism according to which persons are allocated to nation states, citizenship has been characterised by functions of both inclusion and exclusion: the nationals of a state attributed citizenship at birth have been included in the polity as equal members, while the non-nationals, who can acquire citizenship by naturalisation provided that they meet certain criteria, have been excluded. The challenge that growing ethnic diversity thus poses to notions of national citizenship revolves precisely around its inclusionary/exclusionary dynamics and brings into light the problem of a universal citizenship vis-à-vis particular cultural identities. On the one hand, as is presently theorised and practised, citizenship claims universality by virtue of including all members of the political community on equal terms. It reflects national concerns and practices. On the other hand, there are large numbers of people within contemporary polities who do not share in the majority's national identity and who wish to have their particular identities publicly recognised. Can a national citizenship accommodate, without assimilating, difference? What multiculturalism therefore problematises in the first instance is the terms in which non-nationals are included in the practice of citizenship.

To further elucidate this problem, we need to recall that, in both its liberal and civic republican formulations, citizenship has been depicted as a homogeneous, universal and egalitarian status or activity. All the citizens of the community would share in a common identity (homogeneous), transcend or suppress their own particularities (universal) and have access to equal rights (egalitarian citizenship). However, the growing number of non-national citizens within contemporary societies puts into question all three features of a national citizenship: first, these citizens do not share in the community's national identity; second, they seek public recognition of their particularity; and third, their equal rights entail, in some instances, differential treatment. Squires clarifies and stresses that the universalism of national citizenship, which in the final analysis is what multiculturalism challenges, has been theorised either as assimilation or as integration (2000: 5–7). Civic republican citizenship assimilates, as we have seen, particularity and liberal citizenship integrates it. And this is precisely where, in a nutshell, the problem lies, where the limitations of the dominant understandings of national citizenship come to the fore. On the one hand, a liberal and/or civic republican citizenship needs to be revised so as to accommodate, but without either assimilating or overriding, particularity – especially in the light of arguments stressing the importance of culture for individual well-being. On the other hand, by uncoupling the citizenship/nationality link and dispensing with citizenship's claims to homogeneity, universality and egalitarianism, claims inextricably bound with national identity, we unavoidably also put into question the centrality of citizenship as an institution. This is a first implication of multicultural politics for national citizenship. A second implication arises when we consider the prospect of differentiating citizenship along ethnic lines – an idea often seen as a solution to the problems confronting national citizenship.[3]

Kymlicka comments:

> The demands for differentiated citizenship pose a serious challenge to the prevailing conception of citizenship. Many people regard the idea of group-differentiated citizenship as a contradiction in terms. On the orthodox view, citizenship is by definition a matter of treating people as individuals with equal rights under the law . . . It seems unlikely that differentiated citizenship can serve an integrative function in this context. If citizenship is membership in a political community, then in creating overlapping political communities, self government rights necessarily give rise to a sort of dual citizenship and to potential conflicts about which community citizens identify with most deeply.
>
> (1994: 39)

What Kymlicka thereby directs our attention to is whether a differentiated citizenship could in fact provide the members of the polity with a common and binding experience. It is around this issue that the second implication for national citizenship revolves. This is the following: if a universal, homogeneous and egalitarian citizenship can no longer hold on to its defining properties in the light of multiculturalism, can it still serve a common and integrative function?

To clarify the sense in which the integrative and common function of citizenship might, in the face of ethnic politics, appear inadequate, we need to emphasise that democracy, as we have already mentioned in passing, requires a certain degree of unity, a 'we consciousness' or civic solidarity, which holds the society together and facilitates the identification of the good common to all. Now, according to civic republicans, it is through their participation in public affairs that people constitute themselves as citizens and define the common good. The affairs that are common, public and national determine the participants' 'we consciousness'. By contrast, according to liberals, it is as national citizens, as 'we', that people have the right to participate in public affairs and legitimate the state to act on their behalf. Because national citizenship is seen to ensure the homogeneity necessary for integration, stability and democratic action, differentiating it along ethnic lines, it is feared, would have negative effects. The conflicting demands that different ethnic groups will make to the state would render impossible, or even irrelevant, the delimitation of a good common to all.[4] At the same time, it is feared that, in the absence of some commonality among the members of the *demos*, democratic politics would be considerably weakened – if not made impossible. Could common humanity perhaps serve as the basis of commonality in a democracy? As we will show in the next section, some political theorists certainly consider this a viable option.

From this section, we need to retain the idea that, in the face of demands for differential rights, societal integration and democratic unity, national citizenship, conceived either as a status or an activity, appears at best weakened and at worst inadequate to address the currents that put its national boundedness into question. Or, as Balibar puts it, 'the current debates are haunted by the search for a paradigm in which cultural pluralism will no longer be residual or subordinate, but constitutive'. Hence there is the need, as he stresses:

> . . . to re-examine each implication, each justification, of the equation (citizenship = nationality) = sovereignty. Even if this equation is no longer considered sacrosanct by everyone, it nonetheless operates at the basis of the organisation of civic rights, and dominates even the prospect of an evolution.
>
> (2002: 107)

Yet the case is not only that we need to re-examine the link between citizenship and nationality, it is also that we need to rethink citizenship's territorial boundedness.

In particular, two interrelated challenges are posed to the citizenship/ territoriality link: the first concerns the emergence of so-called multiple citizenships, which, in implying conflicting loyalties, potentially lead to the desacralisation of citizenship; the second concerns the democratic deficit that arises when states decide their policies in international institutions in which citizen participation is lacking. Both challenges put into question the reach of democratic citizenries, their ability to shape and legitimate decisions and issues escaping territorial borders. We look at each of these challenges in turn.

According to Veit Bader:

> Citizenship is developing in two ways into a multiple and multilayered concept: political citizenship is complemented by economic, industrial and social citizenship (many spheres of citizenship) and political citizenship is gaining importance on different, increasingly supra-state levels of political integration (many levels of political citizenship).
>
> (1995: 212)

One supra-state level of political integration is the European Union. Citizens of Europe enjoy, for example, both nation state and European citizenship. Likewise, we notice that, in the face of the growing institutionalisation of issues and the transnationalisation of political actors, individuals have more opportunities to participate and acquire citizenship identity in different fora. These fora range from the state to the regional, and even the global, levels. What does this mean for the territorially bound citizenship? In a first reading, it appears that the liberal and civic republican conceptions of citizenship are concomitant with the development of a multiple citizenship. As Squires puts it:

> The participatory approach emerging from the civic republican tradition is perhaps not so tightly bound to the state. Emphasis on political participation as a civic duty shifts the emphasis to obligation to one's community. Whilst usually also a territorially bound notion, with community frequently assumed to be equivalent to the nation, it is perhaps easier to conceive of communities operating at more multiple and cross-cutting levels than states. It is possible that as the notion of communities is less closely tied to a notion of sovereignty it is therefore better able to provide a basis for citizenship in an era of fluidity and deterritorialisation.
>
> (2000: 4)

Likewise, liberal citizenship with its emphasis on the rights of the individual can adjust to the challenge of multiple communities. 'Rights are more mobile than states' (Cairns 1999: 114) and are not necessarily tied to state territory.

However, both understandings of citizenship appear, in a second reading, to be problematic. Liberal citizenship does not denote a multiplicity of communities, but the territorial state. As Delanty explains, 'the evolution of rights was related to the rise of the nation state and reflected the formal nature of modern law. Civil, political and social rights were formal entitlements granted by the state to its citizens' (2000: 126). Deterritorialised or multi-territorialised rights challenge thereby the liberal understanding of citizenship. Likewise, civic republican citizenship confronts the problem of conflicting loyalties and responsibilities. As an overriding political identity, civic republican citizenship cannot be multiple. In the light, moreover, of globalisation, citizen responsibility, a notion fundamental for civic republicans, seems to have acquired new meanings. 'The classic model of citizenship often stressed the duties or responsibilities of citizens, that is, the duty to be a good member of society', says Delanty:

> Now a new idea of responsibility has arisen which bears very little resemblance with this older way of thinking ... The idea of co-responsibility totally changes the entire discourse of responsibility. This has come with the recognition that individual responsibility is no longer able to find a solution to many problems facing society, in particular those emanating from technology.
>
> (2000: 127, 128)

Although therefore the liberal and civic republican conceptions appear, in the first instance, to tally well with the prospect of multiple citizenships, on closer inspection, there are certainly some theoretical difficulties that need to be addressed if we are to consider seriously the possibility of multiple citizenships. At the same time, we could argue that it is one thing to be political in different contexts and quite another to be a citizen, not only because citizenship, as we have been stressing throughout, presupposes the state as the locale in which it is being practised, but also because citizenship is, by virtue of its universality, which both the liberal and civic republican conceptions stress, a central political identity. Would this centrality not be undermined once we conceive it as multiple?[5] Of course, an implication of the idea of multiple citizenships is that while it strengthens the ability of citizenries to shape politics, it also puts this ability into question. For would multiple (and therefore dispersed) citizenries be able to secure the necessary legitimacy for decisions taken at the global level – a question that indicates that a global *demos*, as we will later see Held to be arguing, might perhaps be a better option for bringing citizenship into line with current developments? This last point brings us to the second interrelated[6] challenge confronting the notion of a territorially bound citizenship.

According to Davidson, there are two effects of globalisation for territorial citizenship:

> The sovereignty of the nation state is affected and the power of its citizens to make their own destiny in that context declines. Second, a new realm of law is created for the latter where they can only be empowered if a global level of citizenship is created to replace what is lost within the nation state.
>
> (2000: 9)

Specifically, citizenship, as is currently understood, is bound with the right or practice of a people to determine their affairs within a delimited territory. In this sense, citizenship defines and furthers democratic coexistence – if by 'democracy' we understand the right of a people to self-determination. However, in the face of both globalisation and European integration, there are issues and concerns (such as the economy or the environment) that cannot be confined within territorial borders. Yet these issues directly impact on citizens' lives. Moreover, as a result of the growing institutionalisation of world politics and the transnationalisation of political actors, both state governments and citizens are subject to the authority and sometimes interference of international organisations. Citizens have no access to the decision-making structures of such organisations. In effect, we are confronted with a situation in which domestic citizenries cannot alone deliberate on global issues or hold their governments accountable for them. Also territorial states cannot handle such issues on their own and they have to cooperate extensively with other states and international institutions. Therefore, the democratic idea of self-determination appears to be challenged: territorial sovereignty appears to be diminishing, accountability sidestepped and citizen participation lacking. Heater notes:

> Globalisation . . . raises questions about the nature of citizenship in our own times. If a government is reckoned legitimate in so far as it can be held accountable to the citizenry (and this is the democratic principle), then legitimacy is weakened as accountability is undermined.
>
> (1999: 162)

Heater gives an example:

> If a government can blame the failure of businesses and unemployment on transnational financial difficulties or manipulations over which it truly has no control, then what is the price for citizenship? The state has failed to honour one element of its side in the reciprocal relationship –

namely, to ensure its citizens' economic rights; yet it cannot be held responsible for this dereliction. Accountability is impossible; legitimacy and citizenship are consequently impaired.

(1999: 162)

According to Davidson, quoted earlier, a second, related effect of globalisation is 'the creation of a new realm of law where citizens can only be empowered if a global level of citizenship is created to replace what is lost within the nation state' (2000: 9). This sets forth a double problem. The first concerns the state's ability to determine access to citizenship. Civil, political and social rights are granted by the territorial state. Given, however, changes in international law concerning the status and rights of refugees, asylum seekers and guest workers, the question arises as to whether the state still has the authority to decide who will enter its territory and how he/she is to be treated. States' jurisdiction faces limitations in this respect and one area from which these limitations derive is, as we have seen, the emergence of codified normative concerns. This brings us to the second problem, which refers to the growing codification and salience of human rights.

We have already mentioned that, as a result of changes in international legislation, states have been placed under new types of regulation regime. These regulation regimes, which revolve around transnational issues, contest and monitor state authority. Human rights are one issue that has grown salient because of such changes at the global setting. The challenge that human rights therefore pose to territorial citizenship goes right to its core: in a global village, should foreigners temporarily or permanently residing in state territory be excluded from state membership? Is their exclusion morally legitimate? Squires comments that 'it could be that confronting issues of civil, political and social rights is best done directly without invoking the notion of citizenship, which carries with it the close association with the territorial state and therefore presumes exclusion' (2000: 4). On one side, therefore, it appears that territorial citizenship is no longer adequate as an institution to deal with increasing numbers of foreigners who require access to rights. Partial access to rights moreover can potentially weaken citizenship, as we saw in the first chapter. On the other side, it seems that exclusion, a prime function of a territorial citizenship, is no longer considered to be morally legitimate.

To be sure, civic republican citizenship cannot be reconciled with overriding moral concerns. Oldfield explains:

> [Civic republican] citizenship is exclusive: it is not a person's humanity that one is responding to, it is the fact that he or she is a fellow citizen, or a stranger. In choosing an identity for ourselves, we recognise both who our fellow citizens are, and those who are not members of our community, and thus who are potential enemies . . . This simply means

that to remain a citizen one cannot always treat everyone as a human being.

(1998: 81)

Although liberal citizenship fares better in this respect, since 'rights based liberalism disconnects citizenship to some extent from territory and formal legal status and thereby sets into motion a dynamic of inclusion of non citizens which implies a yet largely unrecognised reshaping of the boundaries of democratic politics' (Bauböck 1997: 8), liberal citizenship still presupposes the state, which grants citizenship rights.

The situation that therefore confronts citizenship, in either its liberal or civic republican formulations, shows that there is a need to revise the underlying premises of the concept. Moving beyond the remit of the nation state and privileging human rights, basic and all-inclusive rights, is seen by some to address the problems currently facing citizenship. The third section of the chapter thus concentrates on and examines the argument that privileges human rights in the belief that they address the problems currently confronting citizenship.

The argument that privileges human rights

In order to explore the argument that privileges human rights, this section focuses on the writings of Held, Bohman and Benhabib, who unite around their deliberative approach to democratic politics.[7] Influenced by the work of Jürgen Habermas, all three authors suggest that a deliberative account of democracy that gives centre stage to processes of communication, to public exchanges of reason, could apply to settings other than the nation state. This is partly because rational exchanges presuppose neither national nor territorial borders. But it is also because public reasoning is *eo ipso* empowering. Public reasoning could serve as a means for challenging relations of domination, according to Bohman. It involves justifying exclusions, according to Benhabib. And is the vehicle for promoting legitimacy in institutions of global governance, according to Held. More notably, public expressions of reason promise an intersubjective agreement on the terms of democratic cooperation beyond nation state borders. Notwithstanding their significant differences and disagreements about (global) democracy, therefore, Held, Bohman and Benhabib agree that public reasoning, by virtue of its inclusivity, potential for empowerment and intersubjective results, holds the key to reinvigorating democratic practice. This is one marker of the deliberative approach to a global or transnational democracy.

The second marker of deliberative proposals for universal democratisation is that they have a strong proceduralist orientation. Institutionalised processes of deliberation, impartial and all-inclusive, conducted at diverse levels and settings, are seen to consolidate democratic practice by facilitating global decision-taking and agreements about common concerns. Moreover, according to Held, Bohman and Benhabib, a cosmopolitan framework of law secures both justice and democracy. This is because law and democracy are co-original, as we have seen Habermas to be arguing: processes of deliberation (democracy) give birth to constitutional principles (basic legal rights) and constitutional principles (the legal system) entrench such processes of deliberation (democracy). The implicit and sometimes explicit endorsement of the co-originality thesis provides the third marker of the deliberative approach to a global or transnational democracy. It leads Held, Bohman and Benhabib to recast citizenship in very similar terms – that is, to retain citizenship as a notion, yet paradoxically to dissolve it into those legally codified human rights with which it is co-original – precisely because, as discussed below, they disentangle citizenship from dynamics of exclusion.

Of course, the perspectives of these authors differ with respect to the suggestions they make. While Held speaks of a global citizenship, which denotes the idea that self-determined citizens deliberate at a variety of settings for issues directly affecting their lives, Bohman and Benhabib disagree with the idea of a global *demos* and suggest that we renegotiate inclusions and exclusions through processes of democratic iteration (Benhabib) or through the formation of transnational *demoi* (Bohman). But what are the concrete suggestions that the three authors make, leading us to argue that they end up identifying citizenship with human rights? While the rest of this section delves into their conception of citizenship with the aim of showing that, despite claims to the contrary, they all envision it in universal terms, the last section of the chapter demonstrates why this all-inclusive conception of citizenship lapses into human rights.

David Held's notion of global citizenship

Held's conception of global citizenship comes as part of his project for a cosmopolitan or global social democracy, which aims at recovering legitimacy in institutions of global governance in which participation, transparency and accountability are often seen to be lacking (1995, 2004). Aligned, therefore, to his proposals for further institutionalisation and a cosmopolitan framework of law, citizenship plays a central role in his project as a means to securing democratic legitimacy. How then does Held approach citizenship?

On the surface, there is little doubt that citizenship, which Held understands both as rights and participation, becomes dissociated from dynamics of national and territorial exclusion. This is besides what the cosmopolitan model of democracy promotes: deliberations open to all, in a variety of settings. On closer inspection, however, we notice that Held in fact employs three different, yet interrelated, conceptions of citizenship.[8] On the one hand, he speaks explicitly of a global citizenship, a new conception that reconfigures democratic practice in the face of growing interdependence. A global citizenship, *pace* nation state citizenship, is 'built on the fundamental rights and duties of all human beings . . . recognising their capacity for self governance at all levels of human affairs' (2004: 115). It follows that a global citizenship, which draws on common humanity, unavoidably subsumes the member/non-member distinction characteristic of democratic practice.

On the other hand, however, Held is more ambivalent about approaching citizenship in universal terms; rather, he speaks of empowering rights, which provide for equality of status and, in effect, for equality of deliberation (1995: 222–223). According to Held, empowering rights can be identified neither with citizenship nor with human rights. While citizenship is no longer relevant because it remains confined to the nation state, human rights seen by some as Western constructs, give rise to disagreements over their exact content and definition. Empowering rights by contrast, argues Held, are not necessarily tied to the nation state and do not make any claim to universality, but to democracy. Here, we notice that Held refrains from using the term 'citizenship'. Sensitive to citizenship's historical link to the nation state, he settles with the notion of empowering rights. However, on a third level, Held is unwilling even to concede as much as the idea of empowering rights concedes. Instead, he speaks of multilevel or multiple citizenships, which, in the light of 'overlapping communities of fate', develop along with nation state citizenship. 'People would come to enjoy multiple citizenships', he says – that is, 'political membership in the diverse political communities which significantly affected them' (1995: 233).

If we now look closely at these related accounts, we could delimit the three minimum features of Held's approach to citizenship: first, it denotes the autonomy and equal status of each and every human being; second, it is a process of deliberation, a participatory activity enabling citizens to exchange reasons for (global) issues affecting their lives; and third, it is not exclusively tied to the nation state. In a nutshell, citizenship is construed in Held's account as an all-inclusive notion: all-inclusive in terms of who participates (all autonomous agents), where they participate (in different arenas) and how they participate (under a cosmopolitan framework of law that secures autonomy and impartiality). In Held's words:

> The new conception of citizenship is based on general rules and principles . . . [Its] meaning shifts from membership in a community which bestows, for those who qualify, particular rights and duties, to an alternative principle of world order in which all persons have equivalent rights and duties in the cross cutting spheres which affect their vital needs and interests.
>
> (2004: 114)

Although it could be objected that Held's conception of global citizenship, in so far as it coexists with and adds to nation state citizenship, does not directly entail universal inclusion, we could argue that this appears to be the case only in the short or medium terms. In the long term, Held does anticipate, as the last citation clearly indicates, that a global citizenship would override exclusive democratic practices. But is a global, all-inclusive, citizenship possible?

Seyla Benhabib's case for democratic iterations

In her latest effort to rethink political membership in the face of transnational migration and a multicultural politics, Seyla Benhabib astutely points out that democracies require borders and thus relations of both inclusion and exclusion (2006: 33). This is partly because democratic legitimacy presupposes representation of a specific people and accountability to a specific constituency. But it is also because the tension between the practices of the particular *demos* and cosmopolitan norms, such as human rights principles, is not something that we could do away with, according to Benhabib, but is constitutive of liberal democracies. Rather than developing therefore the idea of a global *demos*, which by implication undermines that which is constitutive of liberal democratic politics – the tension between sovereign self-determination and universal norms – Benhabib suggests that, through democratic iterations, we can renegotiate relations of inclusion and exclusion, and thus mitigate the tension between the two.

At its most basic, the idea of democratic iterations denotes that deliberations,[9] which require that participants give justifications for exclusions, open the way for the *demos* to reiterate the conditions for just membership. Benhabib explains:

> Democratic iterations are linguistic, legal, cultural and political repetitions in transformation, invocations that are also revocations. They not only change established understandings but also transform what passes as valid or authoritative precedent ... [By engaging therefore in such processes] a democratic people, which considers itself bound by certain guiding norms and privileges, reappropriates and reinterprets these.
>
> (2006: 49–50)

What Benhabib suggests therefore is that, through processes of democratic iteration, the citizenry progressively revises relations of inclusion and exclusion. More importantly, she expounds that, through rational argumentation in acts of democratic iterations, new norms emerge with respect to nation state practices and these new (universal) norms would be incorporated into democratic processes of will formation, thereby acquiring positive legal status. In this way, the spread of cosmopolitan norms, all the more prominent today, comes to be reconciled with popular sovereignty. No longer referring 'to the physical presence of a people gathered in a delimited territory', popular sovereignty would now refer to 'the interlocking in the global public sphere of the many processes of democratic iteration in which peoples learn from one another' (2007: 32).

Certainly, Benhabib does not seem, in the first instance, to reassert citizenship, the vehicle of democratic politics, in all-inclusive terms. A tension in her argument, however, reveals that she actually does. The tension surfaces once we consider that while democratic iterations uphold the idea of the citizenry, which decides on its own affairs, they *necessarily* lead to, if not presuppose, revision of (exclusive) practices and legalisation of human rights norms – otherwise, they would be short of 'iterations' in the Derridean sense that Benhabib uses. But if the point of democratic iterations is to renegotiate and revise exclusive nation state practices, so to reconcile cosmopolitan norms with particular politics, then their *implication* is that the citizenry, which iterates such potentially universal norms, comes unavoidably to embrace everyone. Because if the citizenry were not to embrace all human beings who are of equal moral worth, then there would be little point in processes of democratic iteration. Since Benhabib does not, therefore, justify why the second or third-generation citizenry that comes into being *after* iterative acts have taken place is not all-inclusive, we are led to the conclusion that Benhabib does embrace, if not anticipate, the possibility of a universal citizenry. What, however, for Benhabib is only an implicit suggestion, for Bohman appears to be the objective, as the following passages demonstrate.

James Bohman's transnational democracy of demoi

In his latest work, *Democracy Across Borders: From Demos to Demoi*, James Bohman, much like Held and Benhabib, attempts to reconfigure democratic practice in the wake of a changed political landscape. Like Held, Bohman places emphasis on deliberations in settings and arenas across state borders. And like Benhabib, he resists the idea of universal inclusion, of a global *demos*, on the grounds that the tension between universal norms and particular politics is constitutive of modern democracy. These two premises, which inform Bohman's proposal for a transnational democracy, lead him to suggest that we retain the idea of the *demos*, yet we reconceptualise it in the plural, as *demoi* engaged in democratic deliberations across state borders. Moreover, what further distinguishes Bohman's position from Held's and Benhabib's is that he grounds his suggestion for a transnational democracy of *demoi* in the republican ideal of non-domination – rather than self-determination. To have non-domination, he says, 'is to have a particular kind of normative status, a status allowing one to create and regulate obligations with others. This is the status of being a citizen. It is a status of non domination rather than self legislation; it is to be not ruled by others' (2007: 9).

It follows that, for Bohman, citizenship plays a pivotal role in his account of transnational democracy. Understood as the capacity to deliberate, citizenship is precisely that primary status which enables and empowers collectivities to challenge relations of domination. This is partly because communicative freedom, which citizenship embodies and secures, is the most pertinent means available to individuals to expose their rule by another. But it is also partly because the political right to initiate deliberation denotes the democratic minimum necessary for global democratisation, according to Bohman. As he puts it, 'the democratic minimum permits meaningful political activity to emerge, since it attributes to each citizen the capacity to initiate deliberation and thus to take up the common activity of deliberating about common concerns' (2007: 47). By thus tying citizenship with the democratic minimum, Bohman is able to sustain and defend the idea of cross-border democratic practices. Yet if Bohman valorises citizenship in *demoi*, on the grounds that it is that basic, minimal, status guarding against instances of domination, all the more possible in the context of an interconnected world, then how exactly does he reformulate the concept in universal terms, as this chapter suggests?

In order to dissociate citizenship from the nation state, and thus from dynamics of national and territorial exclusion that today appear problematic, Bohman anchors citizenship in the human political community. Humanity, *pace* nation state membership, carries several advantages for Bohman. In representing the perspective of the 'generalised other', humanity emerges as the horizon against which we test (and change) exclusive norms and practices. By virtue of its magnitude therefore, humanity appears to be a more relevant anchoring point than state membership in challenging relations of domination. At the same time, humanity, far from being an individualistic notion, secures the solidarity necessary for politics. This is because Bohman understands humanity in a way that implies a relation to others. He understands it as a 'second person', rather than 'first person', status. And 'when taken as a second person status, humanity', says Bohman, 'captures the strong connection between rights and political status in a just political community called to be responsive to claims of justice and injustice' (2007: 108). Notably, therefore, humanity denotes a political community, because it is the addressee of claims to justice – a point that reveals that justice and democracy are, for Bohman, co-original, 'one cannot be realised without the other' (2007: 38). Consequently, by anchoring citizenship in humanity on the presupposition that (political) humanity directly enlarges the scope of political practice, Bohman ensures that he reformulates both citizenship (in more inclusive terms) and human rights (as something more than an individualistic inscription). Of course, the question that arises at this point is what exactly is left from citizenship. Because is it not the case that, by so recasting citizenship, we end up privileging human rights? The following section addresses this question.

Privileging human rights?

Human rights are different from citizenship. Human rights, according to Delanty:

> ... are based on an ethical and legal concept of the individual; citizenship is based on a political and legal understanding of the individual. They share a legal conception of the individual but differ with respect to their universality. Human rights are basic ... rights that all individuals enjoy by virtue of their common humanity, whereas citizenship is specific to the members of a particular community.
>
> (2000: 69)

Five basic differences can thus be delineated between citizenship and human rights. Although these differences are familiar to us from the first chapter, it is worth briefly recalling them here. First, whereas human rights pertain to all human beings irrespective of membership in a political community, citizenship is accorded exclusively to the members of nationally and territorially delimited communities. Second, while human rights are conceived as universal, citizenship is particular because the rights and privileges it confers remain confined within particular nation states.[10] Third, and notwithstanding the political role that human rights often take on, they are, in principle, moral and legal rights. As Habermas notes:

> Human rights are Janus-faced, looking simultaneously toward morality and the law. Like moral norms, they refer to every creature 'that bears a human face', but as legal norms they protect individual persons only insofar as the latter belong to a particular legal community.
>
> (2001: 118)

Citizenship, by contrast, has, as we have already seen in the previous chapter, strictly political connotations. It is the primary political means embodying democratic self-determination. Fourth, while citizenship is exclusively granted by states, human rights override the capacity of states once 'protection is their prime function' (Heater 1999: 160). Finally, whereas human rights are often viewed as passive rights, by virtue of their protective function, citizenship is viewed as a dynamic set of entitlements that could be exercised.

In the light, therefore, of these five differences between citizenship and human rights, it becomes apparent that, by envisioning democratic practice in universal terms, Held, Bohman and Benhabib risk effacing citizenship's distinctiveness and identifying it with human rights. All the indications are here: a citizenship that pertains to all human beings by virtue of their deliberating capacity would negate national and territorial boundedness and overrule exclusions (difference one). It will certainly be a universal principle, designating the democratic minimum, as Bohman astutely argues (difference two). Moreover, a universal citizenship will principally involve and encourage further legalisation – the cosmopolitan framework of law that Held, for example, privileges – on the grounds that law *pace* particular politics is consensual, rational and inclusive, and therefore suitable as a vehicle for global democratisation (difference three). And a universal citizenship will, inevitably, override the capacity of states (difference four). Finally, given that human rights are, as we have seen, increasingly viewed as dynamic and empowering in the light of their consolidation in international law, it becomes apparent that a citizenship that takes on human rights' universality[11] would be, as Held, Bohman and Benhabib anticipate, a dynamic notion (difference five).

Yet an objection arises at this point. If we are, in the first instance, correct in our suggestion that a universal citizenship collapses into human rights, then why do Held, Bohman and Benhabib retain the term 'citizenship', resisting to recast democratic practice in human rights terms? To be sure, within the literature there have been such arguments, notably Goodhart's, which claim that, in the face of a global politics, we should reconceive democracy in terms of human rights (2005). Or Brysk and Shafir express the hope, in their article for *Citizenship Studies*, that human rights could perhaps be eventually transformed into citizenship (2006). Why is this not the case with the three authors examined here? To address this question, we need to return to the emphasis that Held, Bohman and Benhabib place on deliberation. For it is their deliberative approach to democratic practice that provides us with cues as to how exactly they end up identifying citizenship with human rights.

Two underlying assumptions of the deliberative perspective that we have already examined are relevant for us here. The first is that a procedural understanding of democratic practice, which gives centre stage to public reasoning, could secure global democratisation – since, as we have seen, public reasoning is inclusive and empowering. The second assumption is that human rights, which entrench processes of democratic deliberation, cofound the democratic order with citizenship. Both of these assumptions, we are now in a position to show, lead Held, Bohman and Benhabib to effect the same theoretical move: first, to empty citizenship of all substantive bonds, by identifying it with public exchanges of reason – a necessary step in the process of dissociating the concept from the exclusive nation state politics that today appear problematic; and then to embrace the prospect of such a minimal citizenship that differs little from human rights, on the implicit presupposition that human rights that co-found the democratic order could come to reinvigorate it. For example, this seems clearly to be the case with Bohman, who ultimately privileges human rights when he argues that citizenship, understood minimally as the status that secures the right to initiate deliberation, could, now that nation state politics appear problematic, be anchored in humanity, precisely because humanity is political (and thus co-original with citizenship).

Likewise, something similar could be shown in the case of Benhabib, whose deliberative approach leads her to privilege human rights at two circular moments. First, at the moment of democratic will formation when she identifies democratic practice with rational revisions of established norms, reserving thereby nothing distinctive that this conception of citizenship can lay claim to and nothing that human rights cannot secure.[12] This suggestion appears likely when we recall that popular sovereignty, for Benhabib, no longer refers to the actions of a particular *demos*, but to 'interlocking processes in which *peoples* learn from one another' (2007: 32). Second, we might suggest that Benhabib privileges human rights at the moment of will crystallisation, when peoples 'open to learn from one another' become rationally convinced to iterate new, more inclusive norms. At this moment, human rights *could* again be taking priority over citizenship, precisely because nation state citizenship appears problematic while universal human rights, which cofound the democratic order, appear more relevant and compelling.

Similarly, Held's conception of citizenship, which denotes that self-reflecting individuals would rationally deliberate and decide for those (global) affairs impacting on their lives, could also easily lead to an argument that privileges human rights. For why could basic human rights, which valorise common reason among other humane properties, not secure public exchanges of reason at the global level – which is how Held defines citizenship? The point, therefore, is not that Held implicitly envisions human rights as the main principle of politics, nor that he simply effaces the difference between citizenship and human rights, and identifies the former with the latter; rather, it is that his conception of citizenship is, like Bohman's and Benhabib's, so minimal that human rights *could* assume its role.

To return therefore to the question posed earlier in the section – namely, why citizenship is still used as a term – we can now explain that this is because Held, Bohman and Benhabib understand democracy in very specific terms. By postulating that democratic practice involves procedural exchanges of (an intersubjective) reason, which secures legitimacy (Held), tackles exclusions (Benhabib) and challenges relations of domination (Bohman), they are able to retain citizenship as a term, yet approach it so indistinctively that it *could* be identified with human rights. Of course, this is not to say that the deliberative understanding of democracy leads one to undermine citizenship and privilege human rights; rather, it is to say that, *when* applied to the case of a problematic nation state citizenship, such an understanding of democracy is likely to lead to arguments that end up shadowing citizenship with human rights.

But a question arises at this point: what is the problem with arguments that identify citizenship with human rights? There are two conceptual difficulties with such arguments. The first difficulty surfaces when we consider that neither Held nor Benhabib, for example, clearly explain *why* exactly individuals would deliberate at the global level (Held) or why they would iterate cosmopolitan norms (Benhabib). Although common reason dictates so, surely rationality could not be enough for grounding participation at levels other than the state, or promoting legitimacy. Might it not, therefore, be the case that democratic practice, at the global age to be certain, requires something more, some sort of *common* allegiance? This brings us to the second difficulty confronting deliberative arguments that appear to privilege human rights. Envisaging citizenship in universal terms is possible, theoretically, only if we play down the need for a collective 'we consciousness', democratic unity, or what Habermas calls 'civic solidarity' (2006: 139). Curiously, both Held and Benhabib do not explore this in detail. Although Bohman appears, in contrast, to recognise this need for 'civic solidarity' when he reconceives humanity as a second-person status, we could question whether humanity could engender the type of solidarity that drives democratic participation.[13] Thus the following question arises at this point: can human rights actually take us out of the problems currently confronting citizenship? The next chapter addresses this question.

Chapter 3

The illusive promise of human rights

The aim of this chapter is to examine whether human rights, which presuppose neither national nor territorial membership, could in fact take us out of the problems confronting citizenship. To this aim, the chapter engages in a theoretical investigation by enquiring into the notion of human rights: first, it problematises the type of subject, which human rights presuppose; second, it explores whether human rights could, by virtue of their legal codification, be privileged over citizenship. In differing respects, this is the view that Held, Bohman and Benhabib express in the light of their deliberative understanding of democratic politics that reconciles political participation with law. By viewing democracy in deliberative terms, we have argued in the previous chapter, all three authors are led to privilege human rights on the presupposition that, as legal rights that are co-original with citizenship, they could reinvigorate democratic practice in the face of the problems currently confronting it. The chapter takes issue with this view and argues that as a rights and legalistic discourse, human rights are paradoxical means for making politics – if they are privileged, of course, over citizenship. Moreover, and by virtue of the type of subject that they presuppose, human rights appear to be inherently limited. They cannot therefore simply take on the political function of citizenship.

This two-sided argument is made from a Lacanian standpoint. Although Lacan does not write explicitly about human rights, his account of subjectivity provides us with a vantage point for demonstrating the limitations of the type of subject that human rights presuppose. This is first a transparent subject. Donnelly explains:

> Human rights are *equal* rights: one either is or is not a human being, and therefore has the same human rights as everyone else (or none at all). They are also *inalienable* rights: one cannot stop being human, no matter how badly one behaves nor how barbarously one is treated. And they are *universal* rights, in the sense that today we consider all members of the species Homo sapiens 'human beings', and thus holders of human rights.
> (2003: 1)

Everyone therefore transparently human is entitled to protection by right, irrespective of his/her national or territorial membership. At the same time, it is not only that the human subject is transparent, according at least to the human rights literature, but it is also fixed around certain Enlightenment presuppositions of what exactly it means to be a human being. Panikkar[1] delineates four such presuppositions: (i) rationality (that there is a universal human nature that can be known by rational means[2]); (ii) superiority (that human nature is essentially different from and higher than the rest of reality[3]); (iii) dignity (that the individual has an absolute and irreducible dignity that must be defended against society or the state[4]); and (iv) autonomy (the autonomy of the individual requires that society be organised in a non-hierarchical way, as a sum of free individuals[5]). As an example, consider here how Held and Benhabib, for example, draw implicitly in these Enlightenment presuppositions when they ground political participation in the inherent rationality and autonomy of individual agents. Further, and in the light of these Enlightenment presuppositions, it appears that the subject that human rights presuppose is unified and centred. Rationality, dignity, autonomy and superiority combine and make him/her a specifically human subject. They provide him/her with an identity that is united and consistent. At the same time, they make its inner core the centre around which this identity revolves. The inner core of humanness, of dignity, rationality, superiority and autonomy, is what human rights are called on to protect. This is also what Lacan precisely questions. By demonstrating that this fixed and centred subject is unavailable, by revealing, that is, that the rational, autonomous, dignified and superior subject is 'not there', he provides us with some insight to problematise the notion of human rights.

The Lacanian perspective is explained in the first section of the chapter. In the second section, we look at the psychoanalytically informed argument of Douzinas and draw explicitly the implications of Lacanian psychoanalysis for human rights. Douzinas' argument is interesting because it brings into focus the fantasy scenario that legally codified human rights bring into play, their role in sustaining the desire for a whole and complete legal system. By thus stressing the incompleteness and subjecting aspect of law, Douzinas' account enables us to justify why the problems currently confronting citizenship cannot be resolved through legally codified human rights. The second section concludes by suggesting that a shift to law, to human rights codification, as a means for addressing political issues such as those facing nation state citizenship, can have negative repercussions for democracy – a point that later chapters explore in more detail.

The Lacanian perspective on subjects and rights

Copjec's comment gives us a first insight into the Lacanian approach that we here use to problematise the notion human rights. 'For Lacan,' notes Copjec, 'no position defines a resolute identity. Non-knowledge or invisibility is not registered as the wavering and negotiations between two certainties, two meanings or positions, but as the undermining of every certainty, the incompleteness of every meaning and position' (1994: 18). To explain therefore this Lacanian approach, which, as we see here, denies the possibility of a resolute identity, we need to start by noting that, for Lacan, human experience unfolds along two registers: the imaginary and the symbolic. But what exactly happens in these two registers leading Lacan to argue that human subjectivity is uncertain and unavailable? The register of the imaginary comes first.

The register of the imaginary

The imaginary level consists in the mirror stage. This refers to the period between the 6th and 18th month of an infant's life, during which the self perceives itself for the first time as an image in the mirror. The mirror image represents the infant as a total and unified entity. By identifying with it, the self experiences its first sense of totality, of identity. It is formed as an ego, according to Lacan. Stavrakakis explains:

> [B]efore this phase the self as such, as a unified whole, does not exist. In the mirror stage . . . the fragmentation experienced by the infant is transformed into an affirmation of its bodily unity through the assumption of its image in the mirror. This is how the infant acquires its first sense of unity and identity, a spatial imaginary identity.
>
> (1999: 17)

Two indications as to the challenge that Lacanian psychoanalysis poses to the subject of human rights come herein to the fore. The first concerns the fact that, for Lacan, identity is spatial and imaginary, as Stavrakakis puts it. It emerges at the mirror stage and is not something already pre-given, total and unified, as proclaimed by human rights. Whereas the latter emerge as the means protecting the immutable and thereby superior identity of humans, Lacan's mirror stage opens us to the possibility that this identity might be constructed and imaginary. The second challenge refers to the differentiation between the ego and the subject, a necessary first point to note about Lacan and psychoanalysis in general. To understand what this move amounts to for human rights, we need to reflect on the Freudian discovery of the unconscious. By distinguishing between the unconscious, which obeys its own laws, and the conscious ego, which is being subverted by the repressed desires and functionings of the unconscious, Freud decentred subjectivity. In Lacan's words: 'Freud suggested that the very centre of the human being was no longer to be found in that place assigned to it by a whole humanist tradition' (cited in Dufresne 1997: 8). This is the place of consciousness, of transparency and fixity of identity.

Frosh explains further:

> The view that each individual possesses a fundamental core of selfhood from which all her/his attributes arise is a dominating notion in Western perceptions of what constitutes basic humanity. In a general way, it is reflected in the philosophy of the 'cogito' ('I think therefore I am') that at the centre of being is a rational source of meanings (wishes, desires, attributes, etc.) . . . It is precisely in challenging this notion of the existence within each of us of a central, directing consciousness that the psychoanalytic revolution inheres. Freud's formulation of the unconscious makes all human behaviour and experience comprehensible only through reference to 'another site' than consciousness.
>
> (1987: 85)

Since the subject that human rights presuppose seems to be reduced to the 'cogito', at least in the writings of Held, Bohman and Benhabib – that is, to the rational and autonomous individual identified with his/her ego – it is being challenged by psychoanalysis. In fact, as Stavrakakis notes, 'it is the subversion of the subject as cogito which makes psychoanalysis possible: psychoanalysis opposes any philosophy issuing directly from the cogito' (1999: 15). In pursuing further, therefore, and radicalising the Freudian insight into the subversive laws of the unconscious, Lacan shows us a subject that can neither be pinned down nor reduced to consciousness. Rather, it first emerges as an imaginary ego, at the mirror stage, and then as a split subject, at the register of the symbolic. In exploring further these two challenges, the section draws the implications of the Lacanian 'ego' for the human rights idea.

In particular, the notion of the 'ego' that Lacan says develops at the mirror stage is traced back to Freud. This is a point to which we have already referred. Freud distinguishes between three parts of the human experience: the id, which refers to the unconscious and follows the pleasure principle, which seeks to avoid pain; the ego, which represents consciousness and functions in accordance with the reality principle, the principle of common sense; and the super-ego, which consists in an ensemble of idealised images to which the subject attempts to conform. For Freud, the ego, which he conceives as an active agency representing reality, 'is closely connected with the organisation of perception since it first develops as a result of stimuli from the external world impinging upon the senses . . . it depends upon the perception of one's own body as a separate entity' (Storr 2001: 62). For Lacan, the ego, which is also related to perception, constitutes an object of illusory mastery. It is an imaginary and alienating alter ego. It is imaginary because its constitution depends on an external, mirror image. It is alienating because it is a reflected image with which the ego will never coincide. An insight into the phases of the mirror stage elucidates the imaginary and alienating character of the ego.

In the process of ego formation, says Lacan, the self experiences a diversity of feelings. These range from jubilation and insufficiency to fragmentation and alienation. Or, as he puts it:

> [T]he mirror stage is a drama whose internal thrust is precipitated from insufficiency to anticipation – and which manufactures for the subject, caught up in the lure of spatial identification, the succession of fantasies that extends from a fragmented body-image to a form of its totality that I shall call orthopaedic – and, lastly, to the assumption of the armour of an alienating identity, which will mark with its rigid structure the subject's entire mental development. Thus to break out of the circle of the Innenwelt into the Umwelt generates the inexhaustible quadrature of the ego's verifications.
>
> (2001: 5)

Specifically, in seeing herself in the mirror for the first time, the infant feels joy and jubilation. Because she realises that the image therein, which moves whenever she does, is hers, the infant experiences joy. This is the self's first sense of unity and identity. Then jubilation gives way to a feeling of insufficiency and fragmentation. Insufficiency commences the moment that the infant acknowledges that what it sees is only an image, an exteriority, or Gestalt, which cannot really touch, master or reproduce herself – she depends on others, for example, for reproducing the experience. Due to her sensory motor development, moreover, which precedes her bodily integrity, she realises that what she sees in the mirror is only a fragmented and uncoordinated 'version' of herself. When compared to the image of the (m)other next to her, the infant is not a 'whole' self. A feeling of alienation therefore ensues. Benvenuto and Kennedy explain:

> There is a fundamental alienation in this act. The infant's master is in the mirror image, outside herself, while she is not really master of her movements. She only sees her form as more or less total and unified in an external image, in a virtual, alienated, ideal unity that cannot actually be touched. Alienation is this lack of being by which her realisation lies in another actual or imaginary space.
>
> (1986: 55)

The infant feels alienated because it realises its incompleteness, the fact that it is neither a total nor a unified entity. In effect, it anticipates the moment that it will be an 'I'. For Lacan, however, as we will shortly see, the 'I', although precipitated, can never be complete and total.

Stavrakakis suggests that the Lacanian ego 'can only be described as a sedimentation of idealised images which are internalised during the mirror stage' (1999: 17). It is neither fixed nor pre-given; rather, it is a construction:

. . . a kind of 'not me' which is obliged to conform to a 'me' in order to attain self-consciousness, but which at the same time seems to disappear or at least to be misunderstood ('meconnaissance) in this very process of objectification.

(Nobus 1999: 118)

What are the implications of this Lacanian ego for the subject underpinning human rights? To address this question, we need to recall the type of subject that, at the beginning of the chapter, we suggested human rights presuppose – namely, the rational, autonomous, dignified and superior agent. The Lacanian conception of subjectivity challenges each one of these properties of selfhood. In contrast to the rational subject who, by virtue of its capacity for reason, accurately reflects the structures of its mind and the world, Lacan brings to the fore the imaginary subject. Although the ego appears to be thinking rationally when it realises that its image is fragmented and uncoordinated, it is not rationality that sanctions existence for Lacan, but imagination. The ego is constituted by the image and not the other way around. Nobus explains:

Claiming that the Gestalt is constituted by the child would presuppose that it functions ab initio as a relatively integrated agency, which is exactly what Lacan wanted to counter. To Lacan, relative integration (in the form of a 'me') was an effect rather than a cause of the mirror stage.

(1999: 114–115)

Of course, this Lacanian insight into the formation of the supposedly rational subject carries some implications for the arguments of Held, Bohman and Benhabib. It reveals that the type of self-deliberating individuals they talk about, the inherently rational beings, who see advantages in (re)iterating and codifying cosmopolitan norms (Benhabib) or exercising their rights at the global level (Held), are not available. Lacan demonstrates, moreover, that the inherent autonomy, which these subjects are seen to practise, is unattainable. The ego imagines but does not actually attain its autonomy. It anticipates the moment that it will no longer be dependent on others for the repetition of the mirror experience, the moment when its Gestalt will be truly its own and its identity complete and distinct. Yet this moment remains imagined, alienating and anticipated. According to Lacan, the self can never be fully and completely individuated, he/she can never display an autonomous identity; rather, its only experience of selfhood consists in acts of identification, which strongly depend on its social surroundings.

Acts of identification that, as we will later see, continue at the register of the symbolic are already considered important at the imaginary level. They are instrumental to the ego's first sense of 'identity', of unity and wholeness. Because the infant identifies with an external object, the mirror image, which it compares with the image of the others surrounding it, acts of identification are both socially mediated and alienating. Their social dimension is explained by the fact that they always take place within a social context – the infant depends on others for the experience at the mirror stage but also identifies with others. Because the image of the other with whom the infant identifies is complete and different from that of its own, imaginary identifications are, however, alienating. They posit the ego in a state of permanent conflict with its social surroundings, since, as Nobus elaborates, 'apart from a "me", the mirror image also installs a rival other, on whom one can never steal a march and whose good looks are often discordant with one's own feelings of discomfort' (1999: 113). A state of permanent conflict, therefore, and sociality, as conceptualised at the mirror stage, are the two Lacanian insights that do not only challenge the notion of the inherently autonomous subject of human rights, as argued by Held for example, but also attest to the constitutivity of both conflict and a *topos* for subjects. Indeed, what is considered the stuff of a problematic citizenship, exclusion and the territorial state, are, according to Lacan, the permanent features of subjectivity. He shows us that a rationally constructed and harmoniously reached agreement with others, the alternative, which theorists of deliberative democracy suggest, cannot be realised.

Further, Lacan demonstrates that if the self is neither inherently rational nor autonomous, it can also not originate. Instead of being a transparently superior and fixed entity, the subject on which human rights are based is always on the making, anticipated and imagined. But if the subject is always on the making, how can it be said to be inalienably dignified? The Lacanian ego neither has nor has not a dignified essence. The idea of dignity central to the human rights discourse is perhaps the effect of something external, not something naturally pertaining to human beings. Because Lacan empties the subject of all essence, he hints to the idea that both its dignity and superiority are constructed. In contrast therefore with the idea of the subject as unified and centred, as an individual agent with a fixed identity and a core of selfhood consisting in all of its specifically humane properties – rationality, autonomy, dignity and superiority – Lacan's mirror stage brings to the fore a 'disunited' and decentred ego. For Lacan, it is an anticipated but never achieved unity. Although the ego identifies with others and/or objects, it does not and cannot attain a full and complete identity. It is, moreover, a decentred ego in the sense of being insufficiently individuated – that is, an ego that does not revolve and, as we will see, will never revolve around an essential centre, a core of humanness.

What we should therefore keep from the Lacanian mirror stage is that the fixed and transparent subject, which human rights presuppose, is shown to be an illusory ideal, an object of imaginary mastery. It is a subject that, although not 'dead', it is never complete. Although it always anticipates, it does not achieve totality and unity. In the light therefore of this type of subject, are human rights an adequate substitute to citizenship, to its political function? The following section continues with the ways in which Lacan problematises the idea that the subject has an identity. It focuses on the account he gives of the subject as this becomes constituted at the register of the symbolic.

The register of the symbolic

We concluded the foregoing passages by arguing that the ego, which emerges at the mirror stage, is an object of imaginary mastery, an incomplete and therefore alienated ego, which anticipates the moment of its completeness. This moment, however, is not part of the experience at the imaginary register. In search of totality and unity, the child enters the register of the symbolic. Lacan understands the symbolic as the field of linguistic representations. Language enables the subject to move away from the realm of illusions, the mirror stage, and to express concretely her thoughts and wishes. As Stavrakakis puts it, 'the symbolic "binds and orients", it gives consistency to the imaginary instances of human experience' (1999: 19). Therein, in the social dimension of language, emerges the Lacanian subject.

This is a subject that comes into existence precisely because of the symbolic order. Its reality is the reality of the symbolic order (Benvenuto and Kennedy 1986: 90). What Lacan means by this is that prior to the introduction of language, with which thinking and representation of wishes and desires begins, there is no existence. Both reality and existence are the effect of the order of linguistic representations that the child enters the moment she learns to speak. Fink explains that:

> What cannot be said in language is not part of reality; it does not exist, strictly speaking. In Lacan's terminology, existence is a product of language: language brings things into existence (makes them part of human reality) things which had no existence prior to being ciphered, symbolised or put into words.
>
> (1995: 25)

Might it not therefore be the case that human rights, which are purported to be the rights naturally pertaining to human beings, be the result of a linguistic construction? Lacan aims at demonstrating something more: the Spaltung that language introduces into the subject.

The idea of Spaltung is borrowed from Freud, for whom it expresses the split between the conscious and the unconscious. Lacan, who accepts this insight, makes Spaltung the general, defining feature of the subject. Entrance onto the symbolic involves both a gain and a loss for Lacan: although the subject gains her sense of subjectivity and reality, she emerges as forever split and alienated. She is split between her subjectivity and the discourse of the Other, the symbolic order, which pre-exists and constitutes her. A first challenge to the subject of human rights surfaces herein. The total and centred subject that human rights presuppose is exposed to be not a 'mirage' or unavailable, as was the case at the register of the imaginary, but as a 'fraud', to use Frosh's expression (1987: 137). It is both a split and an alienated subject. It is alienated because although it searches for totality and unity in language, it does not attain it. Alienation thereby does not wane at the register of the symbolic. In fact, as Fink notes, although it is 'the necessary "first step" in acceding to subjectivity, this step involves choosing one's disappearance' (1995: 51). Why? In order to understand how the subject 'disappears' under the laws of the symbolic, we need to shed light on its structure. In doing so, we are in better position to explain the challenge that the Lacanian conceptualisation of the subject poses to the notion of human rights.

In explaining the structure of the symbolic, Lacan turns to Saussurean linguistics. Language is made up of elements, signifiers (sounds-images) and signifieds (concepts), standing in a differential relation to one another. In contrast to Saussurean theory, however, which unites the signifier with the signified and says that they produce a 'sign', Lacan divides them. He prioritises the signifier over the signified (S/s) and argues that there is no 'sign', only signifiers. By forming chains of signification with one another, signifiers produce meaning in their very connections. They are, moreover, anchored in the unconscious, according to Lacan. Stavrakakis explains at length:

> In Lacan's schema, the signifier is not something which functions as a representation of the signified; nor is the meaning of the algorithm S/s that there is a parallelism between the two levels, between that of the signifier and that of the signified. Simply put, meaning is produced by signifiers; it springs from the signifier to the signified and not vice versa (as argued by realist representationalists). It is this idea that Lacan captures with his famous example of the toilet doors. In this case the signified – loosely defined as external reality – is the same – two identical doors presumably leading to two identical toilets. What creates the different meaning in each case, what creates the difference between the 'ladies' and the 'gentlemen's' toilet is the different signifier, that is to say the fact that each door carries a different label ('ladies' and 'gentlemen'). The signifier manifests the presence of difference and nothing else, making impossible any connection between signs and things. In other words, reference to signs implies a reference to things as guarantees of signification, something which Saussure himself was ultimately unable to avoid, while the notion of the primacy of the signifier breaks with such representationalist connotations.
>
> (1999: 25)

What does this mean for human rights?

Benhabib argues that all-inclusive rights, which protect and empower human beings, could be iterated and acquire positive legal status. Likewise, both Bohman and Held, who see nationality and territoriality as too restrictive in the face of global politics, suggest respectively either to anchor citizenship in humanity (Bohman) or to revision it in global terms (Held), making unclear its difference from human rights. Yet might it not be the case that the signifier (human rights) is all there is? That there is no signified (a core of humanity that can practise politics)? Of course, it can be objected that the same argument could also apply to citizenship. However, there is a potentially important difference that, although we will elaborate in a later chapter, it is necessary to indicate here. This is the following twofold idea: first, that citizenship is a dynamic concept, which is not permanently pinned down to a signified, an essentialised subjectivity. In fact, by virtue of its inclusion-exclusion dynamics, it can be depicted as the instantiation of the Lacanian signifier as such. Second, although as is presently conceptualised – that is, as either liberal or civic republican – citizenship appears to be problematic, neither of these accounts exhausts its potential. Human rights by contrast cannot move beyond the idea of the essentialised, fixed and transparent, subject. Perhaps this is their greatest asset. This makes them, however, a rather inadequate substitute to the political function of citizenship – a point that we will revisit in the last section of this chapter.

In returning therefore to the Lacanian conception of the signified, we see further implications for the human rights idea. 'What happens to the signified in the Lacanian schema?', asks Stavrakakis, explaining:

> Lacan understands the signified as an effect of transference. If we speak about the signified it is only because we like to believe in its existence. It is a belief crucial for our construction of reality as a coherent, 'objective' whole; a belief in something that guarantees the validity of our knowledge, sustaining the fantasy of an adaequatio between language and the world.
>
> (1999: 25)

Lacan situates the signified in the Real. This is the register that lies beyond the imaginary and the symbolic. It refers to that which resists symbolisation or, as Lacan puts it, 'the real is the impossible' (2001: xii), although in the order of the Real and thus impossible, the signified is being imagined through the interplay of signifiers. Applying this insight into the notion of human rights leads us to question the argument that suggests that they can take us out of the problems currently confronting nation state citizenship in the light of a postnational and deterritorialised politics. We make the following parallelism: the signifier (human rights) is what makes us imagine that there is a signified, a core of humanness, when in fact there is nothing, as such. The subject that human rights presuppose, the purportedly fixed and transparent human entity, always slips away and lies beyond symbolisation, in the Real.

On the one hand, this means that Lacan conceptualises the subject as the subject of the signifier. It emerges in the symbolic order, the order of the signifier, and signifiers are preponderant. There is no signified, for Lacan. On the other hand, arguing that there is no such thing as a 'concrete' subject, because it always slips away, means that Lacan 'hypothesises the subject – that is, he only ever supposes it' (Copjec: 1994: xi). Yet he does not erase it; rather, he reveals it to be the subject of a lack. Stavrakakis elucidates the Lacanian position on lack. '[T]his lack', he says:

> . . . can only be thought as a trace of the ineliminable act of power, at the root of the formation of subjectivity, as the trace of an *ex nihilo* decision entailing the loss of certain possibilities or psychic states (the imaginary relation with the mother for example) and the formation of new ones . . . The subject can only exist on the condition that it accepts the laws of the symbolic. It becomes an effect of the signifier. In that sense it is a certain subordination, an exercise of power that constitutes the condition of possibility for the constitution of subjectivity.
>
> (1999: 20)

In a certain respect, therefore, it is because it 'chooses' to abide by the laws of the symbolic order that it is the subject of a lack. These laws are represented by the Name-of-the-Father, a primary signifier, which the subject encounters upon its entrance onto the symbolic. In Lacan's words, 'it is in the Name-of-the-Father that we must recognise the support of the symbolic function which, from the dawn of history, has identified his person with the figure of law' (2001: 74) – the Name-of-the-Father that demands from the self to give up on its wholeness and totality in order to become a subject signifies the advent of the split and lack in subjectivity. But there is another aspect to this lack: a lack of jouissance.

'Jouissance' refers to the real enjoyment experienced prior to the introduction of the laws of the symbolic order. This 'real, pre-symbolic enjoyment' is only an ideal, however, because the wholeness and unity to which it refers – for example, the ideal of unity with the (m)Other – cannot be attained. The subject is split and permeated from the start by a constitutive lack. Jouissance moreover is also a social affair. Evans explains that what Lacan means by this is that it is:

> . . . impossible for us to conceive of enjoyment except in relation to a cultural Other. The phenomenon is thus intimately linked with another contemporary social phenomenon, namely multiculturalism. But as soon as we are forced to have recourse to the Other in order to mark the position of our own jouissance (a feature which is a fairly recent

development according to Lacan, suggesting that in previous historical epochs jouissance was enclosed in some kind of interiority, defined only in relationship to itself), a curious paradox results. On the one hand, we need to preserve the jouissance of the Other in order to be able to define our own; but on the other hand, we seek to destroy that Other enjoyment because we suspect it may be more superabundant than our own.

(1999: 20)

This insight can also be applied to human rights. In the previous chapter, we read Held, Bohman and Benhabib to be arguing in their different ways that the all-inclusive notion of humanity could take us out of the problems posed to national citizenship. Lacan, by contrast, shows us that the desire to destroy the Other's jouissance in order to preserve our own is always there. The tension between 'our' jouissance and 'theirs', which citizenship, in fact, connotes with reference to its dynamics of inclusion/exclusion, appears through the Lacanian lens to be constitutive. This is a point to which we will return and elaborate in greater detail in Chapter 5.

Meanwhile, on the subjective level, as we have already pointed out, jouissance can never be attained. It is a forbidden ideal because the Name-of-the-Father, the laws of the symbolic order, demands that we abandon totality and wholeness for the sake of subjectivity. Because jouissance, however, is lost/prohibited/impossible, desire emerges. According to Stavrakakis:

> Desire is the element that keeps everything going. It is animated by the quest for a lacking/impossible fullness around the promise of encountering jouissance – and jouissance always has the 'connotation of fullness'. Whenever we reach the object of our desire, any jouissance we get is nothing compared to what we were expecting . . . If no object can provide us with our lost/impossible jouissance, it follows that the fragile equilibrium of desire can only be maintained by the continuous displacement from object to object: strangely enough it is the prevention of jouissance that sustains desire as a promise to attain the mythical jouissance; if the realisation, the full satisfaction of desire is impossible, then the promise of this realisation becomes necessary; without it no desire can be sustained.

(1999: 45)

The advent of desire is therefore intimately related with the law of the symbolic order and can be loosely conceived as an effect of the signifier. Since the symbolic law, which institutes both the split and lack in the subject, prohibits jouissance, desire both aims at and is sustained by jouissance. It has no object of its own and is insatiable. It revolves moreover around the promise of unity and totality, and therefore relies on fantasy. Fantasy, as Žižek notes:

. . . is the very narrative of the primordial loss, since it stages the process of this renunciation, the emergence of law. In this precise sense, fantasy is the screen that separates desire from drive. It tells the story that allows the subject to (mis)perceive the void around which drive circulates as the primordial loss constitutive of desire. Or, to put it in yet another way: fantasy provides a rationale for the inherent deadlock of desire.

(1999: 209)

Because it therefore resorts to fantasy, the subject keeps desiring. Fantasy stages an imaginary scenario, it makes the subject imagine that its constitutive lack will be covered. It does so through the objet a.

On the one hand, the objet a, which derives from the field of fantasy, is what promises to cover over the lack in the subject, it is the object that causes desire. On the other hand, the objet a is a remnant of wholeness and unity, a remainder of the subject after it has entered the symbolic order. Fink explains:

The objet a can be understood as the remainder produced when the hypothetical unity breaks down, as a last trace of that unity, a last remainder thereof. By cleaving to that remainder the split subject, though expulsed from the Other, can sustain the illusion of wholeness; by clinging to objet a, the subject is able to ignore his/her division. That is precisely what Lacan means by fantasy.

(1995: 59)

Through the objet a, therefore, to which we will later see Douzinas liken human rights, the subject sustains its desire for an impossible jouissance. The desiring subject is Lacan's alternative to the cogito.

These Lacanian insights put into question the type of subject that human rights presuppose. By arguing for its split, prioritising the signifier and sanctioning desire, Lacan challenges both the idea of the rational agent, underpinning human rights and the notion of rationality as a whole. First, he disassembles the subject and shows us why the latter is not a pre-given rational entity. The fixed subject who, by virtue of its reason, accurately reflects on and constructs the structures of the world does not exist as such, says Lacan. Instead, we have a split subject determined by the order and rules of the signifier. Second, as the subject of the signifier, it always slips away. It can never be pinned down to an essence, let alone to a rational core, according to Lacan. The certainty of the cogito, 'I think therefore I am', is thereby shaken. Or as Benvenuto and Kennedy put it: 'Gone is the never ending quest for knowledge as such; instead, one is left with the available signifier, whose laws must be followed, if one is to uncover knowledge and discover meaning' (1986: 110–111). Third, by exposing it as a lacking and thus desiring subject, Lacan questions the centrality accorded to rationality. The subject exists and acts, he says, not because it rationally decides to, but because it has no other option but to obey the rules of its desire. This is, according to Frosh, 'one of the sources of the subversive impact of psychoanalysis: it overturns the western view that the distinguishing mark of humanity is reason and rationality . . . the true sources of being lie not in "cogito" but in desire' (1987: 25).

By tracing the 'sources of being in desire', Lacan challenges therefore the deliberative case for privileging human rights. He makes us think twice. Would these rights not be the result of a desire for something impossible, a forever harmonious and total coexistence – the result, in other words, of a desire for jouissance, which, as we have seen, always connotes the ideal of a lost/impossible fullness? The Lacanian conceptualisation of the subject challenges moreover the idea of the autonomous agent who engages in rational deliberations. In contrast, the subject that Lacan argues for is both split and socially determined. It is the subject constituted by the symbolic order, the field of linguistic and thus shared representations. As such, it is always socially determined, it depends on Other(s). The symbolic order however, the Other or the objective level, is also lacking according to Lacan. In Stavrakakis' words:

> If the subjective is no longer 'subjective', the objective is also no longer 'objective' in the sense of a closed structure, of an entity capable, under certain circumstances, of filling the lack in the subject. The field of representation is itself revealed as lacking because it attempts the impossible, that is to say, the representation of something ultimately unrepresentable. Representation is the representation of a real fullness, which is always beyond our grasp.
>
> (1999: 38)

But if the Other (the 'universal' with which Held and Bohman are concerned, for example) is shown to be lacking, how can the subject who is also lacking find therein a total and final solution to the problems confronting citizenship? The Lacanian perspective exposes this as an impossible ideal.

In conclusion therefore to this section, we need to keep the idea that the subject that Lacan brings to the fore is shown to have only a failed 'identity' – precarious, split and lacking – neither rational nor superior as the idea of human rights postulates. This subject, which in the final analysis is only being hypothesised, attempts to fill in its constitutive lack through acts of identification. Although these are always failing, because the objective level, as we saw, is also lacking, they are the subject's only option for precariously satisfying its desire for an impossible/lost unity. Identification (not identity) and lack (not totality) are therefore the Lacanian insights into the type of subject that human rights presuppose. These Lacanian insights expose moreover human rights as an inadequate alternative to citizenship. Human rights are inadequate, because the idea of prioritising the rights of a subject, which is in fact not there, cannot be seen as a solution to the problems that the nationally and territorially bound citizenship faces in the wake of deterritorialised issues and denationalised demands. The next section, which looks at Douzinas' psychoanalytically influenced account of human rights, reaches a similar conclusion. Douzinas, who focuses on and problematises the idea of legally codified human rights, justifies from an additional angle why such rights cannot take on the political function of citizenship.

Douzinas' psychoanalytically influenced account of human rights

In his paper 'Human Rights, Humanism and Desire', Douzinas takes issue with 'the unstoppable proliferation of human rights' (2001: 183) – that is, with their increasing codification and contextualisation in international law. Although in the previous chapter, the emphasis that Held, Bohman and Benhabib place on legalisation remained only implicit and secondary to the objective of showing how their deliberative approach to democracy leads them to privilege human rights, this emphasis has been ever-present. For Bohman, for example, common humanity, on which he anchors citizenship, is a political community in so far as it is the addressee of claims to justice – an idea that indicates that law is for him, as for Habermas, co-original with politics and therefore an alternative means to addressing political problems. At the same time, if we recall Benhabib's position, we notice that democratic iterations lead precisely to a jurisgenerative politics within which new, more inclusive norms acquire a positive legal status. And for Held, like Bohman and Benhabib, it is again legally entrenched all-inclusive rights that meet the challenges arising from globalised issues and demands. More than that, the case is not only that all three authors end up privileging human rights as legal rights, co-original with citizenship, but that they also draw inspiration from what exactly Douzinas describes as the 'unstoppable proliferation of human rights' in international law. In this particular respect, therefore, Douzinas' investigation is useful for the purposes of this chapter. By showing what is exactly involved behind the increasing salience of legally codified rights, he responds to the arguments of Held, Bohman and Benhabib.

Douzinas starts his investigation by noting the shift from natural rights to internationally entrenched human rights. Prior to the Second World War, he says, human rights were justified in terms of their naturalness, as the rights pertaining to a superior, dignified, rational and autonomous human nature. As a response to the Holocaust, however, it is the 'legal universalisation' of human rights that justifies their forcefulness. Their higher status, remarks Douzinas, 'is seen as the result of the triumph of the universality of humanity, of their legal universalisation. The law addresses all states and all human persons qua humans and declares their entitlements to be a part of the patrimony of humanity, which has replaced human nature as the rhetorical ground of rights' (2001: 184). As it has already surfaced, Douzinas' focus on the legal universalism of human rights leads us to approach the notion of human rights from an additional angle. This concerns their legal codification, the idea that legally codified human rights can be seen as an answer to political participation. Because Douzinas' account, moreover, is psychoanalytically influenced, it enables us to effect a transition: from the Lacanian perspective of the previous sections, the implications of which are herein drawn for human rights, to the law/politics equation, which, in the next chapter, we put into question.

Legal universalism is therefore what, according to Douzinas, has replaced human nature as justification for human rights:

> Every state and power comes under the mantle of the international law of human rights, every government becomes civilised as the 'law of the princes' has finally become the 'universal' law of human dignity. However, this is an empirical universality, based on the competitive solidarity of sovereign governments and on the pragmatic concerns and calculations of international politics.
>
> (2001: 184)

In contrast with the 'normative universality' of human nature – that is, in contrast with the idea that human rights ought to be respected and protected universally by virtue of the common nature to which all humans share – 'empirical universality' denotes simply the number of states that have become signatories in international documents. Because national considerations determine the ratification of human rights treaties, human rights are both weakly implemented internationally and in constant tension with the interests of sovereign states. In effect, for Douzinas, 'the legal community of human rights is universal but imaginary' (2001: 184).

It is imaginary because first, it owes its existence to political interests. Second, because it relies on a notion, that does not empirically exist. Humanity has both been shifting as a term across different historical periods and been shaped by state interests. In other words, humanity is a contingent notion, according to Douzinas, arising out of particular philosophical pre-suppositions and relations of power. It is neither universal nor immutable. In his own words:

> Humanity's mastery, like God's omnipotence, includes the ability to redefine who or what counts as human, and even to destroy itself. From Aristotle's slaves to the cyborgs of 'Blade Runner', the boundaries of humanity have been shifting. These shifts can be traced in the history of the legal institution. What history has taught us is that there is nothing sacred about any definition of humanity and nothing eternal about its

scope. Humanity cannot act as the a priori normative principle and is mute in the manner of legal and moral rules. Its function lies not in a philosophical essence but in its non essence, in the endless process of redefinition and the continuous but impossible attempt to escape fate and external determination.

(2001: 189).

Douzinas makes therefore the following claim: although humanity is itself an 'empty' notion, void of moral and legal considerations, it becomes 'objectified' through legalisation. Human rights become the legally entrenched rights of those who are defined as human. At the same time, human rights are supposed to challenge this 'objectification' of humanity. Thus Douzinas observes a paradox: on the one side, codified human rights legitimate the power of states to define and objectify humanity; on the other side, they are the means to challenge this power. He notes:

If rights are the yardstick against which state brutality is to be judged, their inherent historicism makes them vulnerable to the hypocrisy of power and turns them often from protections against domination and oppression into the basis of state legitimacy. But human rights are also used by the oppressed, the exploited and the marginalised, they are the last great discourse of resistance and rebellion. Beyond the discourse of governments, human rights are ways of constructing the self against the demands of power. How can we theorise their paradoxical role?

(2001: 196).

In order to explain the paradoxical and ambiguous role of rights, Douzinas resorts to structural linguistics and approaches humanity as a floating signifier. In the previous section, we explained that, according to Saussure, language consists of differential elements, signifiers (sounds-images) and signifieds (concepts). Floating signifiers are those sounds-images that, because they do not attach to any particular concept, are empty of meaning and thus potentially attachable to a variety of signifieds. By conceiving humanity as a floating signifier, Douzinas justifies first its emptiness. Because it is lacking meaning, humanity is being constantly redefined. Second, he justifies its excess and overdetermination, the fact that humanity carries a surplus of meaning through centuries of redefinition. It is to this latter effect that rights have been instrumental. By arresting the meaning of the floating signifier, of the 'human', legal rights have afforded him/her protection and recognition. However, by functioning only as constructs, which partially fixate meaning, rights are shown to 'belong to the symbolic order of language and law'; they are open and artificial. As Douzinas puts it:

Rights do not refer to things or other material entities in the world. They

are combinations of legal and linguistic signs, words and images, symbols
and fantasies . . . Any entity open to semiotic substitution can become
the subject or object of rights, while any right can be extended to new
areas and persons or conversely withdrawn from existing ones. Nothing
in the ontology of potential subjects or in the nature of objects inherently
stops them from entering the hallowed space of rights.

(2001: 196)

Their linguistic and legal constructivism sanctions, in effect, their ambiguous
and paradoxical function.

What Douzinas thereby argues is that neither humanity nor rights can be
permanently fixed or determined. While humanity as a floating signifier has
been repeatedly emptied and filled in with meaning, the rights that have
arrested its meaning have been changing and expanding. A clear implication
of this argument is that rights construct humans. They do not naturally
pertain to humanity. This insight challenges the idea that legally entrenched
human rights are an adequate alternative to a problematic citizenship. Their
legal codification, which Held, Bohman and Benhabib promote and valorise,
is revealed to be a force both objectifying humanity and affixing the meaning
of humans through the construction of rights. Human rights appear therefore to be inherently limited as a notion that can simply take on the political
function of citizenship. Moreover, they appear to be opening a whole new
range of problems for us.

'Rights work for the subject by turning individual or group wishes into
publicly recognised and protected institutions. One could argue therefore',
says Douzinas, 'that rights legalise desire' (2001: 197). At this point, he
takes recourse to Lacanian psychoanalysis. He shares Lacan's conceptualisation of the subject as constitutively split and lacking. As we have already
seen, the subject is split between its subjectivity, which it gains upon
entrance onto the symbolic level, and the Other, the order of language and
law represented by the Name-of-the-Father. By virtue of its Spaltung, the
subject is revealed as lacking. Because it lacks an essence, a total and
unified identity, it lacks and always searches for jouissance, for a real pre-
symbolic enjoyment, connoting its lost/unattainable/prohibited fullness.
Lacanian desire, which Douzinas says rights legalise, both aims at jouissance and sets its search into motion. The objet a, a remainder according
to Lacan of the subject after it has entered the symbolic order, a remnant
of the lost/impossible wholeness, causes desire. It promises the subject that
its lack will be covered. Human rights function, for Douzinas, like the objet
a, as a remnant, that is, of an impossible totality and unity. They present a
fantasmatic scenario, which promises the subject that its lack will be
covered. This is, however, impossible. As the object-cause of an insatiable
desire, the objet a always defers the realisation of jouissance, of wholeness
and totality.

Douzinas explains further:

> Rights give the impression that the subject and society can become
> whole: only if all the attributes and characteristics of the subject were to
> be given legal recognition, would he be happy; only if the demands of
> human dignity and equality were to be fully enforced by the law, would
> society be just. But like the objet a, rights both displace and fill the lack
> and make the desired wholeness impossible. The other's desire escapes
> the subject, always seeking something else, but the little that remains
> allows the subject to exist as a desiring being. Rights, like the objet a,
> become a fantasmatic supplement that arises but never satiates the sub-
> ject's desire. Rights always agitate for more rights: they create ever-new
> areas of claim and entitlement, but these always prove insufficient. We
> keep demanding and inventing new rights in an endless attempt to fill
> the lack, but this only defers desire.
>
> (2001: 197)

The argument that therefore Douzinas makes here follows and further rad-
icalises his earlier insight into the nature of rights. From his constructivist
view of rights as linguistic and legal signs affixing the meaning of humanity,
constructing humans, he moves into a view of rights as fantasmatic means
necessary for sustaining and legalising desire.

This Lacanian account of human rights challenges the standpoint of Held,
Bohman and Benhabib. It shows us that human rights, which all three
authors prioritise, present a fantasmatic scenario, a promise for an unattainable totality just like the objet a. As a kernel of fantasy, however, can human
rights take us out of the problems confronting the nationally and territorially
bounded citizenship? Although a fantasy is instrumental in articulating and
reinforcing promises of emancipation, it is one thing to argue for its necessity
and quite another to envision it as a substitute to citizenship. In other words,
it is one thing to search for totality, for an ideal, and quite another to realise
this ideal. In the latter case, realisation might also entail closure. By privileging therefore human rights and by realising the fantasy scenario that they
bring into play, we risk closure – a point that the next chapter explores in
more detail.

Of course, Held, Bohman and Benhabib do not simply argue, as we have
seen, that human rights should take on the function of citizenship; rather,
they all take recourse to, or privilege, law and the legal entrenchment of these
rights. However, as Lacan earlier showed us and Douzinas here demonstrates, the Other, the symbolic order or the law to which subjects turn in
order to attain unity and totality, is also lacking. It cannot provide them with
a full representation of themselves, and it cannot give them a full and stable
identity. Douzinas elaborates:

The desire of the subject is the desire of law: the person takes his march-ing orders from law and, for this operation to succeed, the law must be seen as non-lacking, as a complete whole that has the answer to all pro-blems of conflict. The desire of the other as complete and non-lacking is therefore a function of the subject; he needs the law to be gapless, to be the 'seamless web' of liberal theorists like Ronald Dworkin, in order to accept his subjection. But the symbolic order and law cannot be complete.

(2001: 201)

The point that Douzinas is making, the point that answers the arguments of Held, Bohman and Benhabib, is that law and its privileging cannot be seen as an alternative to politics. On one side, law is necessary but lacking. On the other side, it subjects. Human rights are not therefore those transcendental principles that, by becoming legally entrenched, realise justice and meet the challenges confronting citizenship; rather, they are the compensatory means for an incomplete and subjecting legal system.

What we should therefore keep from this Lacanian argument of Douzinas is the twofold nature of human rights. As a fantasmatic scenario, human rights, says Douzinas, legalise desire. Yet desire never becomes satisfied nor do human rights, as the object-cause of desire, ever attain the ideal at which they aim: unity and totality, harmony and/or closure. As legal principles, however, human rights promise to fill in the lack of an incomplete and subjecting legal system. In the light of both of their functions, as fantasy and compensatory legal principles, they cannot be seen as a substitute to citizenship. As a fantasy, they are inherently limited and limiting. As a legal alternative to citizenship, they raise important stakes for both democracy and democratic politics. The next chapter explains these.

Chapter 4

Politics and legalism

So far in the book, we have seen that human rights is a notion that cannot simply be privileged over citizenship. While citizenship appears currently problematic, it is a rich and dynamic notion. The citizen makes politics and challenges politics. By contrast, the type of subject that human rights presuppose appears to be a subject forever split and lacking. Lacan showed us that identifying a rational and autonomous subject, as the human rights idea does, is impossible. Subjects never attain a complete and stable identity, and precarious acts of identification are their only option. As a rights and legalistic discourse, moreover, human rights are also limiting according to the Lacanian perspective, which we explored in the previous chapter. They are a fantasy scenario necessary as compensation for a subjecting legal system. Of course, an important clarification is due at this point. Problematising the legalistic discourse and type of subject on which human rights draw by no means implies a complete rejection of the concept. As we explored in Chapter 1, human rights, an inextricable tenet of modern liberal democracy, play a central role in challenging and exposing relations of power and subordination. However, this political role, the book has been arguing, not only is different to that of citizenship, but also needs to be recognised and valorised as different – otherwise we risk impoverishing and weakening democratic politics by reducing it to one principle. Human rights, therefore, are not *eo ipso* limiting according to the argument of this book; rather, it is only and in so far as they substitute for citizenship, therefore undermining democratic practice, that they are shown to be limiting. But there is a further implication to the case of privileging human rights and it is the aim of the present chapter to examine this in more detail. It concerns the anti-politics of the human rights argument.

The chapter examines this anti-politics from two related angles: first, from the angle of privileging law over democratic politics; second, from the angle of privileging liberalism over democracy. Although the reasoning underpinning the use of the first angle is clear, given our focus on human rights as legal rights, the use of the second angle needs to be further explained. In particular, and dormant so far in our exposition of the argument that privileges human rights, has been the idea that defenders of an all-inclusive politics based on human rights do not simply end up prioritising law over politics on the assumption that they are co-original, but they are also led to privilege the liberal over the democratic tenets of modern democracy – since inclusion, law and human rights are all liberal presuppositions. To be sure, by framing his suggestion for a democracy of *demoi* in terms of the republican ideal of non-domination, Bohman resists and insists that he does not privilege liberalism over democracy. However, if we consider that the deliberative conception of politics that he defends leads him precisely to negate frontiers and prioritise common humanity, then we have enough reason to doubt whether Bohman actually succeeds in his objective.[1] From a different perspective therefore on politics, a perspective that brings into focus its conflictual rather than con-sensual character, as is the case with the deliberative perspective, the chapter argues that privileging human rights/liberalism/law over politics can lead to depoliticisation, an unalterable status quo and potentially anti-pluralistic effects.

To justify this argument, the first section of the chapter takes recourse to the writings of Christodoulidis, Schmitt and Rancière. In particular, Christodoulidis' critique of republican constitutionalism, a vision that iden-tifies politics with law, shows us through a legal lens why it is problematic to collapse politics into law. From a different angle, Schmitt's critique of liberal-ism enables us to show the incapacity of a liberal politics to think in political terms. And Rancière's critique of postdemocracy puts us in a better position to discuss the implications of depoliticisation. All three accounts show clearly not only that the human rights argument raises important political and democratic stakes, but also that it is risky to turn to law in order to address political problems. Subsequently, the second section of the chapter gives centre stage to the idea that unites the critiques of Christodoulidis, Schmitt and Rancière – namely, that democratic politics involves contestation, not consensus. The section takes this idea further by introducing Mouffe's agon-istic conception of democracy. Returning thereby to the focus of the first chapter, the section shows exactly why, from Mouffe's agonistic standpoint, legally codified rights cannot be seen as a solution to the limitations facing nation state citizenship. Although Mouffe shares Rancière's perspective and accepts Schmitt's critique of liberalism, she moves beyond Schmitt's undemocratic conclusions and shows us a strictly political way of thinking. This leads to an argument for reasserting citizenship, for an agonistic concep-tion of citizenship, which the next chapter develops further.

Anti-politics

In his essay 'Republican Constitutionalism and Reflexive Politics', Christodoulidis takes issue with what he calls the republican vision of constitutionalism – a vision that, among other theories, encompasses the deliberative perspective of Habermas, which we explored in the first chapter. More specifically, republican constitutionalism, which according to Christodoulidis 'attempts to marry politics and law or democratic will and constitutional reason' (2006: 2), puts forward two main arguments. First, it stresses the integrative role that deliberative processes play in democratic societies. Opposing the economic view of politics as a process of bargaining that precludes the possibility of identifying an 'objective public interest in politics', republican constitutionalists emphasise that democratic deliberations open the way for the formation of a good common to all. Second, they argue that the constitution is not something external to politics, but the very instantiation of politics, since it 'hosts the political process' on the assumption that it 'contains the deliberative practice of a community, the dialogue of all about all' (2006: 4). Although these arguments are familiar to us from the first chapter, the way in which Christodoulidis reads and critiques them is interesting and relevant for the purposes of this chapter. For Christodoulidis views this marrying of law with politics, or better put, the containment of politics in law, as a dangerous attempt to 'domesticate politics', 'an imperialistic *legal* move to set the terms of *political* discourse' (2006: 5). Could we not argue along similar lines that a 'domestication of politics' is the inevitable implication of the turn to law, to legally codified human rights as a means to addressing the problems confronting democratic practice?

Of course, it is essential here to grasp that the dangerous 'domestication of politics' that issues from the deliberative case for privileging human rights is a *political* implication in a twofold sense: first, because it opens the question of what politics and even more so democratic politics is all about. Is it just a process that furthers societal cooperation, a procedure that once applied secures an as far as possible harmonious (and potentially closed) coexistence, or is it something more – which we need to nurture and sustain, rather than simply domesticate? Second, the implication is political because it gives rise to strictly political questions that the deliberative perspective, by virtue of its emphasis on law, tends to underplay. To illustrate these political questions, Christodoulidis uses the example of debates over a European constitution. Arguing that, from a legal angle, it is impossible to tackle questions of communal identity, since the law has to assume as given the identity of the *demos* (rather than as something to be constructed through politics), he claims that the republican (deliberative) emphasis on legal institutionalisation tends to avoid and ignore that which is most fundamental to politics. In the case of the European constitution, this is the political question of how to construct a *demos*. Operating necessarily on the assumption that the *demos* is given legalism, according to Christodoulidis, closes rather than opens the debate. He notes:

> Making something 'political' means claiming that there are other options too, that there can be other explanations; politics invites actors to contest

given aims, given representations, symbols, relations, causal links and necessities and must represent them *in that* undertaking. In a word, politics invites us to contest the determinations at the meta-level of what counts as aim, function and causation for purposes of representation. In that, every determination is forever postponed, every causal link identified and every constellation of meaning forever contested, no representation ever exhaustive. Politics is driven by the contingency of determinations, and the surrender of certainty that entails; but for law that very surrender is debilitating.

(2006: 7)

Starting therefore from the assumption that law and politics are different, rather than co-original, Christodoulidis makes two concrete arguments against the republican case of marrying the two. Although, to be sure, Christodoulidis only considers the co-originality thesis, not the case of privileging law over politics, his arguments can also be used to show the risks involved in valorising legally codified human rights over democratic practice. More specifically, his first argument is that, *pace* republican constitutionalists, law and politics are significantly incommensurable. While politics is contingent and presupposes contestations that question given identities and representations, law not only attempts to tame these contestations but also to reduce contingency. By means of narrowly constructed and limiting categories,[2] law, argues Christodoulidis, reduces complexity and disciplines conflicts in a double sense: first, through a selective representation of (conflictual) issues; second, through mechanisms and procedures that are devised precisely to resolve conflicts. Law is, in short, a 'reduction achievement' according to Christodoulidis. This is his second argument against republican constitutionalists. 'By setting the thresholds of valid dissensus, the *when* and *how* of possible conflict', law reduces, represses, and limits (2006: 8). It reduces political conflicts to legal disputes, which can then be rationally resolved by taking recourse to legal criteria. It represses those conflicts that do not follow the legal logic. And it limits political contestations:

> Constitutional processes *do* allow for constitutional deliberation and self determination *but* in a significantly limiting and limited way; they simultaneously lend resilience and opacity to what remains unchallengeable. If there is one formula to encapsulate the claim I make against subordinating politics to law it is this: what is political is a political question; what constitutes a political community, a political 'we', is a question for the community to answer. The process is dynamic and cyclical: the concept cannot be pinned down at the outset.

(2006: 8)

Along similar lines we could therefore argue that, in the face of the problems confronting democratic practice today, it is perhaps best to take recourse to politics rather than law – revising citizenship instead of privileging legally codified human rights. Thus the question that arises at this point is this: what is this politics to which we should take recourse?

For Christodoulidis, politics is reflexive in that it is open (and therefore revisable), reflective (about exclusions) and contestatory. As he puts it:

> Grounding our identity in politics, in the act of suspending binding determinations, of countering law's closure, of resisting the finality of law's representations involves seeing ourselves as political actors for whom a radical openness to the future is not 'always already' called into line by constitutional pre-commitments and limitations.
>
> (2006: 9)

Reflexivity, therefore, a defining feature of politics for Christodoulidis, involves an ethos of vigilance regarding closures and exclusions, collective contestations aiming at challenging such exclusions, and a critical recognition and respect for political openness and incompletion. Christodoulidis identifies three aspects of reflexivity: reflexivity as self-reference; contingency; and constituent power. Reflexivity as self-reference points to the idea that politics has to reflect back on itself in order to find answers to political questions, to serve as the referent point for such questions. 'By being reflexive,' argues Christodoulidis, 'politics refers everything back to its own possibilities' (2006: 10). Reflexivity as contingency indicates that politics is dynamic, not static, giving rise to ever-new sites for politicisation and alternatives. Finally, a reflexive politics, according to Christodoulidis, necessarily presupposes a constituent power – that is, performative actors who challenge and contest what at a given moment is designated as politics. Whereas, however, for Christodoulidis, politics is reflexive and contestatory, for Schmitt, to whom we now turn, politics is outrightly conflictual. The friend/enemy distinction designates the specifically political criterion for Schmitt and thus distinguishes politics from all other areas of human activity. More than that, by refusing to see the conflictuality constitutive of politics, deliberative theorists, Schmitt shows us, are incapable of thinking politically. In effect, their argument for privileging the all-inclusive rights of humanity is, through the Schmittian lens, anti-political, as we will shortly see.

Schmitt notes:

> Let us assume that in the realm of morality the final distinctions are between good and evil, in aesthetics beautiful and ugly, in economics profitable and unprofitable. The question then is whether there is also a special distinction, which can serve as a simple criterion of the political and of what it consists. The nature of such a political distinction is surely different from that of those others. It is independent of them and

as such can speak clearly of itself. The specific political distinction to which political actions and motives can be reduced is that between friend and enemy. This provides a definition in the sense of a criterion and not as an exhaustive definition or one indicative of substantial content.

(1996: 26)

The friend/enemy distinction therefore defines the realm of politics for Schmitt. Because it distinguishes politics from other areas of human activity, it has an objective nature and autonomy. Moreover, it denotes the intensity of a union or separation between two collectivities. These collectivities, it transpires, the friend/enemy units, are not separated from one another because of their aesthetic, moral or economic differences – differences, that is, which draw upon distinctions from other spheres of human activity. Rather, they are two similar units that, in a specific situation, disagree in a broad sense and fight each other. The moment that the political emerges therefore, a moment that is both ever-present and decisive for Schmitt, pure differences become subordinated 'to the conditions and conclusions of the political situation at hand' (1996: 38). This is why Schmitt argues that the autonomous political designates the intensity of a friend/enemy relation. And to further clarify his argument, Schmitt explains that the political enemy, the other, is someone similar who, at a given situation, is excluded and thus seen as an enemy with whom one conflicts. It follows that since conflict and antagonism constitutively define friend/enemy relations, they also constitutively define politics, according to Schmitt.

By therefore suggesting that politics rests on conflict and antagonism, Schmitt provides us with a vantage point from which to problematise the argument that privileges human rights. In one respect, Schmitt shows us its anti-political implications. Arguing for the effacement of frontiers and the resolution of antagonisms leads, on his standpoint, to the negation of politics, to the undermining and disappearance of friend/enemy distinctions – a point to which we will return shortly. In another respect, Schmitt's ideas show us the limits of the case for human rights. A consensus that is not based on an act of exclusion is impossible for him, precisely because politics presupposes and rests on distinctions between friends and enemies. Such distinctions prevent the emergence of an all-inclusive consensus. Suggesting, moreover, that procedures and a Rechtsstaat are means that facilitate and reinforce a consensual coexistence entwines with liberal politics in his view. And liberal politics, claims Schmitt, is not only incapable of thinking in political terms – while the political rests on an exclusion, a liberal politics argues, as we have seen, for inclusion – it also contradicts the logic of democracy, its strictly political logic.

Indeed, at the beginning of this chapter, we pointed out that the priority that the deliberative approach to democratic politics accords to the legal system, to legally codified human rights, weighs in favour of a liberal politics

– a politics that focuses on the rule of law and which approaches democracy as a model of procedures that facilitates cooperation. On the standpoint therefore of Held, Bohman and Benhabib, democratic politics is first reconciled with liberal premises, and then underplayed, precisely because it is seen in liberal and thus minimal terms – as a means, that is, for legitimating law, a consensual and legally entrenched coexistence. Because democratic practice presupposes, moreover, only rationality and impartiality, it is emptied of all distinctiveness. Schmitt's critique of liberalism enables us to substantiate this argument and show the implications of identifying democracy minimally, as discussion and law. Although both emphases, discussion and Rechtsstaat, are identical in a sense with the democratic premises of a public opinion and a rule of law that is expressive of the people's will, they are not equivalent, argues Schmitt. To see why, we first look at his approach to liberalism; second, we look at his understanding of democratic politics.

Specifically, a fundamental premise of liberalism is that through discussion and openness, which resolves conflicts of opinions and reinforces justice, a general or public good will emerge. This is, according to Schmitt, liberalism's claim to legitimacy. In this claim, rational argumentation and persuasion play an instrumental role. They reveal the truth and lead to justice. It proceeds that, within the context of a liberal theory, what a universally applicable law does is to 'unite truth and justice through the balance of negotiations and public discussion' (1988: 48). The universal criterion of law, continues Schmitt:

> . . . is deduced from the fact that law (in contrast to will or the command of a concrete person) is only reason, not desire, and that it has no passions . . . it is general and already promulgated, universally valid without exception, and valid in principle for all times . . . This conception of law is based on a rationalistic distinction between the (no longer universal but) general and the particular, and representatives of Rechtsstaat thinking believe that the general has a higher value, in itself, than the particular.
>
> (1988: 42)

Under this belief that 'the general has a higher value than the particular' falls also the priority that Held, Bohman and Benhabib accord to legally codifying human rights. First the focus on discussion, then on truth and justice, and third, on a universally valid law, all premises interrelated with one another, lead Held, Bohman and Benhabib to argue for human rights – rights that draw on what people share in common, which connect with justice and which are the cornerstone of the legal system.

As Schmitt argues, however, the idea of a universal suffrage implies that 'every adult person, simply as a person, should *eo ipso* be politically equal to every other person. This is a liberal, not a democratic idea' (1988: 11). And significantly, this idea contradicts the democratic logic. Why? Democracy rests on homogeneity, says Schmitt. By 'homogeneity', he understands a kind of unity, which is marked by relations of substantive political equality. Equality is substantive if it contains the possibility and risk of inequality. And it is political, it belongs, that is, to the political sphere, if it revolves around the distinction between 'equals' (the *demos*) and 'unequals' – and here we can notice the link between his approach to the political and his understanding of democracy. In contrast therefore with deliberative theorists who approach democracy minimally, as a process of rational discussion that legitimates the legal system, Schmitt argues that democracy presupposes a particular *demos*, a unit of equals who are necessarily differentiated from the 'unequals', the non-members. The idea of a particular 'we consciousness', a delimited *demos*, is precisely what Held and Benhabib, for example, downplay. They argue, as we have seen, that, in the face of global and postnational developments, people will just rationally deliberate to confer legitimacy to institutions of global governance (Held) or reiterate cosmopolitan norms (Benhabib).

Of course, Schmitt, who helps us question this argument, is not a democrat – and, later in the chapter, we will revisit and elaborate on his insights from Mouffe's democratic standpoint. Yet although not a democrat, it is from his conflictual perspective on (democratic) politics that we can show why the argument for liberalism, for discussion, law and human rights, does not resolve the problems confronting exclusive citizenries. Schmitt helps us to show, in other words, the limitations of a liberal politics and its inherent contradiction with the logic of democracy (with the idea of popular sovereignty). Specifically, the contradiction that he brings to the fore is the following: while democracy presupposes a homogeneous entity of equals, who are always differentiated from the unequals, liberalism presupposes, according to Schmitt, that all human beings can be made politically equals – that is, that liberals assume that an absolute human equality is not only just and feasible, through discussion, but also that law, a general medium, can facilitate this. Because the liberal logic presupposes therefore inclusion and the democratic logic exclusion, Schmitt argues that they are irreconcilable and contradict each other.

Moreover, says Schmitt:

> [W]here a state wants to establish general human equality in the political sphere without concern for national or some other sort of homogeneity, then it cannot escape the consequence that political equality will be devalued to the extent that it approximates absolute human equality. And not only that, the sphere of the political and therefore politics itself would also be devalued in at least the same degree, and would become something insignificant. One would not only have robbed political equality of its substance and made it meaningless for individual equals, but

politics would also have become insubstantial to the extent that such an indifferent equality is taken seriously ... Substantive inequalities would in no way disappear from the world and the state; they would shift into another sphere, perhaps separated from the political and concentrated in the economic, leaving this area to take on a new, disproportionately decisive importance.

(1988: 12)

We can thus identify two arguments here that are suggestive as to the implications of the argument which prioritises human rights: the first shows its depoliticising effects; the second, the implications of such effects. In particular, the prospect of a democracy of mankind, within which everyone is included and rationally convinced as to their preferred terms of coexistence, is depoliticising in so far as it renders irrelevant any kind of distinction between friends and enemies. More than that, it leaves no space for politics. If, by (democratic) politics, we therefore understand what Schmitt does, a frontier between those who partake in the *demos* and those who are not, then the prospect of all inclusion via human rights depoliticises. But there are further implications. As Schmitt points out, substantial inequalities would not simply disappear with the realisation of an absolute human equality, but be transferred into another sphere that would come to dominate politics – which means in turn that other kinds of exclusion, say of a moral nature, will be proclaimed and legitimated. William Rasch explains and takes this point further.

Rasch notes, à la Schmitt, that every configuration depends on a permanent outside – equality on inequality, norm on the exception, inclusion on the exclusion and friend on the enemy. Given thus that the outside cannot simply be eliminated (but only rendered invisible), Rasch poses the question of what would actually serve as the outside of humanity. Moreover, given that humanity is the horizon within which all sorts of distinctions are being made, according to Rasch, then its negative pole might indeed 'be something that lies beyond that horizon, something completely antithetical to horizon and positive pole alike – it can only, in other words, be the inhuman' (2004: 142). The human/inhuman criterion may then come to replace the political distinction between the friend and the enemy. This criterion is moral, because distinguishing the human from the inhuman, an absolute notion from its absolute other, is to distinguish the good, now posed in absolute terms as that which all humans rationally see, experience and agree on, from the evil – inhumanity. In such a case, politics is emptied of all specificity and comes to be dominated by morality – a point that, as we will see in the next section, Mouffe also explores. Morality is moreover potentially imperialistic.

This brings us to a further implication of the argument that, in the name of politics, privileges human rights. In *The Concept of the Political*, Schmitt highlights the imperialistic purposes of humanitarian wars, wars that, under the name of humanity, advance the objectives of particular states. Rasch draws and elaborates on Schmitt's point. He says:

> In the past, we/they, neighbour/foreigner, friend/enemy polarities were inside/outside distinctions that produced a plurality of worlds, separated by physical and cultural borders. When these worlds collided, it was not always a pretty picture, but it was often possible to maintain the integrity of the we/they distinction, even to regulate it by distinguishing between domestic and foreign affairs. If 'they' differed, 'we' did not always feel ourselves obliged to make 'them' into miniature versions of 'us', to Christianise them, to civilise them, to make of them good liberals. Things have changed . . . The inner/outer distinction has been transformed into a morally and legally determined acceptable/unacceptable one, and the power exists (or is thought to exist), both spiritually and physically, to eliminate the unacceptable once and for all and make believers of every-one. The new imperative states: The other shall be included. Delivered as a promise, it can only be received by some as an ominous threat.
>
> (2004: 144–145)

Specifically, the idea here is, again, that an all-inclusive (and thus disagreement-free) politics, based on common humanity, is ultimate. When this ultimate idea becomes therefore 'usurped' or 'misused', as Schmitt says, then the potential effect is not far from the 'threat', as Rasch puts it, of making the same out of everyone. This prospect does not only suggest that human rights, which a deliberative politics prioritises, can potentially serve as imperialistic means, but that they can also serve as a means for legitimating the status quo, since an all-inclusive consensus would be impossible to challenge once it has been rationally decided and legally entrenched – thereby representing all rational human beings. We are thus brought back to the absoluteness of humanity as a political principle. While citizenship, by virtue of its inclusion/exclusion dynamics, ensures that friend/enemy groupings will always be recreated anew, human rights, if privileged, entail closure – because consensus and inclusion cannot but also reinforce content with how things are, or will be, the moment that human rights become prioritised over citizenship.

This is also why the argument that prioritises human rights impacts on pluralism. Unconditional inclusion under the name of humanity would undermine any kind of particularity. But can we seriously envisage this pros-pect? For Schmitt, the international system is a pluriverse. On his view, therefore, the idea of a human, as opposed to a political, equality is far removed from reality. Indeed, the world might be coming closer together as a result of globalisation and developments such as European integration, but this world however is still marked by a plurality of cultures, nationalities and value systems. To believe that disagreements and conflicts between them can be resolved, as deliberative theorists seem to suggest, does not only seem unrealistic from an antithetical perspective on politics but also undesirable – since the idea of 'politicising' humanity has the effect of 'neutralising' and suppressing particularity and plurality. Rancière, who also speaks from a conflictual perspective on politics, reinforces these conclusions – albeit this time from a democratic perspective.

In *Disagreement: Politics and Philosophy*, Rancière undertakes a critique of 'postdemocracy'.[3] He explains:

> The term will simply be used to denote the paradox that, in the name of democracy, emphasises the consensual practice of effacing the forms of democratic action. Postdemocracy is the practice and conceptual legitim-isation of a democracy after the *demos*, a democracy that has eliminated the appearance, miscount and dispute of the people and is thereby reducible to the sole interplay of state mechanisms and combinations of social energies and interests.
>
> (1999: 101–102)

From this quote, we can derive three interrelated features of postdemocracy: first, that it is a practice understood in consensual terms; second, that this kind of practice effaces the *demos*; and third, that it reduces politics to 'combinations of social energies and interests'. In the course of examining these three features of postdemocratic politics, we suggest that the deliberative/consensual approach underpinning the human rights argument has a point of contact with postdemocracy. It shares, that is, in certain postdemocratic premises. In exploring moreover these postdemocratic premises, we elucidate Rancière's criticisms and show how, from his conflictual standpoint, postdemocratic politics is seen to have anti-political implications.

In particular, postdemocracy rests, according to Rancière, on the idea that consensual processes of participation regulate plural passions and lead to a reasonable agreement on the terms of common coexistence. Consensus informs democratic action, on this view. On the one hand, democratic action presupposes and rests on consensus. As Rancière notes, 'before becoming the reasonable virtue of individuals and groups who agree to discuss their problems and build up their interests, consensus is a determined regime of the perceptible, a particular mode of visibility of right as *arkhe* of the community' (1999: 107). On the other hand, consensus is precisely what issues from democratic participation approached as a consensual practice:

> A determined regime of opinion and a determined regime of right are posited as regimes of the community's identification with itself, with nothing left over. As a regime of opinion, the principle of postdemocracy is to make the troubled and troubling appearance of the people and its always false count disappear behind procedures exhaustively presenting

the people and its parts and bringing the count of those parts in line with the image of the whole.

(1999: 102–103)

In both respects, we can see how the consensual approach, which, as we have seen, underpins the human rights argument, shares in this feature of postdemocracy. A prior and net agreement on the advantages and results of processes of deliberation is, as we have already pointed out, precisely what underpins the deliberative understanding of democracy. And this emphasis on consensus is what, in effect, leads deliberative theorists to prioritise human rights – the basic and all-inclusive rights that draw on what people share in common. At the same time, both approaches, postdemocratic and delibera- tive, share in their orientation towards the legal system. In the rule of law, stresses Rancière, postdemocracy finds its most expressive manifestation of consensus. Or as he puts it:

> The rule of law is always the rule of a law, that is, of a regime of unity among all the different senses of the law posited as a regime of identity of the community. Today, the identification between democracy and the legitimate state is used to produce a regime of the community's identity as itself, to make politics evaporate under a concept of law that identifies it with the spirit of the community.

(1999: 108)

By identifying therefore law with politics, postdemocracy effaces the political, because, as Rancière understands it, politics is 'neither the consensual regula- tion of the plural passions of the multitude of individuals nor the reign of a collectivity unified by law under the shadow of Declarations of Rights' (1995: 32). Rather, politics is contentious, as it is for Schmitt. It rests on the idea of a dispute, of a constitutive conflict. This constitutive conflict Rancière calls by the name of 'wrong'. The moment that a wrong becomes declared, that a dispute arises between parts of society, politics begins, for Rancière. He stresses 'politics occurs wherever a community with the capacity to argue and to make metaphors is likely, at any time and through anyone's intervention, to crop up' (1999: 60). A 'wrong', a conflict and politics go therefore hand in hand.

By contrast, postdemocracy approaches disputes and 'wrongs' as mere problems that can be rationally resolved. 'This is actually the great transformation that the people's dispute undergoes', says Rancière and he continues, 'any dispute in this system becomes the name of a problem. And any problem can be reduced to a simple lack – a simple holding up – of the means to solve it. Identifying and dealing with the lack must then be substi- tuted for the manifestation of wrong' (1999: 107). By suggesting therefore the legal resolution of all disagreements, postdemocracy effaces politics, according to Rancière. The first indication as to the anti-politics of the argument that privileges human rights surfaces herein. For human rights, the case for privileging them over citizenship could be seen as a 'symptom' of the postdemocratic logic – aspiring to realise exactly what, according to Rancière, cannot be realised: to redress the constitutive wrong of politics. Precisely because they include everyone on equal terms, human rights eliminate the prospect of a 'wrong', of a dispute between parts of society that would mark the beginning of politics. They efface all disputes, all 'wrongs' and, in effect, all politics. Although it can be objected that, to the extent that human rights challenge or address wrongs, they have a political role, the wrong of politics, as Rancière explains,

> . . . cannot be regulated by way of some accord between the parties. It cannot be regulated since the subjects a political wrong sets in motion are not entities to whom such and such has happened by accident, but subjects whose very existence is the mode of manifestation of wrong . . . But though the wrong cannot be regulated, this does not mean that it cannot be processed . . . it can be processed through the mechanisms of subjectification that give it substance as an alterable relationship between the parties, indeed as a shift in the playing field.
>
> (1999: 39)

Subjectified performers, a *demos*, is therefore necessary, according to Rancière, in order to process the constitutive wrong of politics.

This brings us to the second feature of postdemocracy – that, as a consensual practice, it is a democracy after the *demos*. Specifically, by identifying the whole community with itself under the legal system, postdemocracy breaks with the democratic idea that there is a concrete people, a *demos*, that is necessarily differentiated from those who do not belong to it and who are thus considered unequals – and here we can see the link between Schmitt's and Rancière's perspectives. Of course, on the other hand Held, Bohman and Benhabib retain, as we have already mentioned, the idea of a democratic practice. They are not, therefore, postdemocrats in the strict sense of the term. On the other hand, however, they so minimally approach democratic participation as to empty it of all distinctiveness. What remains of it, rationally and consensually conducted processes, can simply be reconciled with the idea of legally codified human rights. In this second sense, therefore, all three authors tend to identify 'the whole community with itself' and thus share in postdemocratic politics. In contrast, Rancière argues that democracy rests on the actions of a concrete entity of equals, actions that challenge an established order. It rests, in other words, in an 'act' of undoing. And this act presupposes that 'those who have no part' are distinguished from 'those who have a part'. In Rancière's words:

> Politics exists because those who have no right to be counted as speaking beings make themselves of some account, setting up a community by the fact of placing in common a wrong that is nothing more than this very confrontation, the contradiction of two worlds in a single world: the world where they are and the world where they are not, the world where there is something 'between' them and those who do not acknowledge them as speaking beings who count and the world where there is nothing.
>
> (1999: 27)

If there are therefore no distinctions between parts of society and if there is no 'wrong' that facilitates the act of undoing, then there is no politics, according to Rancière. There is only a set order of identification, which he calls 'police'. Police is a realm of law in which bodies and their functions become identified. *Pace* this order, politics is dynamic and contingent. It implies subjectification, not identification. Subjects who have priory been identified as unequals become subjectified, equals, and make politics.

This strictly political process of subjectification is precisely what post-democracy, with its emphasis on law, eliminates: first, it effaces the *demos*, the idea of subjectified political performers, because law is general, it includes all and excludes no one; and second, it eliminates the act of undoing because the legal system is final, it entrenches a permanent consensus on the terms of common coexistence. Rancière comments that, within a postdemocratic context:

> Any interval between law and fact becomes eliminated. On the one hand, the law now divests the state of the politics of which it once divested the people; on the other, it now latches on to every situation, every possible dispute, breaking it down to its components as a problem and transforming the parties to the dispute into social performers, reflecting the community's identity with itself as the law of their acting.
>
> (1999: 112)

In eliminating therefore the process of subjectification and collapsing politics into law, postdemocracy stops change. Because of this, it potentially leads to a legitimisation of the status quo. The argument that privileges human rights might indeed have the same effect – legitimating the status quo.

Precisely because consensus, via legally codified human rights, leaves no one to be excluded and thus subjectified, it seals off the prospect of changing an established order. If, by politics, we therefore mean an act of undoing, then human rights cannot be prioritised over political participation/citizenship. Citizenship rests, as we have seen, on dynamics of exclusion and inclusion. It is a political means that, to put it in Rancière's terms, presupposes a distinction between equals, 'those who have a part', and unequals, 'those who do not have a part'. Human rights, by contrast, suggest only inclusion. This idea encloses, however, a threatening prospect: replacing subjectified political performers, subjects who undo the set order, with inhumans, those who do not conform to this order. Rancière explains at length:

> The consensus system announced a world beyond the *demos*, a world made up of individuals and groups simply showing common humanity. It overlooked just one thing: between individual and humanity, there is always a partition of the perceptible, a configuration that determines the way in which the different parties have a part in the community. And there are two main modes of division: counting a part of those who have no part and not counting such a part – the *demos* or the *ethnos*. The consensus system thought its expansion was boundless: Europe, the international community, the citizenry of the world, and, finally, humanity – all so many names for a whole that is equal to the sum of its elements, each having the common property of the whole. What it discovers is a new, radical figure of the identity between all and nothing. The new figure, the non-political figure of the all identical to nothing, of an integrity everywhere under attack, is also, from now on, called humanity. Man 'born free and everywhere in chains' has become 'man born human and everywhere inhuman'.
>
> (1999: 125)

Identifying everyone as human and claiming that this simply 'expands' on the *demos* can potentially have also anti-pluralistic effects. Whereas democratic politics, as Rancière approaches it, ensures that new disputes will give rise to different performers, who will then be subjectified and challenge the set order – the identity therefore of these performers is always contingent – human rights revolve around one fixed identity – that of a common humanity. Humanity is moreover such an all-inclusive term, as we have seen, that can be taken either as a notion that encompasses national and cultural particularities, or as a notion that demises these. With reference to a consensual politics, the case appears to be rather the latter – only if particularities are undermined or suppressed can consensus be realised. This is, however, precisely what, in Rancière's view, 'cleanses the world of surplus identities'. These anti-pluralistic effects of the human rights argument are, however, disguised by the way in which they are approached – as legally codified rights, that is. Rancière notes:

> [T]he law/spirit of the community today reveals itself in a movement between two poles of identity: at one end, it represents the stable essence of *dikaion* through which the community is itself; at the other, this essence comes to be identified with the multiple play of *sympheron*, which constitutes the dynamism of society.
>
> (1999: 108).

Is this not what the argument that privileges human rights in fact suggests? On the one hand, that it is dikaion, only fair, to include everyone in politics under the concept of humanity – because exclusion transpires as a simple relationship and not as something constitutive of politics? On the other hand, that it is to the sympheron of political subjects, to their advantage, to extend democracy (the rule of law) to the global level?

This last idea, however, reveals a specific approach to politics, an approach that reduces it to a simple combination of social energies and interests regulated through the legal system – this is the third and final feature of postdemocracy. On one side, there is the deliberative conception of politics, which, as we have seen, approaches democracy as a model that rationally organises coexistence, an institutionalised process of deliberation that aims at legitimating the legal system. On the other side, there is Rancière's conception of politics. This is collective – unequals become equals and act in common. It is contingent – subjectification ensures that politics is always recreated anew. It is dynamic – it interrupts an established order. And it is contentious – it rests on a dispute as the unequals challenge the right-holders, the equals. Democracy, is on this view, 'politics' mode of subjectification – it is not a set of institutions or one kind of regime among others but a way for politics to be' (1999: 99). While therefore deliberative theorists reduce democratic politics to something secondary, Rancière approaches democratic politics as a distinctive and rich notion on its own accord.

The next section of the chapter takes this line of argumentation further, probing deeper into the conflictual approach to democratic politics. The section introduces Mouffe's agonistic conception of democracy and suggests that, in contrast with the deliberative approach, Mouffe shows us a strictly political way of thinking. Because Mouffe takes into account the antagonistic dimension of the political, her perspective on democracy does not lead to anti-politics; neither does it lead to an argument for prioritising human rights. Within the context of an agonistic pluralism, suggests the section, it is citizenship that needs to be reformulated in the light of a deterritorialised and postnational politics, not human rights prioritised.

The agonistic conception of democracy

To explain Mouffe's agonistic conception of politics, we need first to look at what she understands by the political. 'The political', she says, 'always has to do with the formation of an "us" as opposed to a "them", with conflict and antagonism; its differentia specifica, as Schmitt puts it, is the friend-enemy distinction' (2002: 5). The political rests therefore on the delimitation of a frontier for Mouffe, on a distinction between friends and enemies, and on conflict and antagonism – as the friend/enemy distinction is always constitutively antagonistic. Mouffe explains the constitutivity of antagonism through the notion of the 'constitutive outside'.

'The constitutive outside', she elucidates, is something that is 'present within the inside as its always real possibility . . . Because every object has inscribed in its very being something other than itself and that as a result, everything is constructed as difference, its being cannot be conceived as pure "presence" or "objectivity" (2000: 21). Specifically, the idea that the notion of the constitutive outside illustrates and which Mouffe uses to explain the ineradicability of antagonism is that no object or objectivity is ever purely present. It is constructed instead as difference – that is, difference, an outside that is incommensurable with the inside, both conditions the emergence of objects/objectivity and prevents their full realisation. That the outside, or difference, is incommensurable with the inside is important, because it indicates that we are not talking about the simple opposite of a concrete content but about something that, while determining 'concreteness', also puts it into question. For example, there is an 'us' because there is a 'them' and there can never be a pure 'us' because there is always a 'them', a constitutive outside, which makes any 'us' impossible. It proceeds that because us/them differences can always become political – constructed, that is, as friend/enemy relations – antagonism is potential and ineradicable. It arises at precisely the moment in which simple relations of difference are constituted in terms of the friend/ enemy distinction. Acts of power, of exclusion, are decisive in this passage from difference to antagonism. On the one hand, the exclusion of certain differences from the emergent objectivity or configuration is a matter of politics – a point that we will explore in more detail in the next chapter when we will see that, in a structurally undecidable terrain, the political involves a necessarily exclusive decision, an act of power, according to Mouffe. On the other hand, the moment that an exclusion takes place, antagonism emerges. It follows that, while the political is constitutive of objectivity, exclusion and antagonism are constitutive of the political.

In contrast therefore with deliberative theorists, Mouffe places power and antagonism right at the centre of her approach. 'If we accept', she says, 'that relations of power are constitutive of the social, then the main question for democratic politics is not how to eliminate power but how to constitute forms of power more compatible with democratic values' (2000: 100). The main question for a democratic politics is, in other words, how to trans- form, and not eradicate, power and antagonism. This is exactly at what agonistic politics aims. And to develop her argument, Mouffe distinguishes between politics and the political. While the political expresses, as we have seen, a constitutive antagonism, politics consists of all those discourses and institutions that attempt to 'domesticate' hostility, to tame and sublimate antagonism. Although, therefore, antagonism is ineradicable according to Mouffe, it is through politics that this ineradicable antagonism is being 'domesticated'. Of course, the liberal democratic politics, to which Mouffe refers and conceptualises as agonistic, differs from what deliberative theorists such as Held, Bohman and Benhabib understand by liberal democracy – a procedural model that organises a consensual coexistence. In contrast, for Mouffe:

> Liberal democracy in its various appellations: constitutional democracy, representative democracy, parliamentary democracy, modern democracy – is not the application of the democratic model to a wider context, as some would have it; understood as a regime it concerns the symbolic ordering of social relations and is much more than a mere 'form of government'.
>
> (2000: 18)

Thus what we notice here is that Mouffe understands liberal democracy as a regime that concerns the symbolic ordering of social relations and not as a model of procedures that simply facilitates cooperation through an exchange of reasons. That this regime concerns the symbolic ordering of social relations suggests further that modern democracy is constitutive of our way of life, it is not a type of government that depends on rational justifications.

A non-rationalistic understanding of democratic politics distinguishes therefore Mouffe's agonistic approach. She takes recourse to the writings of Wittgenstein and argues that:

> Allegiance to democracy and belief in the value of its institutions do not depend on giving them an intellectual foundation. It is more in the nature of what Wittgenstein likens to 'a passionate commitment to a system of reference'. Hence although it's a *belief*, it is really a way of living or of assessing one's life.
>
> (2000: 97)

This is the idea that Mouffe borrows from Wittgenstein: that a practice is always ingrained in a specific form of life. It is because a collectivity shares in a common life that it agrees on what is and constitutes liberal democratic practice. By emphasising therefore the connection between practices and ways of living, Mouffe suggests that rational and universal justifications are not needed for liberal democratic politics, because the principles of the latter are part and parcel of our way of life. Moreover, it is the same emphasis on the practices/forms of life connection that enables Mouffe to counter the view of procedures as impartial means for furthering coexistence. Because procedures are complex ensembles of practices, they cannot simply be imposed on a constitutively pluralistic community. They require some agreement on the language used, and this is an agreement in forms of life points out Mouffe. Herein a further aspect of her understanding of democratic politics surfaces: modern liberal democracy is a constitutively pluralistic regime.

With the democratic revolution and the dissolution of the markers of certainty, argues Mouffe à la Lefort,[4] there is indeterminacy division and conflict among plural and different conceptions of the good. There is indeterminacy and division because power and knowledge are empty. They are no longer concentrated on the body and person of the king. And there is conflict and antagonism precisely because the conceptions of the good are many and different. Conflicts, moreover, among these many conceptions of the good cannot be resolved rationally, suggests Mouffe – a point that indicates that she follows Weber's understanding of pluralism, according to which conflict among plural values cannot be rationally resolved since plural values are incommensurable with one another. The shift, therefore, from a single conception of eudaimonia to pluralism signifies for Mouffe, as for Lefort, a transformation in the symbolic ordering of social relations. This transformation is something specifically modern – that is, the novelty of modern democracy as a regime consists precisely in its irreducible and irreconcilable pluralism, a pluralism that inevitably sometimes results in conflict. By returning, moreover, to the writings of Wittgenstein, Mouffe shows us precisely how the axiological principle of pluralism can be both acknowledged and respected in a democracy: that is, by finding family resemblances among the many language games that define modern democracy and not by seeking to establish a rational consensus on coexistence, which reduces democratic practice to one 'right' version. Through family resemblances, therefore, we can secure both a common basis for democratic participation and respect for plurality, for multiple ways of understanding and following the rules of democracy. As Mouffe puts it:

> If we follow his lead [Wittgenstein's], we should acknowledge and valorise the diversity of ways in which the 'democratic game' can be played instead of trying to reduce this diversity to a uniform model of citizenship. This would mean fostering a plurality of forms of being a democratic citizen and creating the institutions that would make it possible to follow the democratic rules in a plurality of ways.
>
> (2000: 73)

Thus Wittgenstein's perspective is conducive to two important ideas for Mouffe. The first has to do with the fact that a liberal democratic practice is constitutive of our way of life. The second concerns the ways in which allegiance to democratic values can be secured within a constitutively pluralistic democracy – by finding family resemblances between complex ensembles of practices, plural language games, and not by entrenching a rational consensus. We will return to this last point and explain it in more detail in the next chapter. Now, we need to turn our attention to the connection between Mouffe's account of modern democracy and her understanding of the political.

We have just said that modern democracy consists of a plurality of language games, an irreducible pluralism, which necessitates coming to terms with both conflict and antagonism – because if conflict among plural values is to be rationally resolved, pluralism will either be suppressed or superseded. And the political is, as we have seen, the moment of a decision when frontiers become delineated and antagonism emerges. Mouffe's understanding of democracy has thereby the following point of contact with her understanding of the political: the political emerges when relations of difference are constituted in terms of the friend/enemy distinction and become antagonistic; and modern democracy, which is constitutively pluralistic, accepts that antagonism and conflict among these differences are ineradicable. It proceeds that Mouffe argues, as we earlier mentioned, for the transformation of antagonism and conflict through (an agonistic) politics, precisely because conflict and antagonism are, in a constitutively pluralistic democracy, ever present. In Mouffe's words:

> Politics aims at the creation of unity in a context of conflict and diversity; it is always concerned with the creation of an 'us' by the determination of a 'them'. The novelty of democratic politics is not the overcoming of this us/them opposition – which is an impossibility – but the different way in which it is established. The crucial issue is to establish this us/them discrimination in a way that is compatible with pluralist democracy.
>
> (2000: 101)

To this end, Mouffe differentiates between antagonism and agonism, and says that, within the context of an agonistic politics, antagonism should be transformed into agonism. While antagonism takes place between enemies, agonism takes place between adversaries. The category of the 'adversary' is essential to Mouffe's conception of democracy as agonistic. An adversary is not an economic competitor but someone with whom we share something in common, the symbolic framework of liberal democracy, yet with whom we disagree on the way we interpret this framework and the way in which we want to organise it. Through the notion of the adversary, therefore, Mouffe is able to account for conflict and antagonism, for their potentiality in a democracy, but also to provide for their expression through an agonistic confrontation which is a democratic outlet. That Mouffe argues, however, for an agonistic confrontation and for adversarial politics indicates that, on another level, she also takes into account and respects the democratic logic, which rests on and presupposes frontiers, since the notion of the adversary conceptually precludes the idea of an all inclusive 'us'.

Indeed, arguing for an all-inclusive consensus in politics is not just antipolitical, according to Mouffe, but also conceptually impossible. Because the democratic logic always entails relations of both inclusion and exclusion, it prevents its emergence. At the same time, an all-inclusive consensus for Mouffe can only be the result of a hegemonic articulation. She explains:

> Consensus in a liberal democratic society is – and always will be – the
> expression of a hegemony and the crystallisation of power relations. The
> frontier that it establishes between what is and what is not legitimate is a
> political one, and for that reason it should remain contestable. To deny
> the existence of such a moment of closure or to present the frontier as
> dictated by morality or rationality is to naturalise what should be
> perceived as a contingent and temporary hegemonic articulation of 'the
> people' through a particular regime of inclusion-exclusion. The result of
> such an operation is to reify the identity of the people by reducing it to
> one of its possible forms of identification.
>
> (2000: 49)

And to understand exactly what Mouffe means by this, we need to recollect
that social objectivity never exists as a pure presence for her; rather, it is acts
of power, acts of exclusion, which construct the social world. Mouffe calls the
point of confluence between such acts of power and social objectivity
'hegemony'. Given therefore that a consensus can only owe its existence to
acts of power for Mouffe, acts that disguise and naturalise what they exclude,
it should be understood for what it is: as a temporary and hegemonic stabil-
isation of power relations; not as something that is natural and thus
incontestable. Thus, to ensure democratic contestation through which hegemonic articulations are being challenged, Mouffe puts forward the idea of a
conflictual consensus. This means that while consensus on the ethico-political
principles of liberal democracy is necessary, on liberty and equality, dissent
and contestation is also necessary regarding the interpretation of those
principles.

Democratic contestation is necessary because, in its absence, 'the political
in its antagonistic dimension manifests itself through other channels,' argues
Mouffe and continues, 'antagonisms can take many forms and it's illusory to
believe that they could ever be eliminated. This is why it is preferable to give
them a political outlet within an "agonistic" pluralistic democratic system'
(2000: 114). Hence Mouffe draws here on Schmitt's argument regarding the
implications of negating the political – whereby other spheres, such as
the juridical and moral, come to dominate politics. On the one hand, as the
politics of deliberative theorists epitomise, the law (legally codified human
rights) and the juridical system are increasingly seen as the solution to the
limitations currently facing nation state citizenship. But the idea of 'addressing limitations' through the legal system is only an instance of a wider case –
that, in the absence of or disaffection with politics, it is the law that takes its
place, which is expected to resolve all kinds of conflicts and antagonisms once
and for all. On the other hand, the strictly political differentiation between
friends and enemies gives way to a distinction between good and evil. A
moral criterion comes thereby to dominate the political realm. And morality,
as Schmitt showed us in the previous section, can be potentially imperialistic.

The shortcomings therefore of the consensual and rationalistic approach to democratic politics show the need for a model that, while it recognises the constitutivity of conflict and antagonism, moves also beyond the rationalistic understanding of democracy. Mouffe's model of agonistic pluralism does precisely this. And this is decisive for reinforcing the dynamism of modern democratic politics. Thus within the context of an agonistic pluralism, in which there is contestation among the many and different interpretations of liberal democratic principles, democracy does not rest on harmony. It rests on agonistic contestations among adversaries. This is where the specificity and greatest strength of modern democratic politics lies. To dismiss its specificity by undermining democracy while privileging law and to dismiss its strength by arguing for its realisation, for a harmonious coexistence, is to endanger it. As Mouffe says:

> What is specific and valuable about modern liberal democracy is that, when properly understood, it creates a space in which the confrontation is kept open, power relations are always being put into question and no victory can be final . . . To imagine that pluralist democracy could ever be perfectly instantiated is to transform it into a self-refuting ideal, since the condition of possibility of a pluralist democracy is at the same time the condition of impossibility of its perfect instantiation.

> (2000: 15, 16)

By prioritising therefore human rights, the basic and all-inclusive rights of human beings, Held, Bohman and Benhabib risk transforming democracy into 'a self-refuting ideal'. Within the context of an agonistic politics, by contrast, a politics that, as we have seen, acknowledges the tension between liberalism and democracy, human rights and citizenship, the former cannot be privileged over the latter – because to privilege human rights is, as we will shortly see, to underplay democracy as a constitutively pluralistic and paradoxical regime. How can we therefore renew democratic practice in the face of global and postnational developments? The next chapter suggests that we concentrate on and revise our approach to democratic citizenship. It argues that while we should acknowledge and valorise the role of human rights in a democracy, that they both inform and limit popular sovereignty, we should also move beyond the currently problematic conceptualisations of citizenship and reformulate the concept so as to take into account present global and postnational developments. To this end, the next chapter enquires into the agonistic conception of citizenship.

Chapter 5

Back to citizenship, an agonistic conception

This chapter revisits Mouffe's writings from the early 1990s and argues that, in her work, we find a novel conception of citizenship that could add to and reinvigorate citizenship discourse by addressing some of the challenges confronting it today. Of course, Mouffe in the early 1990s was speaking not of an agonistic but of a radical democratic citizenship. While the agonistic conception of citizenship, which we here bring forward, could certainly be interpreted in radical democratic terms, it is a theoretical and not a political conception – by contrast, the term 'radical democratic' signifies one particular and politicised interpretation of citizenship in tune with the political project of a radical and plural democracy. This difference between the two conceptions explains further that, by rereading Mouffe's conception as agonistic, our intervention aims neither to problematise nor revise it; rather, the aim is, in the first instance, to establish a link between her early work on citizenship and her latest, theoretical, work on agonistic politics, and second, to show that this theoretical conception of citizenship, which has gone largely unnoticed in the literature, could prove particularly relevant today.

This argument unfolds along three sections. In the first section, we contextualise our enquiry into the agonistic conception of citizenship. We focus on Mouffe's early work and examine the anti-essentialist perspective, which she developed in *Hegemony and Socialist Strategy*, together with Ernesto Laclau. Because Mouffe inscribes her arguments within the anti-essentialist framework of discourse theory, the section introduces and elucidates the concepts and ideas that underpin this theory. It shows that its insights inform not only Mouffe's conception of citizenship, but also her approach to politics, which we looked at in the previous chapter. In the second section, we specifically concentrate on and study the agonistic conception of citizenship. Our starting point consists in establishing a link between Mouffe's anti-essentialist perspective, her approach to politics and the way in which she reasserts citizenship. The section suggests that an overarching concern runs through her work: to articulate pluralism with unity in such a way that neither pluralism is asserted at the expense of unity nor unity at the expense of pluralism. Mouffe integrates this concern into her agonistic conception of citizenship. She defines citizenship as a constructed political identity that consists of an identification with the constitutive principles of modern democracy, liberty and equality for all. While her focus on the constructed character of citizenship enables her to attend to pluralism, her emphasis on commonality, on a common identification with the political principles of liberty and equality, enables her, as we show, to attend to democratic unity – without, however, returning us to a premodern view of the political community. By articulating therefore pluralism with commonality, the agonistic conception makes for a distinctive and novel approach to citizenship. This approach, we shall argue, has an important role to play in the face of a changed context. The final section that builds on this argument places the agonistic conception against the background of a deterritorialised and post-national politics. Because the problems that citizenship currently faces derive, as we have seen, from the emergence of such politics, we consider it necessary to conclude this study by showing that the agonistic conception is relevant in their wake. We do this by first indicating why prioritising human rights is inadequate on Mouffe's standpoint, and second, by showing the ways in which her own conception addresses contemporary developments. The chapter concludes by suggesting that we address the citizenship/human rights debate by envisaging citizenship as agonistic, not by prioritising human rights.

An anti-essentialist approach to citizenship

To introduce Mouffe's approach to citizenship, we need first of all to explain that she defines citizenship as a political identity that consists of an identification with the principles of liberty and equality for all. This definition diverges from the dominant approaches in the literature, which depict citizenship either as a unitary and overriding practice (civic republican conception) or as a fixed legal status (liberal conception). To further distinguish Mouffe's approach, we need also to explain that she understands citizenship as a constructed identity, constituted specifically through a process of identification. Citizenship is neither empirically given nor fixed, according to her. It is an articulating principle, an identity, which brings together the different positions of the social agent and is thus open to many different interpretations. The many interpretations of citizenship indicate that its meaning is precarious for Mouffe. The ideas of precariousness, identification and construction reveal an anti-essentialist understanding of the subject – anti-essentialist, precisely because it refuses, as we will shortly see, the idea of a pre-given, self-enclosed and total identity. Elucidating therefore Mouffe's anti-essentialist understanding of the subject and of social objectivity – as the two are inter-related – is the aim of this section. Since it was in the previous chapter that we looked at Mouffe's conception of politics and it is in the next section that we look at her specific approach to citizenship, this first section functions as a stepping stage, in between Mouffe's perspective on politics and her specific approach to citizenship. While it contextualises the former, it gradually introduces the latter.

To both contextualise and introduce Mouffe's approach, we need to stress that she draws on the anti-essentialist insights of discourse theory. Discourse theory claims that meaning is infinitely played and can neither be fixed nor arrested within a total structure. Rather, it is within discourses, ensembles of signifying sequences, that meaning is established. It is established when certain elements, polysemic signs, have come together in a particular way. Because these elements can, however, acquire different meanings and also relate to one another in different modes, the structuration of discourses changes over time. From this initial exposition of discourse theory, we can see how Mouffe's claims differ from those of an essentialist approach to social objectivity. While the latter suggests that social objectivity is empirically present or given, 'out there' to be discovered, Mouffe says the exact opposite. She says that social objectivity is constructed through discourses – it is not predetermined. Because discourses change moreover over time, social objectivity is also contingent and precarious – it is never purely present.

To further clarify this last point, we need to indicate that discourses are articulated within a larger whole or theoretical horizon, the field of discursivity. The field of discursivity is marked by 'surplus meaning', meaning that has not been articulated within discourses and which escapes structuration. Because there are therefore elements that have remained within the field of discursivity, the unity of meaning, of a discourse, is always threatened – the elements can potentially combine in different ways and produce different kinds of discourses. It follows that there is not one way in which meaning can be fixed in a discursive fashion, but there are rather many, yet always partial, precarious and contingent ways in which meaning can be fixed and objectivity constructed. Thus the social, it surfaces at this point, is structurally undecidable according to Mouffe. Torfing explains:

> This does not mean that social meaning and action have no ground, but rather that the ground is destabilised, divided and disorganised to such an extent that it ultimately takes the form of an abyss of infinite play, which turns all attempts to ground social identity into provisional and precarious ways of trying to 'naturalise' or 'objectivise' politically constructed identities. It is this abyss of infinite play, which all signification must necessarily presuppose, that Laclau and Mouffe in a deconstructive style refer to as the structural undecidability of the social.
>
> (1999: 62)

Structural undecidability reveals pluralism as constitutive. There is a plurality of ways in which to constitute meaning, objectivity and social identity, as we will shortly see. At the same time, structural undecidability reveals that decisions are necessary so to institute meaning and partially 'structure' the social. These are political decisions, since they involve acts of power, acts of exclusion, as to which elements will come together and constitute a discourse, and which will remain within the field of discursivity. We can therefore suggest that, for discourse theorists, politics is the instituting moment of all social relations.

Here we have a first indication of a link between Mouffe's conception of politics, which we looked at in the previous chapter, and the theoretical perspective, which we here explore. Specifically, and as we have already seen, what Mouffe calls the dimension of the political presupposes and rests on a constitutively antagonistic distinction between friends and enemies. The moment therefore that simple relations of difference are constituted in terms of the friend/enemy distinction, the political emerges, according to Mouffe. This approach to the political, we are now in a position to see, is informed by the anti-essentialist insight, which we earlier suggested: that the political is an instituting moment that involves a necessary decision taken in an undecidable terrain. This means that Mouffe argues for the constitution of friend/enemy groupings out of simple relations of difference – argues, that is, for a potential and necessary passage from difference to antagonism and thus to politics – precisely because the political is for her a deciding, and thereby necessary, moment for the institution of social relations. The moment therefore that an exclusion takes place, constitutively antagonistic friend/enemy groupings are instituted – they do not pre-exist the political.

At the same time, political antagonism determines that there can never be an all-inclusive 'us'. This suggests that, although politics is an instituting moment, because it rests on an exclusion and a constitutive antagonism, it never issues in total closure – it is never a final moment. In the terminology of discourse theory, the same point reads that antagonism prevents social objectivity from revealing itself as pure presence. Antagonism, explain Laclau and Mouffe, confronts us with a situation in which:

> . . . the presence of the 'Other' prevents me from being totally myself. The relation arises not from full totalities, but from the impossibility of their constitution . . . Insofar as there is antagonism, I cannot be a full presence for myself. But nor is the force that antagonises me such a presence: its objective being is a symbol of my non-being and, in this way, it is overflowed by a plurality of meanings which prevent its being fixed as full positivity.
>
> (2001: 125)

In the next section of the chapter, we will return to the ideas of antagonism and plurality, to the plurality of meanings overflowing identity. At this stage, it is important to point out that these theoretical insights inform the way in which Mouffe reasserts citizenship: as a constructed identity open to many different interpretations. Her focus on the constructed character of citizenship links with her focus on plurality and openness – because there is overflowing of meaning, there can never be a fixed totality. And if there can never be a fixed totality, there can also never be a fixed and pre-given identity. At the same time, Mouffe's understanding of citizenship as an identity that is open to many different interpretations links with her approach to antagonism, as we will shortly see – given that there can never be an all-inclusive 'us', a pure presence because of a potential antagonism, there can also never be one single interpretation that fixates the meaning of citizenship. The meaning of citizenship can only be hegemonised.

Hegemonic practices, explain Howarth and Stavrakakis, are, for discourse theorists, 'an exemplary form of political activity that involves the articulation of different identities and subjectivities into a common project, while hegemonic formations are the outcomes of the projects' endeavours to create new forms of social order from a variety of dispersed or dislocated elements' (2000: 14). For discourse theorists, it surfaces, hegemony is another name for politics. In a structurally undecidable terrain, hegemonic practices decide or determine the formation of social order. They also permeate the social order by presenting as 'natural' that discourse which, in repressing other possibilities, has sedimented different elements into a common project. The idea that a discourse has become hegemonic precisely because it has repressed other, potentially different, formations of the elements indicates that elements, signs that are open to many different articulations, and antagonistic forces between them are necessary for a hegemonic practice to take place. As Mouffe and Laclau elaborate:

> The two conditions of a hegemonic articulation are the presence of antagonistic forces and the instability of the frontiers which separate them. Only the presence of a vast area of floating elements and the possibility of their articulation to opposite camps – which implies a constant redefinition of the latter – is what constitutes the terrain permitting us to define a practice as hegemonic.
>
> (2001: 136)

It follows that if hegemonic practices both determine and permeate (a common) order then what is designated as 'consensual' or 'common' in this order, is their result. This is exactly what we saw Mouffe to be saying in the previous chapter: a non-exclusive consensus in politics always issues from a hegemonic practice. This consensus, we are now in a position to explain, is the result of one hegemonic articulation among others, according to Mouffe – that is, it is a 'consensus' precisely because it has repressed or excluded other possibilities. It proceeds that, because a consensus always rests on an exclusion, it can be challenged – by different articulations of the elements, by other potentially hegemonic articulations.

The notion of articulation, as we have already suggested, is essential to a hegemonic practice – a practice is seen as hegemonic if it articulates different elements into a common project. Articulation is also essential to discourse theory as a whole – articulatory practices fixate meaning, they constitute discourses. In Mouffe and Laclau's words:

> The practice of articulation consists in the construction of nodal points which partially fix meaning; and the partial character of this fixation proceeds from the openness of the social, a result, in its turn, of the constant overflowing of every discourse by the infinitude of the field of discursivity. Every social practice is therefore – in one of its dimensions articulatory. And it is not the internal moment of a self defined totality, it cannot simply be the expression of something already acquired, it cannot be wholly subsumed under the principle of repetition; rather, it always consists in the construction of new differences. The social *is* articulation insofar as 'society' is impossible.
>
> (2001: 113–114)

To grasp what Laclau and Mouffe mean here, we need to recall that the social is structurally undecidable for them. Because meaning can emerge in an infinite number of ways, there is no single centre, according to their theory, which arrests all meaning. A dynamic of decentring is in other words at play in the social field. Yet meaning does emerge, as we have explained, through discourses, which indicates that a dynamic of fixation is also at play in the social field. The practice of articulation lies therefore in between these two dynamics. It is that practice which changes the identity of elements into moments, which constitutes, that is, discourses. It proceeds that articulation is a necessary practice – this is what Laclau and Mouffe mean when they say that 'every social practice is in one of its dimensions articulatory'. In the next section, we will show that citizenship functions for Mouffe as an articulatory principle, a political identity that fixates or articulates the different positions of the social agent. Through chains of equivalence, social agents annul their differences and identify as citizens. To elaborate upon the notion of equivalence, but also of difference, we need to return to the notion of antagonism.

We earlier said that antagonism prevents, according to Laclau and Mouffe, the constitution of any total formation. 'Insofar as there is antagonism,' we have quoted them saying, 'I cannot be a full presence for myself. But nor is the force that antagonises me such a presence: its objective being is a symbol of my non-being' (2001: 125). To account for the construction of antagonism, explain Howarth and Stavrakakis:

> Laclau and Mouffe must provide an understanding of the ways in which antagonistic relations threaten discursive systems. If this is to be shown, then a place must be found for the existence of a purely negative identity

that cannot be integrated into an existing system of differences. To do so, Laclau and Mouffe introduce the logic of equivalence. This logic functions by creating equivalential identities that express a pure negation of a discursive system.

(2000: 11)

According to the logic of equivalence, subjects identify with a common position. The common identification that issues, however, from an equivalential relation is the expression of something purely negative, first, because it rests on an annulment of differences. An equivalential relation splits differences into two camps: those that are annulled and become equivalent; and those that remain differences – a point that brings us to the second reason as to why an equivalential relation is the expression of something negative. Equivalence rests on difference, difference is that which gives equivalence its concrete meaning – otherwise there would be complete sameness and thus no point for equivalential relations. Difference threatens moreover equivalence and can potentially even disarticulate it. And here we are in a position to see precisely how the logics of equivalence/difference account for the construction of antagonisms: '. . . whereas a project employing the logic of equivalence seeks to divide social space by condensing meanings around two antagonistic poles, a project employing a logic of difference attempts to weaken and displace a sharp antagonistic polarity endeavouring to relegate that division to the margins of society' (Howarth and Stavrakakis 2000: 11). It follows that as a project that follows the logic of equivalence, citizenship constitutes, as we will show, an 'us' by determining a 'them'. The 'us' it constitutes, however, is not a fixed totality but a formation, which consists in an articulation among different subject positions. Discourse theorists, it surfaces at this point, hold a specific view of the subject.

Mouffe and Laclau note:

> Whenever we use the category of the 'subject', we will do so in the sense of 'subject positions' within a discursive structure. Subjects cannot, therefore, be the origin of social relations as all 'experience' depends on precise discursive conditions of possibility . . . From the discursive character of all subject positions, nothing follows concerning the type of relation that could exist among them. As every subject position is a discursive position, it partakes of the open character of every discourse; consequently, the various positions cannot be totally fixed in a closed system of difference.

(2001: 115)

Thus, for Laclau and Mouffe, who argue that openness and undecidability permeate the social realm, preventing thereby total closure and fixture, there is no such thing as a subject but only subject positions. On the one hand, this is because for them everything is discursively constructed. They claim that there is no originating subject, and that all meaning, objectivity or identity there is has been constructed within and through discourses. On the other hand, they theorise subject positions precisely because nothing is predetermined or permanently fixed for them, at the 'objective' level. As they put it:

> The category of the subject is penetrated by the same ambiguous, incomplete and polysemical character which overdetermination assigns to every discursive identity. For this reason, the moment of closure of a discursive totality, which is not given at the 'objective' level of that totality, cannot be established at the level of a 'meaning-giving subject', since the subjectivity of the agent is penetrated by the same precariousness and absence of suture apparent at any other point of the discursive totality of which it is part.
>
> (2001: 121)

In the same way therefore that meaning cannot be permanently fixed because it is always overflowing, 'subjectivity' cannot also be fixed, because it is overdetermined. A plurality of subject positions, which constantly subvert and overdetermine one another, make 'subjectivity' impossible.

They also make 'identity' contingent and precarious. In contrast with the essentialist conception of identity, as total, centred and unified, Laclau and Mouffe suggest that we approach 'identity' as temporarily and contingently fixed at the intersection of subject positions. It follows that if the 'subject' emerges as a subject position within the anti-essentialist framework of a discourse theory, the citizen emerges within the same framework as a 'subject' that consists in the articulation of different subject positions. And if the 'identity' of this subject is precarious, then the identity of the citizen is also precarious. But there is an identity, according to Laclau and Mouffe, and this is an important point that we need to explore further. In particular, Laclau and Mouffe follow Lacan and argue that the subject's 'identity' consists in always incomplete acts of identification. In the third chapter, we explained that identification is necessary, according to Lacan, because 'identity' itself is impossible. It is impossible because the Lacanian subject is, as we have seen, constitutively lacking. Through a process of identification, therefore, the lacking subject seeks to attain totality and unity. In fact, its only experience of fullness, totality and unity consists in always incomplete acts of identification. Laclau and Mouffe suggest something similar. But there is an additional explanation why identification is necessary for Laclau and Mouffe: that there is a 'lack' in the structure – not only the subject.

To clarify this point, we need first to differentiate between subject positions and political subjectivity: 'While subject positions account for the multiple forms by which individuals are "produced" as social actors, the concept of political subjectivity captures the way in which social actors act' (Howarth

2000: 108). Laclau writes about political subjectivity. He says that subjects are forced to act or take decisions in moments of crisis when structures are seen as dislocated:

> Dislocation is the trace of contingency within the structure ... There is dislocation not as a result of an empirical imperfection of something which is inscribed in the very logic of any structure. The argument can be put in these terms: no system can be fully protected given the undecidability of its frontiers; but this is tantamount to saying that identities within that system will be constitutively dislocated and that this dislocation will show their radical contingency.
>
> (1996: 54)

It follows that, because discursive structures are contingent due to structural undecidability, as we have seen, and hence constitutively dislocated, they do not confer subjects with an 'identity'. In search of an 'identity', subjects are forced to act, to take decisions as to how they will constitute themselves. And it is to this end that they engage in a process of identification. Laclau comments:

> [There is] an unbridgeable distance between my lack of being (which is the source of the decision) and that which provides the being that I need in order to act in a world that has failed to construct me as a 'modification' (*modus*) of itself. This operation of an adventitious acquisition of being has a name – that name is identification ... So we can assert that identification is an inherent dimension of the decision.
>
> (1996: 55–56)

Identification, we are in a position to suggest at this point, constructs 'identity'. From this follows that if an anti-essentialist approach to 'identity' asserts its constructed character, then an anti-essentialist approach to political identity, to citizenship, can only affirm it as constructed. In the next section, we therefore show that it is precisely Mouffe's emphasis on a constructed citizenship identity that enables her to formulate a conception that respects pluralism. At the same time, her understanding of citizenship as a common identity that consists of an identification with the principles of liberty and equality for all enables her to argue for democratic unity, for an 'us' or 'we consciousness' that identifies with the constitutive principles of modern pluralist democracy. Thus, even at this early stage in our inquiry into the agonistic conception, we can see that Mouffe approaches citizenship in somewhat different terms from those debated in the literature. By virtue of her anti-essentialist understanding of 'identity', she argues for a conception of citizenship that is neither fixed nor pre-given. It is the aim of the next section to examine this conception in detail.

Citizenship as a collective and common political identity

This section of the chapter explores Mouffe's approach to citizenship. It shows that, within the context of agonistic pluralism, a theoretical model, citizenship is understood as a collective political identity. This identity functions as an articulating principle, as we have already indicated; it brings together the different positions of the social agent and establishes between them a bond of commonality. The commonality that citizenship identity embodies consists of an identification with the principles of modern democracy, liberty and equality for all. This approach to citizenship synthesises Mouffe's anti-essentialist perspective with her conception of politics.

With reference to her anti-essentialist perspective, we need to recall the non-fixity/fixation dialectics, which determine, as we showed in the previous section, social objectivity and identity. These dialectics involve a double movement: 'on the one hand, a movement of decentring, which prevents the fixation of a set of positions around a pre-constituted point; on the other hand, and as a result of this essential non fixity, the opposite movement: the institution of . . . partial fixations which limit the flux of the signified under the signifier' (Mouffe 1995: 34). This idea is relevant for us at this stage for two interrelated reasons: the first concerns the fact that determining the subject positions that will fixate identity is a matter of politics, as we have seen – and citizenship involves such politics, as an articulating principle – that is, that approaching citizenship as a political identity that brings together or 'decides' the different subject positions of the social agent follows from Mouffe's anti-essentialist perspective. The second reason concerns the fact that while the dynamic of non-fixity determines that there is no pre-given identity of the subject, so citizenship needs, like any other identity, to be constructed, the dynamic of fixation indicates that the emerging identity, which is always overdetermined, can be constituted only through a process of identification. This suggests that as (an emerging) political identity, citizenship is one such form of identification. Mouffe's anti-essentialism, therefore, her understanding of subjectivity as decentred, informs her understanding of citizenship as a form of identification with a specific interpretation of the principles of liberty and equality for all.

At the same time, it is after grasping the interconnection between identification and decentring, fixation and non-fixity, that we can start drawing a link between Mouffe's anti-essentialism and her approach to politics. Another way of expressing the idea that non-fixity and decentring go hand in hand with partial fixations and identifications is to say that a constitutive pluralism of subject positions goes hand in hand with necessary instances of structuration or unity – instances in which multiple subject positions intersect and produce identity. That non-fixity indicates a constitutive pluralism follows from the argument that nothing is predetermined, that identity emerges at the intersection of multiple subject positions that overdetermine and subvert one another. That decisions and partial fixations suggest instances or moments of unity follows from the way in which they constitute identity – by unifying, establishing bonds of commonality, among the different subject positions of the social agent.

Bringing thus into focus the idea of a constitutive pluralism and of a necessary unity enables us to move into Mouffe's conception of politics and to see the way in which the pluralism/unity pair resurfaces therein. This is not, of course, to say that her anti-essentialist perspective leads her to follow a specific approach to politics, but it is to say that there is a common thread in her work, in the sense of an overarching concern – to entwine pluralism with unity in such a way that neither pluralism is asserted at the expense of unity nor unity at the expense of pluralism. The articulation between (liberal) pluralism and (democratic) unity is also what is specific to modern democratic politics – since modern liberal democracy for Mouffe consists, as we have seen, in the paradoxical articulation between the two. It follows that if modern and agonistic politics rests on and presupposes a paradoxical articulation between liberal pluralism and democratic unity, then a modern and agonistic conception of citizenship has to be formulated in such a way that, while it reflects democratic unity, it makes room for liberal pluralism. It has to be formulated in a way, that is, that neither the individual is sacrificed to the citizen nor the citizen to the individual; rather, both individual liberty and political equality have to be taken into account. This is Mouffe's objective and it is to the end of addressing it that she takes issue with both the liberal and civic republican conceptions of citizenship that we examined in the second chapter.

The liberal and civic republican conceptions of citizenship prioritise either the individual or the citizen. Liberal citizenship is, as we have seen, a formal and legal status that gives to the individual access to a set of civil, political and social rights. These rights protect individual liberty, and they endow also the individual with a capacity to define and further her own conception of the good. Citizen identity does not therefore affect the individual pursuit of self-interest; rather, it is one identity among others, according to liberals. Civic republican citizenship, by contrast, is an overriding activity. It is a practice that constitutes both subjects as citizens and the good that is common to all. Civic republicans do not thereby prioritise the individual. Instead they place emphasis on the political association, the collectivity, which obtains and practises its rights by participating in the affairs of the community.[1]

Now, the problem with these two conceptions of citizenship, according to Mouffe, is that they disregard what is specifically modern in liberal democracy: the paradoxical articulation between the liberal and democratic traditions. This problem is important. In one sense, it is precisely the inability of the dominant approaches to address modern democratic politics adequately that leads Mouffe to formulate a new conception of citizenship – a conception that we will shortly see builds on their strengths and avoids their weaknesses.

At the same time, it is precisely her way of posing or isolating the problem, as one that has to do with the specificity of modern politics, that makes her approach relevant for us because, by reasserting citizenship in a way that is compatible with modern democratic politics, Mouffe adds something to our enquiry into citizenship. She shows us that the problem is not merely with a nation state citizenship that appears inadequate, in both its liberal and civic republican formulations, in the face of postnational and deterritorialised politics, but that the problem is with the way in which we understand modern democratic politics. As opposed therefore to one-sidedly proclaiming either individual liberty or popular sovereignty, we need to integrate both insights into our approach to citizenship. And this last point leads us to the second sense in which it is important to identify that the problem with the dominant conceptions is that they disregard the specificity of modern democracy.

In both the first and second chapters, we saw that, for deliberative theorists who end up prioritising human rights, the issue is how to reconcile liberalism with democracy. Although they therefore accept that modern democracy consists in the articulation of two traditions, they argue that it is in fact possible to completely reconcile one with the other – something that, for Mouffe, is impossible unless one underplays either the liberal or the democratic tenets. And this is exactly what deliberative theorists do, as we have seen. When they say that the democratic tradition can be reconciled with liberalism, they mean the idea of participation. By merely understanding democracy as participation, however, they return us back full circle to liberalism. They end up prioritising liberalism, that is, because they see democratic politics only in terms of individuals who agree on the institutional framework and procedures that best protect their rights and further their interests. They do not see, as we have pointed out, that modern democracy presupposes also unity, a fundamental tenet of the democratic tradition, according to which the *demos* is necessarily bound together by some bond of commonality. It follows that, by disregarding the need for commonality, deliberative theorists tend to undermine also the *demos*. Undermining, however, the *demos*, the necessity for a particular 'we consciousness' and a common bond, is, according to Mouffe, a typically liberal shortcoming that pertains also to the liberal conception of citizenship.

Although civic republicans argue that it is through their inscription in a political community that individuals acquire their rights and sense of identity, so they qualify citizenship as participation in the affairs of a particular political community, it is this same qualification that often carries premodern connotations. As Mouffe puts it, 'the problem [with reviving civic republicanism] arises with the exigency of conceiving the political community in a way that is compatible with modern democracy and liberal pluralism' (1993: 62). By this she means that, although pluralism undercuts modern democracy, some civic republicans argue that, in order to constitute the common good, the political association has to be organised around a substantive and single conception of *eudaimonia*. The focus therefore on a single conception of eudaimonia undermines liberal pluralism.

To understand the point that Mouffe is herein making, we need to recollect that, in the previous chapter, we saw her arguing that modern democracy is a constitutively pluralistic regime because it is characterised by a dissolution of the markers of certainty. At this point, we are in a position to see that the constitutive pluralism of modern democracy, which Mouffe articulates within Lefort's framework, she sees to be deriving from the liberal emphasis on individual liberty. As she explains:

> What I mean by pluralism is the recognition of individual freedom, that freedom which John Stuart Mill defends in his essay 'On Liberty', and which he defines as the possibility for every individual to pursue happiness as he sees fit, to set his own goals, and to attempt to achieve them in his own way . . . Pluralism is linked to the abandonment of a substantive and unique vision of the common good and of the *eudaimonia*, which is constitutive of modernity. It is at the centre of the vision of the world that might be termed 'political liberalism', and it is therefore important to understand that what characterises modern democracy as a new political form of society is the articulation between political liberalism and democracy.
>
> (1995: 35–36)

It follows that, by not recognising the contribution of liberal pluralism, civic republicans often perceive citizenship as an activity practised necessarily by the members of homogeneous communities, by nationals. In the face thereby of multiculturalism, civic republican citizenship appears inadequate either to address or accommodate minorities' issues and demands.

Civic republican citizenship, it appears then, has both a strength and a shortcoming, according to Mouffe. While it focuses on the democratic 'we consciousness', it conceives this in such a way (i.e. as homogeneous) that makes it incompatible with modern pluralistic politics. Something similar applies, of course, to liberal citizenship. While it respects individual liberty, it disregards the necessity for a political association, for a common bond among the citizens, which amounts to something more than a mere agreement in procedures. It proceeds that, in order to formulate a new conception of citizenship that is compatible with modern democratic politics, Mouffe builds on both of the strengths of the dominant conceptions. From the liberal tradition, she retains the emphasis on individual liberty and acknowledges that it is this emphasis that has contributed to making modern democracy a pluralistic regime. From the civic republican tradition, she retains the emphasis on the political association and argues that it is fundamental to recognise that individuals acquire their rights and sense of identity through their inscription in a political community. She retains also the correlative idea of the common good, which she reformulates, as we will see, as a 'vanishing point'.

Of course, here it is important to stress that Mouffe does not seek simply to reconcile the strengths of the dominant conceptions (as Held, Bohman and Benhabib envisage) but to articulate them together. The word 'articulate' is important because, as we have seen, she argues from the start that neither perfect liberty (the liberal tenet of modern democracy) nor perfect equality (the democratic tenet) can ever be realised together. This is therefore the precise sense in which we earlier mentioned that her understanding of politics conditions her approach to citizenship together with her distinctive stand-point in the citizenship/human rights debate. On the one hand, it is because she sees that the specificity of modern democracy lies in the irreconcilability or paradox between liberty and equality that she refuses their reconciliation – a reconciliation that leads us, as we have seen, to prioritise human rights. On the other hand, it is this same insight into democracy that makes her reassert citizenship in a way that articulates liberty with equality, pluralism with unity.

Mouffe articulates pluralism with unity by dispensing with the idea of a citizen identity, which is fixed and unitary. This is because, on a theoretical level, it is precisely the idea of citizenship as a unitary identity that carries the danger of returning us to a premodern view of the political association that does not respect pluralism (civic republican shortcoming). At the same time, it is the idea of citizenship as a fixed identity, one among others, individual and legal, which has the implication of downplaying the 'we consciousness', of constituting and consolidating it (liberal shortcoming). By contrast, Mouffe takes citizenship first as constructed and second as a form of identification with the principles of modern democracy: liberty and equality for all. She notes:

> What we share and what makes us fellow citizens in a liberal democratic regime is not a substantive idea of the good but a set of principles specific to such a tradition: the principles of freedom and equality for all . . . To be a citizen is to recognise the authority of such principles and the rules in which they are embodied, to have them informing our political judge-ment and our action. To be associated in terms of the recognition of liberal democratic principles: this is the meaning of citizenship that I want to put forward. It implies seeing citizenship not as a legal status but as a form of identification, a type of political identity, something to be constructed, not empirically given.
>
> (1993: 65–66)

Taking citizen identity as constructed is important because it enables Mouffe, as we pointed out in the previous section, to change the terms of the debate on citizenship and to approach the latter not as a notion that is given – as nationally bound and hence problematic, for example – but as a construction that can be, at a given moment, hegemonised and articulated differently. It follows that it is Mouffe's anti-essentialist perspective that precisely enables her to advance a conception that respects pluralism. Pluralism is taken seriously in her approach because the constructed character of citizenship ensures that both different articulations and plural interpretations of what it means to be a citizen are always possible. Or, as she puts it in *The Democratic Paradox*:

> Once the identity of the people – or rather, its multiple possible identities – is envisaged on the mode of a political articulation, it is important to stress that if it is to be a real political articulation, not merely the acknowledgement of empirical differences, such an identity of the people must be seen as the result of the political process of hegemonic articulation. Democratic politics does not consist in the moment when a fully constituted people exercises its rule. The moment of rule is indissociable from the very struggle about the definition of the people, about the constitution of its identity.
>
> (2000: 56)

Citizen identity is constituted, according to Mouffe, through chains of equivalence. This is a familiar notion from the previous section and it means that, by annulling their differences and identifying with a common purpose, subjects collectively construct their identity as citizens. A corollary feature therefore of a constructed citizenship is that it is also a collective identity. Politics is a collective activity for Mouffe. It arises the moment when a 'we' becomes constructed and differentiated from 'them'. This us/them relation is moreover potentially antagonistic, as we have seen, and it is within the context of an agonistic democracy that the potential antagonism is being transformed into agonism. Citizenship as a collective identity plays a useful role precisely to this end. On the one hand, it ensures that the emerging citizens, who have collectively identified as 'we', share some common ground. On the other hand, it ensures that these citizens are adversaries – although they collectively identify as citizens, they disagree on how they interpret their identity as citizens. This is besides the defining feature of the agonistic debate: that it is a debate among the different interpretations of democratic citizenship.

This last point leads us to infer a second feature of a citizenship identity, which is conceived as constructed: that it is precariously constituted. In a certain respect, we can say that approaching citizenship as an identity that can never be permanently fixed around a single meaning has a point of contact with approaching democracy as a good, which can never be realised. Democracy, we saw Mouffe to be saying in the previous chapter, 'exists as a good only as long as it cannot be reached' (2000: 137). The reason it cannot be reached has to do with political antagonism, which marks us/them relations and can never be eliminated, according to Mouffe. This ineradicable antagonism prevents therefore the realisation of an all-inclusive 'us'. It follows that the same way in which antagonism prevents an all-inclusive 'us' from realising, it prevents citizenship from being permanently fixed around a single meaning. If democracy is 'the recognition of the constitutive gap between the people and its various identifications' (2000: 56), then democratic citizenship cannot be taken as that identity which permanently fixes the identifications of the people. Rather, within the context of an adversarial politics, it has to be open to many different interpretations. It is therefore the radical democratic, social democratic, conservative and other interpretations of citizenship that sustain the agonistic debate and keep the democratic contestation alive.

At this point, we have a first indication as to how Mouffe's agonistic approach to citizenship counters one of the challenges that multiculturalism poses to the dominant conceptions of nation state citizenship. In the second chapter, we explained that a first implication of a multicultural politics for citizenship concerns the terms of non-nationals' integration – that is, how to accommodate, without assimilating, diversity. And specifically we mentioned that, while a liberal and civic republican citizenship has been conceived as a homogeneous, universal and egalitarian status or practice, there are currently citizens who do not partake in the majority nation, who wish to have their particular identities publicly recognised and who sometimes even need to be treated differentially – so to attain equality. Agonistic citizenship, as an identity that is constructed, collective and precarious, addresses this challenge in the following way: first, the fact that it is constructed, as opposed to being either fixed or unitary, leaves open the possibility that a different kind of citizenship identity can emerge that is not necessarily tied to the nation state – and shortly we will see that it is the political principles of liberty and equality for all that displace the focus on the nation.

Second, the fact that agonistic citizenship is a collective identity articulated through relations of equivalence ensures that both the constitutively pluralistic context of contemporary multicultural societies and the plurality of subject positions making up political agency is taken into account. The pluralistic context is taken into account because the logic of equivalence, which always presupposes difference as we saw in the previous section, both requires and sanctions plurality – that is, that the emerging identity of the citizens articulated through an annulment of their (ever-present) differences, will necessarily be one that has been formulated within a pluralistic context (because of differences) and which can even be potentially subverted by this context – a point that connects, of course, with the earlier idea that different articulations of citizenship can always emerge. At the same time, the plurality of an agent's subject positions, her cultural affiliation for example, are also taken into account in Mouffe's conception – because the political identity, which is constructed through equivalential relations, involves inevitably a collective decision as to which subject positions will be brought together.

Third, by arguing that our citizenship identity can be open to many different and sometimes conflicting interpretations, Mouffe provides us with a useful insight. She suggests that we should both recognise and accept that dissensus and multiculturalism, or irreconcilability and conflict, an agonistic confrontation among the many and different conceptions of the good, go hand in hand – that they are both a defining feature of modern democratic societies. The issue therefore for her is not how to secure a final consensus within a multicultural society via, for example, the legal system, as it is the case for deliberative theorists (and most notably Benhabib), but how to ensure a 'conflictual consensus'.

This insight is important when applied to our inquiry into democratic citizenship, because it shows us that the larger problem confronting citizenship does not, strictly speaking, have to do with the fact that contemporary societies are growingly multicultural, but with the fact that we have not come to terms with the idea that pluralism implies conflict, and that pluralism and conflict are a defining feature of modern democracy. Besides, it is pluralism of sometimes irreconcilable value and cultural systems that is precisely 'what is at stake in the question of multiculturalism' (Burke et al. 2001: 9). The problem therefore, suggests Mouffe, concerns our approach to modern pluralistic politics, not the implications of a supposedly new development – multiculturalism – for citizenship.

To return thereby to Mouffe's democratic politics and to her agonistic conception of citizenship specifically, we need to recall that the second way in which she moves beyond both the liberal and civic republican conceptions is by defining citizenship as a common form of identification with the principles of modern democracy: liberty and equality for all. The idea of identification is familiar to us from the previous section, where we explained that, for Mouffe, as for Lacan, the only option that the subject has for acquiring an identity consists in incomplete and always precarious acts of identification. To this insight, Mouffe adds, as we see here, the idea that the political subject specifically, the citizen, identifies with the principles of liberty and equality. Because liberty and equality are, as we have seen, constitutive of liberal democracy, Mouffe is able to argue that the necessary bondage among democratic citizens, their political association and good can revolve around these principles.

It follows that while the idea of constructing citizenship identity enables Mouffe to attend to liberal pluralism, the idea of a common identification with liberty and equality enables her to attend to democratic unity. She notes, 'what I am proposing is that adherence to the political principles of the liberal democratic regime should be considered as the basis of homogeneity required for democratic equality' (1993: 130). Moreover, it is not only that democratic equality complements liberal pluralism, as we have seen, in the sense that they are both inextricable parts of modern democracy, but also that liberal pluralism requires democratic equality. It requires 'the establishment of a common bond, so that the multiplicity of democratic identities and differences do not explode into a separatism that would lead to the negation of the political community; for without any reference to the political community, democratic politics cannot exist' (1995: 44). How does Mouffe therefore conceptualise the political community, the political association and bond among democratic citizens?

She uses Michael Oakeshott's reflections on civil association. According to Oakeshott, there are two models of political association: the universitas and the societas. The universitas involves a substantive commitment on the part of the citizens to pursue a common purpose. And the societas involves a public concern with the rules of common action, the respublica, as Oakeshott calls it. What holds its members together is not therefore a substantive common purpose, as it is the case with the universitas, but an acceptance of a set of rules that prescribe their conduct. Mouffe, who follows Oakeshott's understanding of the societas, argues that:

> To belong to the political community what is required is that we accept a specific language of civil intercourse, the respublica. Those rules prescribe norms of conduct to be subscribed to in seeking self-chosen satisfactions and in performing self-chosen actions. The identification with those rules of civil intercourse creates a common political identity among persons otherwise engaged in many different enterprises. This modern form of political community is held together not by a substantive idea of the common good but by a common bond, a public concern. It is therefore a community without a definite shape or a definite identity and in continuous re-enactment.
>
> (1993: 67)

It follows that, as a form of identification, citizenship reflects precisely this: it is a common form of political association or political identity that is held together by the principles of liberty and equality for all. The latter provide, according to Mouffe, the rules of our political conduct.

At this point, we have a further indication as to the way in which the agonistic conception addresses multicultural politics and their implications for democratic citizenship. In the second chapter, we pointed out that a second implication of multiculturalism for citizenship concerns democratic stability and, specifically, the fear that differentiating citizenship along ethnic lines might jeopardise democratic stability. Citizenship, as Mouffe reasserts, addresses this fear: first, it provides for a common allegiance to a set of constitutively democratic rules, liberty and equality – that is, that by identifying with the basics of liberal democracy, liberty and equality, subjects otherwise different, can create a common bond between them. This bond revolves around strictly political principles. So Mouffe's conception of citizenship brings us, second, back to politics. As we earlier suggested and here explain, it is precisely her emphasis on liberty and equality and their many possible interpretations (as there are interpretations of democratic citizenship) that allows us to envision citizenship in a way that is not nationally bound.

Of course, the politics that Mouffe talks about is conflictual and this insight is absent from Oakeshott's conception of the *societas*, which she appropriates. In order therefore 'to introduce conflict and antagonism into Oakeshott's model, it is necessary', says Mouffe:

> . . . to recognise that the respublica is the product of a given hegemony, the expression of power relations and that it can be challenged. Politics is to a great extent about the rules of the respublica and its many possible interpretations; it is about the constitution of the political community, not something that takes place inside the political community . . . while politics aims at constructing a political community and creating a unity, a fully inclusive political community and a final unity can never be realised.
>
> (1993: 69)

The reason that it cannot be realised is, as we have seen, because of political antagonism. If, however, a final unity can never be realised, what happens to the correlative idea of the common good?

Together with the focus on the political association, Mouffe argues, as we have seen, that she keeps also the idea of a good that is common to all. So far in the section, though, we have left aside her views on the common good, suggesting that they converge with her standpoint on the political association. Yet an important question arises at this point: does the idea of a political community that can never be reached not contradict the idea that there can be a good common to all? To see how Mouffe tackles this question, we need to follow her argument closely. First, she conceptualises the political association in such a way that she avoids the premodern connotation of a substantive common good. While therefore we still speak of a political association, according to Mouffe, this is not in the strong sense. Liberty and equality do not represent a substantive bond, but a set of rules, a public concern, which is, however, common and strong enough to hold the political community together. Second, she adds that this political community, which the respublica holds together, can never be fully reached because of 'them', the exterior, which always makes its full realisation impossible. It follows that if the political community can never be fully reached, the good that all its members share in common must be somewhat differently conceptualised in Mouffe's standpoint. She approaches the common good as a 'vanishing point'. This means that although there is no such thing as an all-inclusive community that would realise the good of all its members, we still need to make references to a good common to all. So it functions, on the one hand, as a horizon within which we inscribe our demands. On the other, it functions as a 'grammar of conduct'. It determines that we abide by the principles of liberty and equality for all.

Mouffe borrows the expression 'grammar of conduct' from Wittgenstein and Wittgenstein's writings in particular become increasingly important to her work as it later develops. So she writes, in *The Democratic Paradox*, that:

> [Although] Oakeshott's reflections on civil association are very pertinent for envisaging the modern form of political community and the type of bond uniting democratic citizens, the specific language of civil intercourse that he calls the respublica . . . we can also take inspiration from Wittgenstein who . . . has highlighted the fact that in order to have agreement in opinions, there must first be agreement in forms of life. In his view, to agree on the definition of a term is not enough and we need agreement in the way we use it. This means that procedures should be envisaged as complex ensembles of practices. It is because they are inscribed in shared forms of life and agreements in judgements that procedures can be accepted and followed. They cannot be seen as rules that are created on the basis of principles and then applied to specific cases.
>
> (2000: 97)

It proceeds that the rules of the respublica with which democratic citizens identify are not simply procedural specifications of conduct, according to Mouffe. They emerge out of common practices and discourses – not out of procedures and rational argumentation. This point is very important because it enables us to establish a link between Mouffe's agonistic conception of citizenship and her critique of rationalistic models of politics, which we looked at in the previous chapter. It enables us to show, that is, how her standpoint on rationalism, on the rationalistic understanding of politics, shapes her approach to citizenship: both that she reasserts it and that she reformulates it in a way that is directly informed by her critique of rationalism. That Mouffe's critique of rationalism informs her approach to citizenship is clear. *Pace* the rationalists, she argues, as we have seen, that democratic practices are constitutive of our way of life; they are not basic procedural rules that rationally justify coexistence. She suggests moreover that instead of trying to finalise a rational consensus on coexistence, we should accept that there are multiple ways in which the democratic game can be played and that we should find 'family resemblances' among the plurality of 'language games', of the interpretations of democratic rules. When she therefore argues that the rules of the respublica, liberty and equality, are constitutive of our way of life, she says that citizens are those who identify and follow the authority of those rules. Citizens are not simply those individuals who exchange reasons and await to be convinced as to which rules they will obey (see Benhabib). When Mouffe argues moreover that there cannot be a single interpretation of our identity as citizens, she refuses the idea of rationally fixating the meaning of democratic citizenship. As we quoted her in the previous chapter:

> We should acknowledge and valorise the diversity of ways in which the democratic game can be played, instead of trying to reduce this diversity to a uniform model of citizenship ... What Wittgenstein teaches us is that there cannot be one single best, more 'rational' way to obey those rules and that it is precisely such a recognition that is constitutive of a pluralist democracy.
>
> (2000: 73)

In one respect, we can say that privileging human rights in the face of the problems currently facing citizenship does precisely this: it reduces the rules of the democratic game to a single 'rational' interpretation that all human beings, by virtue of their humanity, accept. And here we need to recollect from the second chapter that it is via rationality, a universal medium, that deliberative theorists reconcile a minimal citizenship (understood as public exchanges of reason) with human rights (understood as rationally constructed legal rights). By virtue of this reconciliation, therefore, they see no inconsistency in arguing that, in the face of the problems confronting democratic practice, human rights can take on its political function. Thus particularly interesting for us here is the fact that the force of the deliberative argument hangs precisely on this priority accorded to rationality, on the idea of a rational discourse. And that it is precisely this same priority that, when applied to democratic politics, affects, according to Mouffe, the pluralism of modern democracy – that it effaces the plurality of language games and reduces the ways in which the democratic game can be played.

Moreover, it is precisely because Mouffe detects this anti-pluralistic implication of privileging rationality that her standpoint leads her to reconsider the meaning of citizenship – and here we are in a position to link her critique of rationalistic models with the way in which she rethinks citizenship, with the fact that she refuses to reduce the concept to a mere exchange of reasons. To understand the novelty and importance of this move, we need to recall again that deliberative theorists substitute the focus on the nation with an emphasis on rationality. In this way, they ensure that a 'we consciousness' will be formulated that would not be nationally bound. Mouffe, by contrast, says something else: she says first that the 'we consciousness' emerges out of common practices as we have seen; but importantly she also says that 'allegiance to democracy and belief in its institutions ... is more in the nature of what Wittgenstein likens to "a passionate commitment to a system of reference". Hence although it's a belief, it is really a way of living or of assessing one's life' (2000: 97). Allegiance to democracy presupposes, in other words, according to Mouffe, passion, collective passion.

In another passage, Mouffe makes her position clearer:

> What is really at stake in the allegiance to democratic institutions is the constitution of an ensemble of practices that make possible the creation of democratic citizens. This is . . . a matter . . . of availability of democratic forms of individuality and subjectivity. By privileging rationality . . . [we] leave aside a central element, which is the crucial role played by passions and affects in securing allegiance to democratic values.
>
> (2000: 95)

By bringing in the idea of passion, Mouffe is therefore able to change, yet again, the terms of the debate on citizenship and to ask: what does really make people move in politics and how is allegiance to democratic institutions secured? Of course, emphasising passion does not indicate that Mouffe eschews any reference to reason; rather, it is precisely because she takes reason as plural and discursively constructed that she argues that there can be plural and passionate commitments to different ways of life.

Yet two questions arise at this point: can we claim that a commitment to the nation, with which citizenship is currently tied, is one such passionate commitment – with the implication being, of course, that by reviving Mouffe's conception we are back to square one? That is, that, as opposed to addressing the problem of a national citizenship in the face of multiculturalism, the agonistic conception reinforces it? The second question that arises concerns the following idea: suggesting that passion secures allegiance to democratic institutions is plausible, in the first instance, with reference to state politics and institutions; what happens when deterritorialised processes impact on and even diminish the authority and sovereignty of the state? The next and final section of the chapter, which 'tests' the agonistic conception vis-à-vis those global developments that currently challenge territorial citizenship, addresses both of these questions.

Agonistic citizenship and global politics

This section of the chapter places the agonistic conception of citizenship against the background of processes of globalisation that question state sovereignty to which citizenship is tied. It shows that, within the context of a changed international setting, citizenship, as Mouffe reasserts it, does have an important role to play.

To contextualise our objective, we need to recollect from the first and second chapters the change that there has been in the international setting. As a result of the growing interdependence among states and the institutionalisation of world politics, states no longer decide alone on their policies but have to coordinate their actions, with other states. Supranational organisations have also emerged as arenas in which important decisions are being taken multilaterally. Together with economic institutions, NGOs and social movements, supranational organisations monitor, limit and contest state authority.

While therefore the state used to be an autonomous and sovereign decision-making unit, now that exchanges have intensified across borders, it appears as one layer of governance among others – among the global and regional layers, which contest its centrality. This situation has significant implications for citizenship, as we have seen, since it creates a 'citizenship deficit' (Brysk and Shafir 2004: 8). This means that, while an increasing number of decisions are being taken within global and regional institutions, neither citizens participate therein nor states are accountable for the decisions they multilaterally take within such institutions. In one sense, we can say that it is precisely this situation that has triggered a debate on the future of citizenship. The literature is replete with calls for an approach that would address the gap that has been created between democratic self-determination, currently tied to state territory, and governance at the global and regional levels. In another sense, we can also say that it is precisely this same situation that reinforces the idea of prioritising legally codified human rights – so as to renew democratic legitimacy.

Given thus the relevance of global developments for the citizenship/human rights debate, it is only necessary that we conclude this study with an examination of the ways in which the agonistic conception addresses such developments. By showing that Mouffe's conception is useful in the wake of global processes, we are able to debate citizenship on a new ground – not as a problematic and inadequate notion that can potentially be underplayed by human rights, but as a forceful and necessary tenet of modern democratic politics, exactly on a par with human rights. To this end, we first posit Mouffe's conception of citizenship vis-à-vis those ideas that have so far been debated in the literature and infer from her standpoint a clear argument as to why they are inadequate as a solution to the problems confronting a territorial citizenship; second, we show the strengths of the agonistic conception by placing it against the background of global processes and developments. We show, that is, how, within the context of a changed international setting, citizenship as Mouffe rethinks it is not only adequate, but also has an important role to play.

Within the literature on citizenship, the debate has concentrated, as we have already seen, on two main ideas for renewing democratic legitimacy in the face of global and regional processes: either on a global/cosmopolitan citizenship (Held, Bohman, Benhabib) or a (liberal) legalism most exemplified in Habermas's latest work. That the 'cosmopolitan' or 'global' figures as the obvious solution to what some see as an inadequate territorial citizenship only follows from the impact of global processes on the territorial state. That is, it is precisely because the state is being challenged by global processes that citizenship is often reformulated as global – so to be made compatible with such processes. In another sense, however, we can say that the focus on a global dimension of citizenship is being justified or reinforced by the changes that global developments bring to the fore. Brysk and Shafir explain that:

[The] judicialisation of international relations and the spread of liberal legal norms, a greater autonomy given to courts, and constitutional expansion as well as the enforcement of long dormant international conventions of human rights, greater enforcement of punishment for crimes against humanity, and the creation of an international criminal court [all indicate that] while participatory citizenship seems to decline, NGOs and networks represent a new activist thrust with a clear global dimension . . . These new venues of political influence have created a citizenship surplus.

(2004: 7, 8)

Although the term 'citizenship' is, as we have seen in the course of this study, inaccurate within the context that Brysk and Shafir place it, in the sense that citizenship rests on something more than (rational) input in legal institutions – it rests on and presupposes a *demos* – it is useful to retain from their point the link that they both draw between changes in the legal field as a result of globalisation and the opportunities that these changes create for participatory practice 'with a global dimension', as they note. A clear implication of this link between legalisation and participatory rights at a global level is that it reinforces arguments such as Held's for simply replacing citizenship with universal rights – on the presupposition that legally codifying rights on a world level increasingly challenges the exclusivity of territorially bounded citizenries. The growth in legalisation and practice of rights at a global level moreover gives impetus to arguments, such as Habermas's, for a 'global domestic politics'.[2] This is the second main idea that has been debated within the literature on citizenship. Habermas argues, for example, in *The Divided West*, that within the context of Europe, but also potentially at a global level, legal principles can serve an integrative function. The law or the constitution, a neutral and general medium, can, in the face of global processes, further democratic coexistence and renew democratic legitimacy.[3]

In both cases, therefore, that of a global citizenship and of a global legalism, it is the 'global' and the 'general' that is being privileged. Human rights as a notion have a point of contact, as we have seen, with both the 'global' and the 'general' that the legal system embodies. As rights that pertain to human beings by virtue of their humanity, they apply to everyone. They are basic and global rights. In the absence moreover of a *demos*, there is little to differentiate a global citizenship from human rights, as we showed in the second chapter. At the same time, human rights are rights that are entrenched in international law. Both their salience and applicability derive from their legal codification. In contrast with citizenship rights, which apply only to the members of political communities, legally codified human rights apply to the international community at large. To what extent then does the growing salience and codification of human rights challenge our attempt to revise citizenship in agonistic terms?

To address this question, we need to point out that, within the literature on citizenship, Mouffe is one of the few authors whose approach to democratic politics would not lend itself open to prioritising human rights – either through an argument for a global citizenship or for legalism. It is only necessary thereby to ask whether human rights' extensive codification does not increasingly contradict citizenship and any attempt, in effect, at reasserting it – contradict in the specific sense of questioning the adequacy of citizenship as a notion, in the light of the emergence of global governance. In particular, the idea that human rights might increasingly contradict territorial citizenship in the face of global and regional processes is indicative as to precisely where the problem lies, but also the difference between Mouffe and those who privilege human rights. For someone like Held (or Bohman), for example, who reconciles popular sovereignty with human rights, it appears straightforward to prioritise global and legal rights, in order to renew democratic legitimacy within the context of a changed international setting. For Mouffe, by contrast, human rights are in tension, as we have seen, with popular sovereignty. This tension does not arise specifically from the growing salience and codification of human rights, in the face of globalisation. Moreover, it should be envisaged 'as creating a relation not of negotiation but of contamination, in the sense that once the articulation of the two principles has been effectuated ... each of them changes the identity of the other' (2000: 10).

From Mouffe's perspective, therefore, human rights' extensive codification does not contradict or potentially challenge citizenship, because a tense (and contaminated) relation between the two is specific to and constitutive of modern democratic politics – that is, in so far as human rights' legalisation informs and limits popular sovereignty, they fulfil their role and potential in a democracy. The problem, Mouffe points out, rather arises when human rights 'become a substitute for a truly political discourse' (2002: 93). And, here, we are in a position to see precisely why prioritising them is, through her lens, inadequate and problematic. To see this, we need to recall from previous parts of the book that the political rests, according to Mouffe, on the delimitation of a frontier. It emerges the moment when simple relations of difference are constituted in terms of the friend/enemy distinction. The political rests therefore on acts of power and antagonism. Thus a specific understanding of political discourse issues from this approach to the political. Within a constitutively pluralistic context, in which everything is construed as difference as we have seen, a political discourse is concerned, according to Mouffe, with creating unity, an 'we consciousness', by determining a 'them'. This is, moreover, a discourse in which power and antagonism have not been eliminated but have been made compatible with democratic values. An agonistic citizenship is precisely such a political discourse. As a common form of identification with the principles of liberty and equality for all, citizenship both creates unity, a common bond among the members of the *demos* around liberty and equality, but is also conducive to a conflicting plurality – it is constituted through equivalential relations among different subject positions. An agonistic citizenship is also open to many different interpretations. The many and different interpretations of citizenship challenge potentially hegemonic articulations and they keep an agonistic confrontation alive.

Human rights, by contrast, have a somewhat different function from that of citizenship. Although their function is important and consists in challenging politics, in informing and limiting popular sovereignty, this is complementary to the political function of citizenship and cannot be prioritised over it. It cannot be prioritised because the political, as Mouffe understands it, denotes frontiers, power and antagonism. Human rights, which draw on common humanity, its dignity rationality and autonomy, properties that we debated in the third chapter, negate frontiers, eradicate power relations and refuse antagonism. They designate a non-exclusive consensus on what people share in common – and for Mouffe, there can never be a consensus, a political unity, without exclusion. Prioritising them therefore in the face of deterritorialised processes sits well only with a consensual view of politics. Mouffe, in contrast, not only draws a sharp line between law (human rights) and democracy (popular sovereignty), as we have seen, between a consensual law and a conflictual politics, but she also argues that, as a constitutively pluralistic regime, modern democracy necessitates coming to terms with both conflict and antagonism. Conflict and antagonism, she says, play an integrative role in a democracy. Apart from reinforcing plurality, they sustain contestation and promote change: that is, if conflict among plural values could be resolved – under a common humanity – then pluralism would, on her standpoint, be either suppressed or superseded; democratic contestation would be impossible, if there were no frontiers, no us/them groupings – and everyone is included in the *demos*; and change would be halted if all are content with the way things are. From Mouffe's perspective therefore we could neither prioritise the legal system nor the consensual basic rights of all human beings so to address the problems confronting citizenship.

That deterritorialised processes have implications, of course, for democratic citizenship cannot be disputed. Citizenship remains tied to the territorial state while governance increasingly takes place at global and regional levels. The way one poses and approaches this problem, however, has ultimately to do with what one understands by democracy. So Held, for example, who understands democracy as a reason-giving process, argues, as we have seen, that within global and regional institutions, in which an increasing number of decisions are being taken, citizens' participation is lacking. The problem for him has therefore to do specifically with legitimacy – how to secure democratic legitimacy at the global and regional levels. Precisely because he sees democracy as a model of procedures and citizenship as a participatory practice in which reasons are exchanged, he straightforwardly argues for a global democracy and a global citizenship – straightforwardly, because reason is a universal medium that can simply be exchanged and practised at the global level. Mouffe, by contrast, who understands democracy as a regime in which conflict and antagonism are ever present, is concerned to show that an agonistic confrontation sustains the democratic project. Democratic unity is essential to her and she argues that we cannot, in fact, discuss citizenship without a *demos* who both defines and practises its rights. What holds the *demos* together? How can we envisage the political association in a way that is compatible with modern pluralistic politics? These are some of the questions with which we have seen her to be concerned. Because she is moreover concerned with formulating a nonrationalistic approach to democratic politics, an approach that illuminates the role that passion plays in politics, her work enables us to change the terms of the debate on citizenship.

It enables us to shift the focus to questions about allegiance to democratic institutions, how to secure a *demos* in settings other than the state – but not the globe, as we will shortly see. This is the insight that we can infer from her standpoint. And this is an insight that is missing in the literature on citizenship, dominated, as it currently is, by viewpoints that concentrate on securing legitimacy through rational participation at a global level, but which downplay both the role of the *demos* and the dynamics of passion. How relevant then is her approach today? This brings us to the second objective of the section, which is to show the strengths of an agonistic citizenship by placing it against the background of global processes and politics.

To this end, we need to recall and retain two ideas from the previous section of the chapter. The first is that of passion – that a 'passionate commitment to a system of reference' is what secures allegiance to democratic institutions. In one respect, we can say that passion, understood as a strong commitment to a system of reference, to democracy that is, is precisely that which grounds democratic practice according to Mouffe – that is, that democratic practice does not depend on rational justifications, in her viewpoint, but is ingrained in our specific form of living. The commitment therefore to the democratic way of living (passion) determines that citizens both define and practise their rights. It follows that a *demos*, a collectivity that is bound together by its commitment to the democratic system of reference, is necessary for democratic practice – a point that leads us to the second, interrelated, respect in which we can approach passion in Mouffe's writings. This second respect is also familiar to us from the previous section, where we said that the rules of the respublica, liberty and equality for all, with which the *demos* identifies, are not simple procedural specifications of conduct but emerge out of common practices and discourses. Common practices and discourses bond moreover democratic citizens. Passion describes, within this context, the type of bond that pertains among democratic citizens – that they are not citizens simply because they follow certain procedural rules, but because they collectively and passionately identify with liberty and equality for all. Which means, of course, that they identify with liberty and equality as a way a living – and here we can see the connection with the first sense in which Mouffe uses passion in her writings.

The idea that 'a passionate commitment to a system of reference' secures allegiance to democratic institutions is useful for us at this point because it enables us to isolate an important aspect of Mouffe's work that applies to levels other than the state. Another important aspect of her work concerns a defining feature of agonistic citizenship – that it is a constructed form of identity, open to many different interpretations. This is the second idea that we retain from the previous section of the chapter.

Earlier in our enquiry into the agonistic conception, we mentioned that an overarching concern of Mouffe, which she also integrates in her approach to citizenship, has been to articulate pluralism with unity in such a way that neither unity is asserted at the expense of pluralism nor pluralism at the expense of unity. We can say that while her focus on passion suggests that, when viewed against the background of global and regional processes, an agonistic citizenship has to designate unity, a *demos* that is, and a specific type of bond among its members, her focus on the many different interpretations of citizenship suggests that, against the same background, an agonistic citizenship has to respect pluralism. For Mouffe, pluralism, we need to recall here, implies irreconcilability and conflict; it is that which keeps an agonistic confrontation alive. An agonistic confrontation therefore and a debate among the different and conflicting interpretations of democratic citizenship has also to apply at a wider context than the state. How can we then secure a passionate commitment to a common system of reference, a democratic unity, while respecting at the same time plurality – so to keep the democratic contestation alive, at a level other than the state?

Mouffe notes that 'passion is a double-edged sword: associative and dis-sociative' (Burke et al. 2001: 24). By this, she means that although a common citizenship identity can emerge out of common practices, discourses and language games, out of 'a passionate commitment to a common system of reference', this same passionate commitment has also dissociative effects. On the one hand, it bonds the members of the *demos*, as we have seen. On the other, it does this by determining a 'them', by dissociating the members of the *demos* from the non-members. The argument therefore that passion has both associative and dissociative effects links with Mouffe's approach to the political – it emerges the moment when a frontier is delimited between friends and enemies. The us/them distinction is potentially antagonistic, as we have seen, and it is the aim of an agonistic pluralism to transform the potential antagonism between 'us' and 'them' into agonism. It follows that if, within the context of agonistic pluralism, the objective is to transform the potential antagonism into agonism by 'providing channels through which collective passions will be given ways to express themselves' (Mouffe 2000: 103), within the context of an interconnected world in which agonistic pluralism prevails or should prevail, the objective is, or should be, to multiply passions.

Mouffe explains:

> One of my ideas about how we can [make an agonistic struggle possible] is by multiplying us/them relations. Because the most likely condition for the emergence of antagonism . . . is when there is very strong separation between 'us' and 'them' . . . If on the other hand, the us/them is multiplied, so that for instance you and I constitute an 'us' with respect to 'them', but then a different you and I constitute a different 'us' then it is less likely that there will be antagonism. This is a way to defuse the potential antagonism, which is present in the construction of collective identity. That is what I understand by multiplying passions.
>
> (Burke et al. 2001: 26)

The key to this argument is the idea of multiplying.

There are two reasons why Mouffe's emphasis on multiplying is significant for us at this point. The first reason justifies why an agonistic citizenship is relevant and important, functionally, within a setting in which processes of globalisation and regionalisation have intensified. To see this point through, we need to explain that when Mouffe argues for the multiplication of us/them relations, she suggests that we politicise levels other than the state. We can politicise those levels through democratic practice, through citizenship that is, which, by virtue of its inclusion/exclusion dynamics, creates unity by determining a 'them'. Mouffe does not say that democratic practice needs to be entrenched and legitimated at the global and regional levels, as Held for example does, but that we need to be political also at the regional, sub-regional and other levels, which have come to the fore as a result of global and regional processes. And we are political when we delimit and multiply frontiers – when we become constituted as citizens. But Mouffe does not, of course, view the state as an increasingly obsolete entity, rather, because she sees its functions to be changing, she argues for multiplying the spaces in which politics can take place. This brings us to the second reason as to why the idea of multiplying is important.

We earlier linked Mouffe's point on the associative and dissociative effects of passion with her standpoint on the political, and suggested that she puts forward an argument for politicising spaces other than the state via multiplying us/them relations. But there is another interrelated aspect to this idea and this aspect clarifies further Mouffe's approach to democratic practice. Citizenship has a distinctively political function, as we have seen, for Mouffe: it constitutes unity, a 'we consciousness', by determining a 'them'. It follows that, by arguing for the multiplication of us/them relations, she argues also for the multiplication of 'we consciousnesses', for the multiplication of *demoi* – something that can, of course, be achieved by multiplying the discourses and language games, the passionate commitments in other words, which construct collective identifications, and which have both associative and dissociative effects. So through the idea of multiplying, Mouffe is able to retain the idea of the *demos*, but also to suggest a way in which a *demos* can be defined and secured at additional levels to the state.

She comments:

> [T]he *demos* doesn't need to be the nation state; that's important to understand . . . There will be a plurality of forms of *demos*. Some lower than the nation state, some higher than the nation state. I think that's a way in which we can reintroduce meaning into democratic practice. By multiplying the forms of *demos* in which the citizen could exercise his/her rights of citizenship. But a *demos* is always implied – it could be the European Union, or it might be the region, but it can't be the world.
>
> (Burke et al. 2001: 23)

A global *demos* is an impossibility as we have already seen for Mouffe, because politics and democratic practice always involve frontiers, acts of inclusion/exclusion and power relations. The moment therefore that frontiers are negated, the political evaporates, according to her. This is also the reason why it is problematic, on her standpoint, to prioritise human rights. But equally problematic is also to her the idea of entangling the *demos* with the ethnos. This is important to specify and stress because a potential objection to her work concerns, as we pointed out in the previous section, the emphasis she places on the passionate commitments out of which citizens emerge. Does this emphasis not reinforce the focus on the nation? In other words, is the commitment to the nation not a kind of 'passionate commitment to a system of reference'?

To address this potential objection, we need to recall that Mouffe says that citizenship identity consists of an identification with the political principles that are constitutive of modern pluralist democracy. She talks about liberty and equality – principles of politics, not ethnic principles. Besides, she focuses on political principles precisely in her attempt to move beyond the civic republican conception of citizenship, which often collapses citizenship with nationality, as we have seen. In Mouffe's words: 'I definitely want there to be no link at all between the idea of ethnos and the idea of *demos* . . . citizenship should be linked to the *demos*, to the political community . . . The community should not be based on ethnic principles. That is important' (Burke et al. 2001: 22). At the same time, her argument for multiplying is suggestive as to the way in which she approaches nationality – that is, although she disentangles citizenship from nationality, she does not completely dismiss nationality. Instead she approaches it as a 'libidinal investment', and argues for the creation and, in effect, multiplication of other forms of identification that people could feel strongly about – perhaps as strongly as about their nationality.

Multiplying the forms of identification, however, the *demoi*, needs to be distinguished from an argument for 'multiple citizenships'. There is, of course, common ground between the two arguments: the idea that citizenship can be practised at levels other than the state. Yet Mouffe suggests something more. She suggests that a *demos* is constructed the same moment that it is being multiplied. A *demos* is not a preconstituted unit, which simply practises its rights at the regional sub-regional or state level; rather, it is a unit that is constructed the moment it is being defined. From Mouffe's perspective, the idea therefore of multiplying the *demos* connects with the idea of constituting it. As we have already quoted her saying with reference to democratic politics – from where we take our clues – 'politics does not consist in the moment when a fully constituted people exercises its rule. The moment of rule is indissociable from the very struggle about the definition of the people, about the constitution of its identity' (2000: 56).

Democratic politics involves therefore a struggle about defining the people, according to Mouffe. It also involves a confrontation, an agonistic debate, among the many different interpretations of citizenship. How is an agonistic confrontation secured at additional levels to the state? This is the second idea that we earlier isolated and retained from the previous section of the chapter. Focusing on this idea is necessary, first, because it is important to show that a defining feature of Mouffe's approach applies also to levels other than the state – when we read, of course, Mouffe's approach against the background of an increasingly interconnected setting. Second, an agonistic confrontation that is secured at a variety of levels, as we endeavour to show, provides us with an insight as to the task ahead – keeping the democratic contestation alive instead of resolving it by privileging consensual solutions, such as human rights.

The idea of multiplying is again suggestive as to the way in which Mouffe secures that an agonistic debate will take place in contexts other than the state. As a notion, 'multiplying' implies and presupposes plurality, a plurality of *demoi* that define and practise their rights – otherwise it would be theoretically impossible to sustain an argument for multiplying. Plurality implies, however, irreconcilability and conflict on Mouffe's standpoint, as we have seen. It follows that, by arguing for the multiplication of the *demoi*, Mouffe ensures that a conflicting pluralism will be respected and reinforced in many different settings. That this conflicting pluralism would be conducive to an agonistic confrontation follows precisely from the fact that it is being articulated together with unity. As we have already seen, Mouffe talks specifically about the multiplication of the *demoi*, necessary units for practising democratic politics – that is, the same way an agonistic debate is kept alive through citizenship (an identity that provides both for common ground and dissent), it is also kept alive when, in the face of global and regional politics, there are multiple and competing *demoi* that define and practise their rights. The *demoi* provide for common ground, for unity, and their multiplicity reinforces pluralism, conflict and an agonistic confrontation – and here we need to recall that a defining feature of an agonistic confrontation is that its participants are adversaries, people (units in our case) who are somehow bonded (a *demos*) but who disagree on how they interpret their bond (multiple ways of playing the democratic game).

In reading Mouffe's account of politics against the background of global processes, we can see how her argument for multiplying democratic practices connects with her approach to citizenship. On one level, it provides a link between her focus on citizenship as a collective political identity, which emerges out of 'a passionate commitment to a common system of reference' and her focus on citizenship as a constructed identity open to many different interpretations. In arguing for multiplying passions, us/them relations or the *demoi*, Mouffe tells us in fact to make the emerging layers of governance political – to constitute and delimit collectivities that are bound together by political principles and to pluralise their interactions, to make these agonistic. On another level, her argument for multiplying democratic practices shows us that the articulation between democratic unity and (liberal) pluralism, which defines her approach to citizenship, should also inform our approach to democratic politics at the level of the city, the region or the sub-region.

To concretise her position, Mouffe cites Cacciari's views on 'federalism from the bottom'. Cacciari suggests (and Mouffe very much agrees with this) that, in order to deal with the pressures that the nation state faces from the inside, regionalist and tribalist movements, and from the outside, supra-nationalism and transnationalism, we need to differentiate between the different regions, sub-regions and cities in order to reinforce their autonomy but also to multiply, in effect, their relations of exchange. In this way, we would be in a position to combine unity, because each region or city would be considered unified and autonomous, with a conflictual diversity, as there would be multiple and inevitably conflictual relations of exchange among the different autonomous regions. With reference to Cacciari's views, Mouffe notes:

> Such ideas of course require further development, but I find them very suggestive. If our project is to contest the imposition of a single, homogenising model of society and the parallel decline of democratic institutions . . . it is urgent that we imagine new forms of association in which pluralism would flourish and where the capacities for democratic decision-making would be enhanced. Against the anti-political illusions of a cosmopolitan world governance, and against the sterile and doomed fixation on the nation state, I believe that the type of federalism advocated by Cacciari provides promising insights. By allowing us to envision new forms of solidarity based on recognised interdependence, it might constitute one of the central ideas around which democratic forces could organise in a plurality of democratic public spheres. This would breathe life into the agonistic struggle . . . Moreover, this new federalism should not be seen as being specific to Europe – it could stimulate the

development of other regional units with their specific identities, units in which the global and the local could be articulated in many different ways and in which diverse types of links could be established within a context that respects differences.

(2002: 96)

In this paragraph, Mouffe's intentions are clear: to secure a plurality of democratic public spheres so to breathe life into the agonistic struggle. And the agonistic struggle should indeed continue within the context of increasingly deterritorialised politics. Could this be possible by privileging human rights? This book concludes by suggesting that it is not.

Conclusion
And human rights?

Human rights or citizenship then? On one level, the book certainly rejected the idea that this is an either/or case. As an inextricable tenet of liberal democracy, both citizenship and human rights are constitutive of modern democratic politics. More than that, we cannot envision a better politics, unless we already take into account both citizenship *and* human rights. But there is a caveat here and this concerns the way in which the two principles relate to one other. As the first chapter therefore demonstrated, it is important to recognise and acknowledge the tension between the two principles, not only because their tension, conceptualised in various terms throughout the book, is what defines democratic politics, but also because it is that which precisely drives and strengthens such a politics by promoting contestations and challenges to established hegemonies and given constellations of power. Moreover, in the absence or resolution of the tension between citizenship and human rights, we risk weakening and impoverishing democratic politics by reducing it to one principle. This has been the book's main argument. Motivated therefore by a concern with democratic politics today, the book did suggest that we need to reassert citizenship rather than privileging human rights. Yet this suggestion has been exceptional and conditional.

The suggestion has been exceptional because it issued from an enquiry into the reverse argument – namely, the deliberative case for privileging human rights over citizenship. By problematising this case, the book argued that, in the face of the problems confronting democratic practice today, we should attempt to revise democratic practice – not turn to law and legally codified human rights in order to resolve political problems. Human rights, therefore, have been shown to be limited and limiting from the angle of this book in so far as they are viewed as a substitute for the political function of citizenship – not per se. But the suggestion to reassert citizenship has also been conditioned by three objectives. The first issued from the changes introduced to the international setting, which challenge citizenship while giving impetus to human rights. By showing the turns and shifts in our understanding and expectations of human rights as a result of these changes, the book sought to open a debate about the relation between the two principles, and importantly, to bring into attention the implications of these shifts and turns for democratic practice – an objective that led, in turn, to rethink citizenship. Second, by considering the anti-politics of the argument that privileges human rights, the book highlighted the important political and democratic stakes involved in this move. Finally, by counterpoising citizenship with human rights the book brought into focus the idea that choosing either to reassert citizenship or privilege human rights ultimately hangs on what one understands by democratic politics. If one understands democratic politics in proceduralist and rationalist terms, as a set of processes that reconcile political participation with legally codified rights, then certainly privileging human rights in the face of the problems confronting citizenship is an option. If, by contrast, one understands democracy in agonistic terms, as an ethos or way of living in which strife and contestations play a central role, then the option available is to recast citizenship. Speaking thus from an agonistic perspective on democratic politics, the book concluded by rethinking citizenship as agonistic.

Where then does all this leave human rights? In one sense, it could be argued that by so setting up the citizenship/human rights debate, problematising human rights as political means and concluding with an agonistic conception of citizenship, we leave human rights where they are. Yes and no. Certainly, it has not been the intention of this book to rethink human rights; rather, the reverse has been the case: to show that the role that some political theorists currently reserve and envision for human rights, whether implicitly or explicitly, raises important stakes for democratic politics. In this particular sense, therefore, we do not leave human rights where they are because to leave them where they are implies drawing on a given perception of human rights, as merely protective rights, which the book has shown to have changed in the light of their growing salience and increasing codification in international law. Precisely therefore because the book captures this change and places it within the context of democratic politics, and its implications for this politics, it does not leave human rights where they are – for human rights are no longer just those protective/emancipatory that which inform and limit the actions of citizenries; rather, they transpire as those most empowering and effective rights that could potentially take on the political function of citizenship. Still, the question remains: if we put aside momentarily the argument that privileges human rights over citizenship, is there a role for human rights within an agonistic imaginary?

Mouffe's arguments, which we examined in Chapters 4 and 5, partly addressed this question. In informing *and* limiting popular sovereignty, human rights are part and parcel of modern democratic politics: they set the parameters of democratic contestations and, in a way, we could even argue that human rights are precisely the principle that ensures and secures the agonistic rather than antagonistic character of democratic contestations.

This idea indicates, in turn, that reasserting citizenship as agonistic by no means implies undermining human rights, because for citizenship to be envisioned as agonistic, human rights *already* play a part. The idea of liberty that they exemplify is, next to democratic equality, one of the liberal democratic principles that adversaries in agonic contestations share in common. And their inclusionary and legal dimensions open the way for promoting agonisms rather antagonisms, contestations rather than conflicts.

At the same time we could argue that within the imaginary of an agonistic democracy, human rights play a largely symbolic role. Their role is symbolic in three particular senses: first, in the Lefortian sense, which we mentioned in the first chapter and then revisited when exploring the arguments of Mouffe in Chapter 4. In particular, the idea here is the following: given that modern democracy for Mouffe, as for Lefort, signals a reframing of the democratic idea within the symbolic framework of liberalism, then human rights, a liberal idea, instantiate this symbolic framework. Thus valorising human rights has a symbolic force that not only defines but also ensures that democratic politics takes place. Indeed, as we quoted Lefort:

> Only by recognising in the institution of human rights signs of the emergence of a new type of legitimacy and of a public space, only by recognising that individuals are both the products and the instigators of that space, and only by recognising that it cannot be swallowed up by the state without a violent mutation giving birth to a new form of society, can we possibly hope to evaluate the development of democracy and the likely fate of freedom.
>
> (1988: 30)

The second possible sense in which we could view the symbolic role played by human rights within the imaginary of an agonistic democracy is to follow Wendy Brown and suggest that human rights offer a promise similar to that offered by all other political myths. They are thus symbolic by virtue of the *impossible* promise they hold, the idea(l) of a consensual or harmonious society. As Brown puts it:

> To suggest that rights sought by politicised identities may cut two (or more) ways – naturalising identity even as they reduce elements of its stigma, depoliticising even as they protect recently produced political subjects, empowering what they also regulate – is not to condemn them it is to refuse them any predetermined place in an emancipatory politics and to insist instead upon the importance of incessantly querying that place ... [for] what [human] rights promise may be as elusive, as otherworldly, as unattainable as that offered by any other political myth.
>
> (1995: 121, 128)

Or alternatively we could follow the psychoanalytic insight of Douzinas, which we examined in Chapter 3, and argue that human rights are symbolic within an agonistic imaginary by virtue of the fantasy scenario they bring into play.

A promise and a fantasy scenario then: is this where, in the end, we leave human rights? No, because the symbolic force of human rights, the promise they hold and the fantasy scenario they trigger are central and *necessary* for democratic practice. But equally necessary is the idea of rethinking and revising this democratic practice in the face of the challenges confronting it – not privileging human rights in the belief that, by virtue of their legal codification, they revitalise it. For in this case, as the book has shown, there are important stakes for democratic politics.

Notes

1 Citizenship and human rights in tension

1 The French Declaration of the Rights of Man and the Citizen is particularly relevant because, as an act of founding, it brings to the fore one of the most basic distinctions between citizenship and human rights that not only re-emerges in all acts of refounding but, as we will later see, is also still with us today.

2 Here it is important to explain further that, for Bobbio, it is not only the rights of man that rest on an individualistic conception, but also the rights of the citizen. He notes: 'The modern democracy which was born from the individualistic concept of society, should properly be defined not as the ancients defined it, "power of the people", but as power of individuals taken one by one, of all the individuals who make up society, sustained by a few essential rules' (1996: 104). Although strictly speaking, this author does not disagree with Bobbio on this point, especially since he speaks from the angle of liberal democracy, we would like to add that references to the collectivity, or the common good, which are a distinguishing marker of citizenship, should also be kept into mind.

3 Balibar designates this proposition as 'equaliberty' (1994: 47).

4 Of course, this point echoes Arendt's argument in *The Perplexities of the Rights of Man*.

5 Information on this point has been taken from Seyla Benhabib in *The Rights of Others: Aliens, Residents and Citizens*.

6 Of course, this is a complex issue that lies outside the focus of this section to develop any further. By raising it, we want only to emphasise that discussions and objections to the universality of human rights emerge specifically within the context of debates about the state – both in domestic politics and international relations.

7 Information has been taken from *The Guardian*, 7 March 2009.

8 This expresses the simple point that, although different, the level of the symbolic and the level of practice are always entangled. Citizenship practice always draws on that which is beyond it, the symbolic level on which human rights operate. And the symbolic always informs and initiates changes in practice.

9 The liberal tradition focuses on individual rights, the rule of law, constitutional guarantees and state neutrality. As Dryzek explains: 'liberal politics is mostly and properly about the reconciliation and aggregation of predetermined interests under the auspices of a neutral set of rules: that is, a constitution. A fear that self interested individuals, even if they are in their majority, may turn public power to private advantage necessitates a set of constitutional rights to protect individuals against the government, and against each other' (2000: 9). By contrast, the

democratic tradition focuses on collective rights and popular sovereignty – that is, on the idea that a concrete people, a *demos* of equals, determines and challenges the affairs of government. Bobbio, who suggests that the difference between liberalism and democracy boils down to their different conceptions of the individual, explains further that while liberalism prioritises 'the individual's capacity for self creation, his ability to develop his own faculties and to progress intellectually and morally in conditions of maximum freedom from all externally and coercively imposed constraints', democracy 'joins the individual together with others like himself, so that society can be built up again from their union, no longer as an organic whole but as an association of free individuals . . . Of the two aspects of individuality, liberalism is concerned with that which is inward-looking, democracy with that which is outward-looking. Two different potential individuals are in question: the individual as microcosm or totality complete in itself, and the individual as a particle (or atom) which is indivisible, but which may be combined and recombined with other similar particles in various ways, giving rise to an artificial (and thus always fissionable) unity' (1990: 43).

10 Although we here mainly refer to Habermas's book *Between Facts and Norms*, this same position reappears in most of his writings post-1996.

11 It might be objected that the contrast drawn here between human nature and humanity is misguided. Not only does human nature, or theories of human nature, implicitly underpin what we understand by humanity, but also it is theoretically dubious to attempt to distinguish between the two. Although we partly agree with this objection, we also think it is important to bear in mind that there is a subtle difference between the two terms. While human nature is a more individualist notion, drawing heavily on ideas of rationality or dignity, humanity is a more humanist notion, simple to invoke and easy to empathise with. Of course, as the third chapter demonstrates, when it comes to discussing humanity on its own, it is indeed difficult to escape the philosophical presuppositions underpinning human nature and thus to distinguish theoretically between the two.

12 On the internal relation between law and morality, see Habermas (1998: 256–258).

13 Here we refer to the International Criminal Court created in 1998.

14 Although we could certainly broaden our discussion of global governance to encompass intergovernmental organisations, and how decisions taken therein influence and limit state autonomy, this is not of immediate relevance to the purposes of this section.

15 It is worth noticing that Soysal reaches the same conclusion even in her later work, which examines the participation of diasporas, and specifically of organised Islam, within Europe. There, she points to the emergence of cross-border solidarities and of subnational and transnational public spheres, and argues that 'the referent is no longer exclusively the national citizen, but increasingly an abstract individual entitled to claim the collective and bring it back to the public sphere as her "natural" right' (1997: 510).

16 Although it is in the next chapter that we will explore in more detail the challenges confronting citizenship, here it suffices to notice that, as a result of globalisation and European integration, additional layers of governance have emerged contesting state centrality. Within global and regional institutions, states multilaterally decide on common issues, and such institutions often regulate and limit state actions and policies. This situation carries important implications for citizenship as a territorially bound notion. For example, state citizenries do not currently participate at either the global or regional layers of governance, at which an increasing number of decisions are being taken, and accountability and legitimacy are thus sidestepped. Democratic self-determination, therefore, the fundamental

idea that citizens legitimate their state to act on their behalf, is put into question by deterritorialised processes and politics.

17 Here we allude to the ideological collapse of the left/right distinction.

18 According to Hammar, 'denizens are foreign citizens who have a secure permanent residence status and who are connected to the state by an extensive array of rights and duties. They have their legal domicile of effective residence in the host country; this distinguishes them from other foreign citizens, who lack denizens' well developed ties to persons and institutions in the host country' (1989: 84). Denizens enjoy the privileges of permanent residence. Moreover, as a case in between citizens and non-citizens, denizens weaken the value attached to citizenship. They are privileged non-citizens who usually lack the incentive to acquire formal citizenship rights. At the same time, the fact that denizens are lacking political rights is problematic in so far as it reflects, as Brubaker notes, that a significant fraction of the population is disenfranchised 'and that the interests of disenfranchised groups do not count much in the political process' (1998: 138).

19 Dual citizenship is acquired: by conferment, by virtue of being born of parents of one nationality on the territory of a different nation; by attribution at birth of the nationality of both parents in a mixed marriage; or by naturalisation in a second state while still retaining the original citizenship (Heater 1999: 119). Dual citizens are an anomalous case within citizenship theory. Because they hold a double allegiance, they directly complicate the dominant accounts of citizenship that view it as a singular status. Moreover, in so far as dual citizens remain attached to two different nation states, they challenge the exclusivity of national citizenship.

20 See Bauböck (1994); Held (1995, 2004); Linklater (1998); Delanty (2000); Murphy and Harty (2003); Parekh (2003); Brysk and Shafir (2004, 2006); Bohman (2007).

21 Moreover, we should add here that the only precondition for democratic participation as an impartial reason-giving process is that the rights of the participants be both respected and protected. This can be taken to refer to what Pettit designates as the three constraints that all deliberative democrats share with reference to the procedural practice of democracy – that the procedures be inclusive, judgemental and dialogical in character: inclusive in terms of the equal participation of all; judgemental in terms of the common issues to be deliberatively resolved; and dialogical in terms of the forms and contexts of deliberation (2003: 139). But the precondition can also be taken to refer to particular rights. Habermas, for example, accords priority to autonomy.

22 This Habermasian emphasis on reason explains why the tension between citizenship and human rights is resolved, rather than dismissed on this perspective. The case is not simply that citizenship and human rights are one dual principle, as we earlier saw Balibar to be arguing; rather, rational deliberations, which for Habermas constitute citizenship *and* human rights, are the medium that precisely reconciles the two.

23 As was the case for Carl Schmitt, whose argument on the incompatibility between the liberal and democratic traditions Mouffe here partly borrows.

2 Privileging human rights

1 A slightly different version of this chapter has been published in *Citizenship Studies* (2009).

2 In distinguishing a deliberative perspective to global democracy/citizenship, we draw from Brassett and Smith (2008).

3 Although the idea of a differentiated citizenship has been dominant in discussions in the late 1990s and has since waned in focus in the relevant literature, it is

worth considering here because it provides us with a convenient framework to discuss a core problem confronting national citizenship. Of course, it is common humanity that has today replaced the focus on differentiated citizenship.

4 Cairns astutely states the problem when he says: 'coexistence is not enough . . . We cannot act together unless we have some basis of cohesion. Sharing values is insufficient to provide that cohesion. Francophones and Anglophones in Canada are closer together in values than ever before, and further apart in identity. Finding a basis of cohesion without smothering difference is the task for coming decades. Or, beginning from the other end, finding a way to recognise difference and still preserve a basis for common action is the task for coming decades' (1999: 19).

5 This is similar to the idea we examined in the first chapter, namely – that different statuses of citizenship have the effect of devaluing it.

6 The challenges are interrelated because, in a different reading, a global citizenship could indeed coexist with multiple citizenships.

7 Notwithstanding that Held's account of global citizenship does not explicitly fit into the deliberative perspective that we here sketch, there are two reasons why we consider his proposal to be part of it. The first is that Held's emphasis on securing deliberations in a variety of settings and arenas cannot but also presuppose some exercise of public reasoning – otherwise, there would be little point in promoting such deliberations. Second, the strong proceduralist orientation of Held's proposal is, as we will shortly see, a further defining characteristic of the deliberative approach to global citizenship.

8 Although it appears from the citations used here that Held puts forward the notion of global citizenship in his most recent work (2004), this is far from the case. Already, in his 1995 book *Democracy and the Global Order: From the Modern State to Cosmopolitan Governance*, there are ample references to a global citizenship: for example, when he says that [under a cosmopolitan framework of law] 'the rights and responsibilities of people qua national citizens and qua subjects of cosmopolitan law could coincide, and democratic citizenship could take on, in principle, a truly universal status' (1995: 233).

9 Although Benhabib does not sufficiently elaborate whether democratic iterations involve predominantly deliberations, this appears to be quite likely if we consider that it is discourse ethics that inform her overall approach.

10 Here it needs to be clarified that although citizenship's particularity is a contested property, especially in the light of numerous attempts within the cosmopolitan school of thought to theorise citizenship in universal terms, we could argue that it is precisely in its boundedness that citizenship's particularity, which we here explicate, consists. Moreover, and although it could be further objected, from the other end, that disagreements about the origins, content and validity of human rights raise serious questions about their universality, such objections appear to lose their force when we counterpoise human rights to citizenship. What humanity precisely promotes, if not secures, as an idea is universalisation. Bounded membership, in contrast, precludes this possibility.

11 Of course, it could be objected at this point that the universality that citizenship is seen to appropriate is also infused with the very same inclusionary/exclusionary dynamics that define citizenship discourse (see Edkins 2003). Still, it could be argued that whereas, in the case of citizenship, these dynamics assume a strictly political form, facilitating a contestatory politics, as we will shortly see, in the case of human rights, they thread on moral causes and implications.

12 Here it needs to be clarified that although the way in which Benhabib understands citizenship is undeniably distinctive, questions arise when one brings into the discussion human rights, for it is not exactly clear why basic legal rights could not,

in principle, embody democratic practice, if by democratic practice one understands (rational) deliberations that ensure that democratic norms become revised.

13 This is not to say that humanity is a 'thin' notion, rather, it is to say that it is such an all-encompassing notion that it could certainly 'defuse' civic solidarity. Moreover, it is interesting to notice here that Habermas, whose work greatly influences the arguments of Held, Bohman and Benhabib, explicitly rejects the idea of universal citizenship on the grounds that civic solidarity precisely cannot be secured outside the boundaries of nation states. Instead, what he suggests in *The Divided West* is to reinforce global constitutionalism and domestic public spheres. Next to a global public sphere mobilised by moral outrage against human rights abuses, domestic public spheres could confer indirect legitimacy to institutions of global governance. Of course, Bohman and Benhabib also place emphasis on public spheres. Unlike Habermas, however, they also take the further step of envisioning, as we have seen, a universal citizenship.

3 The illusive promise of human rights

1 Cited in Boaventura de Sousa Santos (1995: 338). See also Panikkar (1982).

2 Although rationality is a contested term, following Nietzsche and Foucault, we can trace references to reason back to the Cartesian *cogito*, to the fusion of thinking and being (e.g. 'because I think, I am'). Holt explains: 'I cannot doubt that I think and to think I must be. Doubt, thought and being (. . . which are known by all by virtue of their doubting, thinking and being and hence require no pre-existing truth and knowledge) coincide to frame an entirely privileged first cause from which other objectivities can be drawn (e.g. one of my ideas is that of infinity, hence there must be a God) but none of which pre-exist the *cogito*' (1997: 8–9). The cogito affirms the accuracy of all that can be rationally proved. Reason constructs the 'real', the 'truth' of the world and the mind and dictates the 'right', as opposed to the 'wrong', course of action. Taking thereby rationality as the universal absolute against which all reflections of the world could be measured, the Enlightenment tradition brought forward the notion of a transparent human nature, a rational human essence knowable by means of its own rationality.

3 The priority accorded to human subjectivity was the result of the Enlightenment privileging of the cogito, of mind and its reason. Man is the originator of all meaning and knowledge because it is he/she who possesses the faculty of reason. Douzinas comments, 'This was the most dramatic effect of the Enlightenment. By the end of the C18th, the concept of "man" came into existence and soon became the absolute and inalienable value around which the whole world revolved' (2001: 188).

4 Belief in the absolute and inalienable dignity of the individual stems originally from the Christian idea of the sacredness of every human being. It was further reinforced by the focus of eighteenth-century liberalism on the individual as the primary unit of political analysis. According to the liberal political philosophies of the eighteenth century, the individual, an isolated and autonomous monad, exists prior to society. He/she is an end in him/herself and has an inherent moral worth and dignity that, in its own turn, derives from his/her prioritisation over societal arrangements. In effect, the state has to respect and safeguard his/her interests. We should add that the liberal emphases on the autonomy and equality of individuals are intertwined with the notion of their inherent dignity.

5 The notion of autonomous individuals, as mentioned earlier, derives also from the liberal political philosophies of the eighteenth century. It means that individuals are enjoying, what Berlin called, 'negative liberty' – that is, 'freedom from' as

opposed to 'freedom to' something. Specifically, individuals who have the right to pursue their own conception of the good as they see fit must be treated as ends, as free and equal. It follows that the state should remain neutral and not be interfering with the individuals' affairs. All that matters is their autonomy and rights to their diverse conceptions of the good life.

4 Politics and legalism

1 It is interesting that Christodoulidis uses the term 'republican constitutionalism' to describe, as we will shortly see, the Habermasian position that identifies law with politics, since it shows that the deliberative approach, which strictly speaking reconciles liberalism with republicanism, does not escape the implication of undermining politics while prioritising law – whether this move is viewed as liberal or republican.

2 Christodoulidis explains further: 'Institutional categories of law account for institutionalisation through complexes of "institutive" "consequential" and "terminative" rules that delineate the realm of institutional facts. Systems theorists map out the world of law – the realm of reduced complexity – by arguing that legal meanings are circumscribed along "temporal", "social" and "substantive" dimensions' (2006: 7).

3 Rancière is not the only theorist who uses the term 'postdemocracy'. Colin Crouch also uses the term to describe a model in which democratic debate has been reduced to a controlled spectacle. 'Under the postdemocratic model,' he says, 'elections certainly exist and can change governments, [yet] public debate is a tightly controlled spectacle, managed by rival teams of professionals expert in the techniques of persuasion, and considering a small range of issues selected by those teams. The mass of citizens plays a passive, quiescent, even apathetic part, responding only to the signals given to them . . . Under these conditions, there is little hope for an agenda of strong egalitarian policies for the redistribution of power and wealth, or for the restraint of powerful interest' (2004: 4).

4 See Lefort (1986: 255–256).

5 Back to citizenship, an agonistic conception

1 We can see that the emphases on individual liberty and citizen participation of the dominant conceptions of citizenship correspond with fundamental tenets of the two traditions that make up modern democracy – that is that, by approaching citizenship as a legal set of rights, liberal theorists uphold the liberal tradition, which focuses, as we have seen, on individual liberty, human rights and the rule of law. Civic republicans, on the other hand, who approach citizenship as an activity that overrides individuals' particularities so to determine the public good, recover a fundamental tenet of the democratic tradition, that of popular sovereignty.

2 A global domestic politics is, according to Habermas, a politics conducted under the framework of cosmopolitan law, implemented by global institutions and legitimated from within national public spheres. See Habermas (2006).

3 For a critique of this Habermasian alternative, see Tambakaki (2009b).

Bibliography

Andrews, G. (1991) *Citizenship*, London: Lawrence & Wishart.

Archibugi, D. (ed.) (2003) *Debating Cosmopolitics*, London: Verso.

——, Held, D. and Köhler, M. (eds) (1998) *Re-imagining Political Community: Studies in Cosmopolitan Democracy*, Cambridge: Polity Press.

Arendt, H. (1958) *The Human Condition*, Chicago, Illinois: University of Chicago Press.

—— (1968) 'The Decline of the Nation State and the End of the Rights of Man', in *The Origins of Totalitarianism*, New York: Harcourt Inc.

—— (2005) *The Promise of Politics*, edited by J. Kohn, New York: Schocken Books.

Arnason, J. P. (2000) 'Globalism, Ideology and Traditions: Interview with Jürgen Habermas', *Thesis Eleven*, 63: 1–10.

Ashenden, S. and Owen, D. (eds) (1999) *Foucault Contra Habermas: Recasting the Dialogue Between Genealogy and Critical Theory*, London: SAGE Publications.

Bader, V. (1995) 'Citizenship and Exclusion. Radical Democracy, Community and Justice. Or What is Wrong with Communitarianism?', *Political Theory*, 23(2): 211–246.

Badiou, A. (2001) *Ethics: An Essay on the Understanding of Evil*, London: Verso.

Balibar, E. (1988) 'Propositions on Citizenship', *Ethics*, 98: 723–730.

—— (1994) '"Rights of Man" and "Rights of the Citizen": The Modern Dialectic of Equality and Freedom', in *Masses, Classes, Ideas: Studies On Politics and Philosophy Before and After Marx*, New York: Routledge.

—— (2002) *Politics and the Other Scene*, London: Verso.

—— (2004a) *We, The People of Europe? Reflections on Transnational Citizenship*, Princeton, New Jersey: Princeton University Press.

—— (2004b) 'Is a Philosophy of Human Civic Rights Possible? New Reflections on Equaliberty', *South Atlantic Quarterly*, 103(2/3): 311–322.

Barbalet, J. M. (ed.) (1988) *Citizenship: Rights, Struggle and Class Inequality*, Milton Keynes: Open University Press.

Barber, B. (1984) *Strong Democracy: Participatory Politics for a New Age*, Berkeley, California: University of California Press.

Barrett, M. (1991) *The Politics of Truth: From Marx to Foucault*, Cambridge: Polity Press.

Bauböck, R. (1994) *Transnational Citizenship: Membership and Rights in the Face of International Migration*, Aldershot: Edward Elgar.

—— (1997) 'Citizenship and National Identities in the European Union', *Harvard*

Jean Monnet Working Paper, No. 4/97, Cambridge, Massachusetts: Harvard Law School.

Baxi, U. (2002) *The Future of Human Rights*, Oxford: Oxford University Press.

Beetham, D. (ed.) (1995) *Politics and Human Rights*, Oxford: Blackwell.

—— (1999) *Democracy and Human Rights*, Cambridge: Polity Press.

Beiner, R. (ed.) (1995) *Theorising Citizenship*, Albany, New York: State University of New York.

Belden Fields, A. (2003) *Rethinking Human Rights for the New Millennium*, New York: Palgrave Macmillan.

Bellamy, E. J. (1993) 'Discourses of Impossibility: Can Psychoanalysis Be Political?', *Diacritics*, 23(1): 24–38.

Bellamy, R. (1999) *Liberalism and Pluralism: Towards a Politics of Compromise*, London: Routledge.

Bendix, R. (1964) *Nation Building and Citizenship: Studies of our Changing Social Order*, New York: John Wiley & Sons.

Benhabib, S. (ed.) (1996) *Democracy and Difference: Contesting the Boundaries of the Political*, Princeton, New Jersey: Princeton University Press.

—— (2001) *Transformations of Citizenship: Dilemmas of the Nation State in the Era of Globalisation*, Amsterdam: Koninklijke Van Gorcum.

—— (2004) *The Rights of Others: Aliens, Residents and Citizens*, Cambridge: Cambridge University Press.

—— (2005) 'Disaggregation of Citizenship Rights', *Parallax*, 11(1): 10–18.

—— (2006) *Another Cosmopolitanism*, New York: Oxford University Press.

—— (2007) 'Twilight of Sovereignty or the Emergence of Cosmopolitan Norms? Rethinking Citizenship in Volatile Times', *Citizenship Studies*, 11(1): 19–36.

Benvenuto, B. and Kennedy, R. (1986) *The Works of Jacques Lacan: An Introduction*, London: Free Association Books.

Berlin, I. (2002) *Liberty*, Oxford: Oxford University Press.

Berting, J. (1990) 'Human Rights: Rights of Individuals – Rights of Collectivities', in J. Berting (ed.), *Human Rights in a Pluralist World: Individuals and Collectivities*, London: Roosevelt Study Centre Publications.

Bhabha, J. (1998) 'Get Back to Where You Once Belonged: Identity, Citizenship and Exclusion in Europe', *Human Rights Quarterly*, 20: 410–451.

Bielefeldt, H. (1996) 'Secular Human Rights: Challenge and Opportunity to Christians and Muslims', *Islam and Christian-Muslim Relations*, 7(3): 311–325.

—— (2000) 'Western Versus Islamic Human Rights Conceptions? A Critique of Cultural Essentialism in the Discussion of Human Rights', *Political Theory*, 28(1): 90–121.

Bobbio, N. (1988) *Liberalism and Democracy*, London: Verso.

—— (1996) *The Age of Rights*, Cambridge: Polity Press.

Bohman, J. (2004) 'Republican Cosmopolitanism', *The Journal of Political Philosophy*, 12(3): 336–352.

—— (2005) 'The Democratic Minimum: Is Democracy a Means to Global Justice?', *Ethics and International Affairs*, 19(1): 101:116.

—— (2007) *Democracy Across Borders: From Demos to Demoi*, Cambridge, Massachusetts: MIT Press.

Bracher, M. (1997) 'Always Psychoanalyse! Historicism and the Psychoanalysis of Culture and Society', *Journal for the Psychoanalysis of Culture and Society*, 2(1): 32–49.

—— , Alcorn, M., Corthell, R. J. and Massardier-Kenney, F. (eds) (1994) *Lacanian Theory of Discourse: Subject, Structure and Society*, New York: New York University Press.

Brady, J. (2004) 'No Contest? Assessing the Agonistic Critiques of Jürgen Habermas's Theory of the Public Sphere', *Philosophy and Social Criticism*, 30(3): 331–354.

Brassett, J. and Smith, W. (2008) 'Deliberation and Global Governance: Liberal, Cosmopolitan and Critical Perspectives', *Ethics and International Affairs*, 22(1): 69–92.

Brown, M. P. (1997) *Replacing Citizenship*, New York: Guildford Press.

Brown, W. (1995) *States of Injury: Power and Freedom in Late Modernity*, Princeton, New Jersey: Princeton University Press.

—— (2001) *Politics Out of History*, Princeton, New Jersey: Princeton University Press.

—— (2002a) 'Suffering the Paradoxes of Rights', in W. Brown and J. Halley (eds), *Left Legalism/Left Critique*, Durham: Duke University Press.

—— (2002b) 'At the Edge', *Political Theory*, 30(4): 556–576.

—— (2004) ' "The Most We Can Hope For . . .": Human Rights and the Politics of Fatalism', *South Atlantic Quarterly*, 103(2/3): 451–464.

Brubaker, R. (1984) *The Limits of Rationality: An Essay on the Social and Moral Thought of Max Weber*, London: George Allen & Unwin.

—— (1989) (ed.) *Immigration and the Politics of Citizenship in Europe and North America*, Lanham, Maryland: University Press of America.

—— (1992) *Citizenship and Nationhood in France and Germany*, Cambridge, Massachusetts: Harvard University Press.

—— (1998) 'Citizenship and the Nation State in France and Germany', in G. Shafir (ed.), *The Citizenship Debates: A Reader*, Minneapolis, Minnesota: University of Minnesota Press.

Brysk, A. and Shafir, G. (eds) (2004) *People Out of Place: Globalisation, Human Rights and the Citizenship Gap*, London: Routledge.

—— (2006) 'The Globalisation of Rights: From Citizenship to Human Rights', *Citizenship Studies*, 10(3): 275 287.

Burke, P., Evans, H. and Tambakaki, P. (2001) 'Interview with Chantal Mouffe', *CSD Bulletin*, unedited version.

Butler, J., Laclau, E. and Žižek, S. (2000) *Contingency, Hegemony, Universality: Contemporary Dialogues on the Left*, London: Verso.

Cairns, A. C., Courtney, J. C., MacKinnon, P., Michelmann, H. J. and Smith, D. E. (eds) (1999) *Citizenship, Diversity and Pluralism: Canadian and Comparative Perspectives*, Montreal: McGill-Queen's University Press.

Campbell, T., Ewing, K. D. and Tomkins, A. (eds) (2001) *Sceptical Essays on Human Rights*, Oxford: Oxford University Press.

Carter, A. and Stokes, G. (eds) (1998) *Liberal Democracy and its Critics*, Cambridge: Polity Press.

Cesarani, D. and Fulbrook, M. (eds) (1996) *Citizenship, Nationality and Migration in Europe*, London: Routledge.

Chambers, S. A. (2004) 'Giving Up (on) Rights? The Future of Rights and the Project of Radical Democracy', *American Journal of Political Science*, 48(2): 185–200.

Chandler, D. (2002) *From Kosovo to Kabul: Human Rights and International Interven- tion*, London: Pluto Press.

Christodoulidis, A. (2006) 'Republican Constitutionalism and Reflexive Politics', *Archives for Philosophy of Law and Social Philosophy*, 92(1): 1–14.

Clarke, P. B. (ed.) (1994) *Citizenship*, London: Pluto Press.

Cochran, C. E. (1989) 'The Thin Theory of Community: The Communitarians and Their Critics', *Political Studies*, 37: 422–435.

Collier, A. (1998) 'Mind, Reality and Politics', *Radical Philosophy*, 88: 38–43.

Connolly, W. E. (1991) *Identity/Difference: Democratic Negotiations of Political Paradox*, Ithaca, New York: Cornell University Press.

—— (1995) *The Ethos of Pluralisation*, Minneapolis: University of Minnesota Press.

Cooke, M. (1997) 'Authenticity and Autonomy: Taylor, Habermas and the Politics of Recognition', *Political Theory*, 25(2): 258–288.

Copjec, J. (1994a) *Read My Desire: Lacan Against the Historicists*, Cambridge, Massachusetts: MIT Press.

—— (ed.) (1994b) *Supposing the Subject*, London: Verso.

Cottingham, J. (1998) *Philosophy and the Good Life: Reason and the Passions in Greek, Cartesian and Psychoanalytic Ethics*, Cambridge: Cambridge University Press.

Cranston, M. (1983) 'Are There Any Human Rights?', *Daedalus*, 112: 1–17.

Critchley, S. (1998a) 'Metaphysics in the Dark: A Response to Richard Rorty and Ernesto Laclau', *Political Theory*, 26(6): 803–817.

—— (1998b) 'The Other's Decision in Me – What Are the Politics of Friendship?', *European Journal of Social Theory*, 1(2): 259–279.

Crouch, C. (2004) *Postdemocracy*, Cambridge: Polity Press.

Crowder, G. (1994) 'Pluralism and Liberalism', *Political Studies*, XLII: 293–305.

—— (2002) *Liberalism and Value Pluralism*, London: Continuum.

Dallmayr, F. (1993) 'Post-Metaphysics and Democracy', *Political Theory*, 21(1): 101–127.

Daly, G. (1994) 'Post-Metaphysical Culture and Politics: Rorty, Laclau and Mouffe', *Economy and Society*, 23(2): 173–200.

Davidson, A. (1997) 'Regional Politics: The European Union and Citizenship', *Citizenship Studies*, 1(1): 33–55.

—— (2000) 'Fractured Identities: Citizenship in a Global World', in E.Vasta (ed.) *Citizenship, Community and Democracy*, London: Macmillan.

Delanty, G. (2000) *Citizenship in a Global Age: Society, Culture, Politics*, Buckingham: Open University Press.

Derrida, J. (2001) *On Cosmopolitanism and Forgiveness*, London: Routledge.

—— (2004) 'The Last of the Rogue States: The "Democracy to Come", Opening in Two Turns', *South Atlantic Quarterly*, 103(2/3): 323–342.

Deveaux, M. (1999) 'Agonism and Pluralism', *Philosophy and Social Criticism*, 25(4): 1–22.

Donnelly, J. (2003) *Universal Human Rights in Theory and Practice*, Ithaca, New York: Cornell University Press.

Douzinas, C. (2000) *The End of Human Rights*, Oxford: Hart Publishing.

—— (2001) 'Human Rights, Humanism and Desire', *Angelaki* 6(3): 183–206.

Dryzek, J. S. (2000) *Deliberative Democracy and Beyond: Liberals, Critics, Contesta- tions*, Oxford: Oxford University Press.

Dufresne, T. (ed.) (1997) *Returns of the French Freud: Freud, Lacan and Beyond*, New York: Routledge.

Dummett, A. (1976) *Citizenship and Nationality*, London: Runnymede Trust.

Dunne, T. and Wheeler, N. J. (eds) *Human Rights in Global Politics*, Cambridge: Cambridge University Press.

Dworkin, R. (1978) *Taking Rights Seriously*, London: Duckworth.

—— (1985) *A Matter of Principle*, Oxford: Oxford University Press.

Dyck, A. J. (1994) *Rethinking Rights and Responsibilities: The Moral Bonds of Community*, Cleveland, Ohio: Pilgrim Press.

Edkins, J. (2003) 'Humanitarianism, Humanity, Human', *Journal of Human Rights*, 2(2): 253–258.

Elliot, A. (1994) *Psychoanalytic Theory: An Introduction*, Oxford: Blackwell.

Enwezor, O., Basualdo, D., Bauer, U., Ghez, S., Maharaj, S., Nash, M. and Zaya, O. (eds) (2002) *Democracy Unrealised: Documenta 11_Platform 1*, Ostfildern, Germany: Hatje Cantz Publishers.

Evans, D. (1996a) *An Introductory Dictionary of Lacanian Psychoanalysis*, London: Routledge.

—— (1996b) 'Historicism and Lacanian Theory', *Radical Philosophy*, 79: 35–40.

—— (1999) 'From Kantian Ethics to Mystical Experience: An Exploration of Jouissance', in D. Nobus (ed.), *Key Concepts of Lacanian Psychoanalysis*, New York: Other Press.

Evans, T. (ed.) (1998) *Human Rights Fifty Years On: A Reappraisal*, Manchester: Manchester University Press.

—— (2001a) 'If Democracy, Then Human Rights?', *Third World Quarterly*, 22(4): 623–642.

—— (2001b) *The Politics of Human Rights: A Global Perspective*, London: Pluto Press.

—— and Hancock, J. (1998) 'Doing Something Without Doing Anything: International Human Rights Law and the Challenge of Globalisation' *International Journal of Human Rights*, 2(3): 1–21.

Falk, R. (2000) *Human Rights Horizons: The Pursuit of Justice in a Globalising World*, New York: Routledge.

Faulks, K. (2000) *Citizenship*, London: Routledge.

Ferrara, A. (2001) 'Of Boats and Principles: Reflections on Habermas' 'Constitutional Democracy', *Political Theory*, 29(6): 782–791.

Fine, R. and Smith, W. (2003) 'Jürgen Habermas's Theory of Cosmopolitanism', *Constellations*, 10(4): 469–487.

Fink, B. (1995) *The Lacanian Subject: Between Language and Jouissance*, Princeton, New Jersey: Princeton University Press.

Fish, S. (1997) 'Boutique Multiculturalism, or Why Liberals Are Incapable of Thinking About Hate Speech', *Critical Inquiry*, 23(2): 378–395.

Fishkin, J. S. and Laslett, P. (eds) (2003) *Debating Deliberative Democracy*, Oxford: Blackwell.

Føllesdal, A. (2002) 'Drafting a European Constitution: Challenges and Opportunities', *Constitutionalism Web Papers*, con web, no. 4.

Forgacs, D. (ed.) (1988) *A Gramsci Reader: Selected Writings 1916–1935*, London: Lawrence & Wishart.

Frank, J. (2005) 'Besides Our Selves: An Essay on Enthusiastic Politics and Civic Subjectivity', *Public Culture*, 17(3): 371–392.

Freeman, M. (1994) 'The Philosophical Foundations of Human Rights', *Human Rights Quarterly*, 16: 491–514.

—— (1995) 'Are There Collective Human Rights?', *Political Studies*, 43: 25–40.

Freud, S. (1998a) *Επίκαιρες Παρατηρήσεις για τον Πόλεμο και τον Θάνατο*, Athens, Greece: Επίκουρος.

—— (1998b) *Μαθήματα ψυχικής Ανατομίας*, Athens, Greece: Ροές.

—— (1999) *Introductory Lectures on Psychoanalysis*, London: Penguin.

Frosh, S. (1987) *The Politics of Psychoanalysis: An Introduction to Freudian and Post Freudian Theory*, London: Macmillan Education.

Galligan, B. and Sampford, C. (eds) (1997) *Rethinking Human Rights*, Sydney: The Federation Press.

Galtung, J. (1994) 'Human Rights and the Western Tradition', in *Human Rights in Another Key*, Cambridge: Polity Press.

Geras, N. (1988) 'Ex-Marxism Without Substance: Being a Real Reply to Laclau and Mouffe', *New Left Review*, 169: 34–61.

Gewirth, A. (1996) *The Community of Rights*, Chicago, Illinois: University of Chicago Press.

Gibney, M. J. (ed.) (2003) *Globalising Rights: The Oxford Amnesty Lectures 1999*, Oxford: Oxford University Press.

Glendon, M. A. (1991) *Rights Talk: The Impoverishment of Political Discourse*, New York: Free Press.

Goodhart, M. (2005) *Democracy As Human Rights: Freedom and Equality in the Age of Globalisation*, New York: Routledge.

Goodin, R. E. (1988) 'What Is So Special About Our Fellow Countrymen?', *Ethics*, 98: 663–686.

Guibernau, M. (2001) 'Globalisation, Cosmopolitanism and Democracy: An Interview with David Held', *Constellations*, 8(4): 427–441.

Gutmann, A. (1993) 'The Challenge of Multiculturalism in Political Ethics', *Philosophy and Public Affairs*, 22(3): 171–206.

—— (1994) (ed.) *Multiculturalism: Examining the Politics of Recognition*, Princeton, New Jersey: Princeton University Press.

Gyandoh, S. O. (1990) 'Human Rights and the Acquisition of National Sovereignty', in J. Berting (ed.), *Human Rights in a Pluralist World: Individuals and Collectivities*, London: Roosevelt Study Centre Publications.

Habermas, J. (1996) *Between Facts and Norms: Contributions to a Discourse Theory of Law and Democracy*, Cambridge: Polity Press.

—— (1999) *The Inclusion of the Other: Studies in Political Theory*, Cambridge: Polity Press.

—— (2001a) *The Postnational Constellation: Political Essays*, Cambridge: Polity Press.

—— (2001b) 'Constitutional Democracy: A Paradoxical Union of Contradictory Principles?' *Political Theory*, 29(6): 766–781.

—— (2005) 'Equal Treatment of Cultures and the Limits of Postmodern Liberalism', *The Journal of Political Philosophy*, 13(1): 1–28.

—— (2006a) *The Divided West*, Cambridge: Polity Press.

—— (2006b) *Time of Transitions*, Cambridge: Polity Press.

Halbert, D. J. (2002) 'Citizenship, Pluralism and Modern Public Space', *Innovation*, 15(1): 33–42.

Hall, S. and Jacques, M. (eds) (1989) *New Times: The Changing Face of Politics in the 1990s*, London: Lawrence & Wishart.

Hammar, T. (1989) 'State, Nation and Dual Citizenship', in R. Brubaker (ed.), *Immigration and the Politics of Citizenship in Europe and North America*, Lanham, Maryland: University Press of America.

Hanagan, M. (1997) 'Recasting Citizenship: Introduction', *Theory and Society*, 26(4): 397–402.

Hastrup, K. (ed.) (2001) *Human Rights on Common Grounds: The Quest for Universality*, Hague/London: Kluwer Law International.

Heater, D. (1990) *Citizenship: The Civic Ideal in World History, Politics and Education*, Harlow: Longman Group.

—— (1999) *What Is Citizenship?*, Cambridge: Polity Press.

Hedetoft, U. and Hjort, M. (ed.) (2002) *The Postnational Self: Belonging and Identity*, Minneapolis, Minnesota: University of Minnesota Press.

Held, D. (1987) *Models of Democracy*, Cambridge: Polity Press.

—— (1995) *Democracy and the Global Order: From the Modern State to Cosmopolitan Governance*, Cambridge: Polity Press.

—— (2002) 'Globalisation, Corporate Practice and Cosmopolitan Social Standards', *Contemporary Political Theory*, 1(1): 59–78.

—— (2004) *Global Covenant: The Social Democratic Alternative to the Washington Consensus*, Cambridge: Polity Press.

Henkin, L. (1990) *The Age of Rights*, New York: Columbia University Press.

Holt, R. (1997) *Wittgenstein, Politics and Human Rights*, London: Routledge.

Holton, R. J. (1998) 'Towards a Global Polity?', in *Globalisation and the Nation State*, London: Macmillan Press.

Hongju Koh, H. and Slye, R. C. (eds) (1999) *Deliberative Democracy and Human Rights*, New Haven, Connecticut: Yale University Press.

Honig, B. (1993a) *Political Theory and the Displacement of Politics*, Ithaca, NY: Cornell University Press.

—— (1993b) 'The Politics of Agonism: A Critical Response to "Beyond Good and Evil: Arendt, Nietzsche and the Aestheticisation of Politics" by Danna Villa', *Political Theory*, 21(3): 528–533.

—— (2001a) 'Dead Rights, Live Futures: A Reply to Habermas' "Constitutional Democracy"', *Political Theory*, 29(6): 792–805.

—— (2001b) *Democracy and the Foreigner*, Princeton, New Jersey: Princeton University Press.

—— (2007) 'Between Decision and Deliberation: Political Paradox in Democratic Theory', *American Political Science Review*, 101(1): 1–16

Howard, D. (1987) 'The Possibilities of a Post Marxist Radicalism', *Thesis Eleven*, 16: 69–84.

Howard, R. E. (1995) *Human Rights and the Search for Community*, Boulder, Colorado: Westview Press.

Howarth, D. (1997) 'Complexities of Identity/Difference: The Ideology of Black Consciousness in South Africa', *Journal of Political Ideologies*, 2(1): 51–78.

—— (2000) *Discourse*, Buckingham: Open University Press.

—— (2008) 'Ethos, Agonism and Populism: William Connolly and the Case for

Radical Democracy', *British Journal of Politics and International Relations*, 10: 171–193.

—— and Norval, A. (1994) 'Negotiating the Paradoxes of Contemporary Politics: An Interview with Ernesto Laclau', *Angelaki*, 1(3): 43–50.

—— —— and Stavrakakis, Y. (eds) (2000) *Discourse Theory and Political Analysis: Identities, Hegemonies and Social Change*, New York: Manchester University Press.

Ignatieff, M. (2001) *Human Rights as Politics and Idolatry*, Princeton, New Jersey: Princeton University Press.

Isin, E. F. and Wood, P. (1999) *Citizenship and Identity*, London: SAGE.

Jacobsen, M. B. (1991) *Lacan the Absolute Master*, Stanford, California: Stanford University Press.

Jacobson, D. (1997) *Rights Across Borders: Immigration and the Decline of Citizenship*, Baltimore, Maryland: John Hopkins University Press.

Jørgensen, M. W. and Phillips, L. J. (2002) *Discourse Analysis as Theory and Method*, London: SAGE.

Julien, P. (1994) *Jacques Lacan's Return to Freud: The Real, the Symbolic and the Imaginary*, New York: New York University Press.

Kahane, D. (1999) 'Diversity, Solidarity and Civic Friendship', *The Journal of Political Philosophy*, 7(3): 267–286.

Kalyvas, A. (2005) 'Popular Sovereignty, Democracy and the Constituent Power', *Constellations*, 12(2): 223–244.

—— (2009) 'The Democratic Narcissus: The Agonism of the Ancients Compared to That of the (Post) Moderns', in A. Schaap (ed.), *Law and Agonistic Politics*, Farnham: Ashgate.

Kant, E. (1997) *Groundwork of the Metaphysics of Morals*, Cambridge: Cambridge University Press.

Keenan, A. (2003) *Democracy in Question: Democratic Openness in a Time of Political Closure*, Stanford, California: Stanford University Press.

Keenan, T. (1997) *Fables of Responsibility: Aberrations and Predicaments in Ethics and Politics*, Stanford, California: Stanford University Press.

Kleinman, A., Das, V. and Lock, M. (eds) (1997) *Social Suffering*, Berkeley, California: University of California Press.

Kostakopoulou, D. (1996) 'Towards a Theory of Constructive Citizenship in Europe', *Journal of Political Philosophy*, 4(4): 337–358.

—— (1998) 'Is There an Alternative to Schengenland?', *Political Studies*, 46(5): 886–902.

Kratochvil, F. (1994) 'Citizenship: On the Border of Order', *Alternatives*, 19: 485–506.

Kristeva, J. (1991) *Strangers to Ourselves*, New York: Harvester Wheatsheaf.

Kroes, R. (2000) *Them and Us: Questions of Citizenship in a Globalising World*, Champaign, Illinois: University of Illinois Press.

Kuan-Hsing Chen (1991) 'Post Marxism: Beyond Critical Postmodernism and Cultural Studies', *Media, Culture and Society*, 13: 35–51.

Kukathas, C. (1992) 'Are There Any Cultural Rights?', *Political Theory*, 20(1): 105–139.

Kymlicka, W. (1992) 'The Rights of Minority Cultures: Reply to Kukathas', *Political Theory*, 20(1): 140–146.

—— (1996) *Multicultural Citizenship: A Liberal Theory of Minority Rights*, Oxford: Clarendon Press.

—— (2001) *Politics in the Vernacular: Nationalism, Multiculturalism and Citizenship*, Oxford: Oxford University Press.

—— and Norman, W. (1994) 'Return of the Citizen: A Survey of Recent Work on Citizenship Theory', *Ethics*, 104: 352–381.

Lacan, J. (1991) *The Four Fundamental Concepts of Psychoanalysis*, London: Penguin Books.

—— (2001) *Écrits: A Selection*, London: Routledge.

Laclau, E. (1990) *New Reflections on the Revolution of Our Time*, London: Verso.

—— (1994) *The Making of Political Identities*, London: Verso.

—— (1996) *Emancipations*, London: Verso.

—— (2001) 'Democracy and the Question of Power', *Constellations*, 8(1): 3–14.

—— and Mouffe, C. (2001) *Hegemony and Socialist Strategy: Towards a Radical Democratic Politics*, 2nd edn, London: Verso.

Lane, C. (1996) 'Beyond the Social Principle: Psychoanalysis and Radical Democracy', *Journal for the Psychoanalysis of Culture and Society*, 1(1): 105–121.

Larmore, C. (1990) 'Political Liberalism', *Political Theory*, 18(3): 339–360.

Latour, B. (2003) 'What If We Talked Politics a Little?', *Contemporary Political Theory*, 2(2): 143–164.

Lefort, C. (1986) *The Political Forms of Modern Society: Bureaucracy, Democracy, Totalitarianism*, Cambridge: Polity Press.

—— (1988) *Democracy and Political Theory*, Cambridge: Polity Press.

Lehning, P. B. and Weale, A. (eds) (1997) *Citizenship, Democracy and Justice in the New Europe*, London: Routledge.

Leledakis, K. (1995) *Society and Psyche: Social Theory and the Unconscious Dimension of the Social*, Oxford: Berg Publishers.

Linklater, A. (1998) 'Cosmopolitan Citizenship', *Citizenship Studies*, 2(1): 23–41.

Lister, R. (ed.) (1997) *Citizenship: Feminist Perspectives*, London: Macmillan.

—— (1998) 'Citizenship and Difference: Towards a Differentiated Universalism', *European Journal of Social Theory*, 1(1): 71–90.

Lupel, A. (2005) 'Tasks of a Global Civil Society: Held, Habermas and Democratic Legitimacy Beyond the Nation State', *Globalisations*, 2(1): 117–133.

Lynch, M. P. (1998) *Truth in Context: An Essay on Pluralism and Objectivity*, Cambridge, Massachusetts: MIT Press.

MacCormick, N. (1996) 'Liberalism, Nationalism and the Post Sovereign State', *Political Studies*, 44(3): 553–567.

MacIntyre, A. (1985) *After Virtue: A Study in Moral Theory*, London: Duckworth Press.

Macpherson, C. B. (1977) *The Life and Times of Liberal Democracy*, Oxford: Oxford University Press.

Marks, S. P. (1998) 'From the "Single Confused Page" to the "Decalogue for Six Billion Persons": The Roots of the Universal Declaration of Human Rights in the French Revolution', *Human Rights Quarterly*, 20: 459–514.

Marshall, T. H. (1973) *Class, Citizenship and Social Development*, Westport, Connecticut: Greenwood Press.

—— (1992) 'Citizenship and Social Class', in T. Bottomore (ed.), *Citizenship and Social Class*, London: Pluto Press.

Mazower, M. (2002) 'The Strange Triumph of Human Rights', *New Statesman*, 4 February.

McClure. K. M. (1990) 'Difference, Diversity and the Limits of Toleration', *Political Theory*, 18(3): 361–391.

McCorquodale, R. and Fairbrother, R. (1999) 'Globalisation and Human Rights', *Human Rights Quarterly*, 21: 735–766.

McManus, H. (2008) 'Enduring Agonism: Between Individuality and Plurality', *Polity*, 40(4): 509–527.

Meyer, W. H. (1996) 'Human Rights and MNCs: Theory Versus Quantitative Analysis', *Human Rights Quarterly*, 18: 368–397.

Mill, J. S. (1996) *On Liberty*, Ware: Wordsworth Classics.

Miller, D. (1988) 'The Ethical Significance of Nationality' *Ethics*, 98: 647–662.

—— (1993) 'In Defence of Nationality', *Journal of Applied Philosophy*, 10(1): 3–16.

—— (1995) 'Citizenship and Pluralism', *Political Studies*, XLIII: 432–450.

Miller, J. A. (ed.) (1993) *The Seminar of Jacques Lacan: Book III, The Psychoses 1955–1956*, New York: Norton & Company.

Milliken, J. (1999) 'The Study of Discourse in International Relations: A Critique of Research and Methods', *European Journal of International Relations*, 5(2): 225–254.

Modood, T. (1994) 'Establishment, Multiculturalism and British Citizenship', *The Political Quarterly*, 65(1): 53–73.

Mouffe, C. (ed.) (1979) *Gramsci and Marxist Theory*, London: Routledge & Kegan Paul.

—— (1992) (ed.) *Dimensions of Radical Democracy: Pluralism, Citizenship, Community*, London: Verso.

—— (1993) *The Return of the Political*, London: Verso.

—— (1995) 'Democratic Politics and the Question of Identity', in J. Rajchman (ed.), *The Identity in Question*, New York: Routledge.

—— (1996) *Deconstruction and Pragmatism*, London: Routledge.

—— (1999) (ed.) *The Challenge of Carl Schmitt*, London: Verso.

—— (2000) *The Democratic Paradox*, London: Verso.

—— (2002) 'For an Agonistic Public Sphere', in O. Enwezor, D. Basualdo, U. Bauer, et al. (eds), *Democracy Unrealised: Documenta 11_Platform 1*, Ostfildern, Germany: Hatje Cantz Publishers.

—— (2005) *On the Political*, London: Routledge

Mouzelis, N. (1988) 'Marxism or Post Marxism?', *New Left Review*, 167: 107–123.

Mulhall, S. and Swift, A. (1996) *Liberals and Communitarians*, Oxford: Blackwell.

Muller, E. N. And Seligson, M. (1994) 'Civic Culture and Democracy: The Question of Causal Relationships', *American Political Science Review*, 88(3): 635–648.

Murphy, M. and Harty, S. (2003) 'Post Sovereign Citizenship', *Citizenship Studies*, 7(2): 181–197.

Nietzsche, F. (1996) *On the Genealogy of Morals*, Oxford: Oxford University Press.

Nobus, D. (ed.) (1999) *Key Concepts of Lacanian Psychoanalysis*, New York: Other Press.

Norris, C. (1991) *Deconstruction: Theory and Practice*, London: Routledge.

—— and Benjamin, A. (1988) *What Is Deconstruction?*, London: Academy Editions.

Norval, A. (2009) 'Passionate Subjectivity, Contestation and Acknowledgement:

Rereading Austin and Cavell', in A. Schaap (ed.), *Law and Agonistic Politics*, Farnham: Ashgate.

O'Keeffe, D. (1995) 'The Emergence of a European Immigration Policy', *European Law Review*, 20(1): 20–36.

Oldfield, A. (1990a) *Citizenship and Community: Civic Republicanism and the Modern World*, London: Routledge.

—— (1990b) 'Citizenship: An Unnatural Practice?', *Political Quarterly*, 61: 177–188.

O'Neil, J. (1997) 'The Civic Recovery of Nationhood', *Citizenship Studies*, 1(1): 19–31.

O'Neill, O. (2000) *Bounds of Justice*, Cambridge: Cambridge University Press.

Oommen, T. K. (1997) *Citizenship, Nationality and Ethnicity*, Cambridge: Polity Press.

Owen, D. (1994) 'Agonal Thought: Nietzsche as a Political Thinker', *Angelaki*, 1(3): 119–128.

—— (2008) 'Pluralism and the Pathos of Distance (or How to Relax with Style): Connolly, Agonistic Respect and the Limits of Political Theory', *British Journal of Politics and International Relations*, 10: 210–226.

Pakulski, J. (1997) 'Cultural Citizenship', *Citizenship Studies*, 1(1): 73–86.

Pannikar, R. (1982) 'Is the Notion of Human Rights a Western Concept?', *Diogenes*, 120: 75–102.

Parekh, B. (1990) 'The Rushdie Affair: Research Agenda for Political Philosophy', *Political Studies*, 38: 695–709.

—— (2000) *Rethinking Multiculturalism: Cultural Diversity and Political Theory*, London: Macmillan.

—— (2003) 'Cosmopolitanism and Global Citizenship', *Review of International Studies*, 29(1): 3–17.

Patten, A. (1996) 'The Republican Critique of Liberalism', *British Journal of Political Science*, 26: 25–44.

Pease, D. E. (1997) 'Critical Response: Regulating Multi-Adhoccerists, Fish's Rules', *Critical Inquiry*, 23(2): 396–418.

Perry, M. J. (1998) *The Idea of Human Rights: Four Enquiries*, Oxford: Oxford University Press.

Peterson, V. S. (2000) 'Whose Rights? A Critique of the "Givens" in Human Rights Discourse', *Alternatives*, 25(4): 303–344.

Pettigrew, D. and Raffoul, F. (eds) (1996) *Disseminating Lacan*, New York: State University of New York Press.

Pettit, P. (1997) *Republicanism: A Theory of Freedom and Government*, Oxford: Oxford University Press.

—— (2003) 'Deliberative Democracy, the Discursive Dilemma and Republican Theory', in J. Fishkin and P. Laslett (eds), *Debating Deliberative Democracy*, Oxford: Blackwell Publishing.

Popper, K. (1945) *The Open Society and Its Enemies, Vol. I*, London: Routledge & Kegan Paul.

Purvis, T. and Hunt, A. (1993) 'Discourse, Ideology, Discourse, Ideology, Discourse, Ideology . . .', *British Journal of Sociology*, 44(3): 473–499.

—— (1999) 'Identity Versus Citizenship: Transformations in the Discourses and Practices of Citizenship', *Social and Legal Studies*, 8(4): 457–482.

Ragland-Sullivan, E. and Bracher, M. (ed.) (1991) *Lacan and the Subject of Language*, New York: Routledge.

Rajchman, J. (1991) *Truth and Eros: Foucault, Lacan and the Question of Ethics*, New York: Routledge.
—— (ed.) (1995) *The Identity in Question*, New York: Routledge.
Rancière, J. (1995) *On the Shores of Politics*, London: Verso.
—— (1996) 'Postdemocracy, Politics and Philosophy: An Interview with Jacques Rancière', *Angelaki*, 1(3): 171–178.
—— (1999) *Disagreement: Politics and Philosophy*, Minneapolis, Minnesota: University of Minnesota Press.
—— (2004) 'Who Is the Subject of the Rights of Man?', *South Atlantic Quarterly*, 103 (2/3): 297–310.
Rasch, W. (2000) 'Conflict as a Vocation: Carl Schmitt and the Possibility of Politics', *Theory, Culture and Society*, 17(6): 1–32.
—— (2004) *Sovereignty and Its Discontents: On the Primacy of Conflict and the Structure of the Political*, London: Birkbeck Law Press.
Rawls, J. (1972) *A Theory of Justice*, Oxford: Oxford University Press.
—— (1996) *Political Liberalism*, New York: Columbia University Press.
Raz, J. (1986) *The Morality of Freedom*, Oxford: Oxford University Press.
—— (1994) 'Multiculturalism: A Liberal Perspective', *Dissent*, 67: 67–79.
—— (1995) *Ethics in the Public Domain: Essays in the Morality of Law and Politics*, Oxford: Clarendon Press.
—— and Margalit, A. (1990) 'National Self Determination', *Journal of Philosophy*, 87(9): 439–461.
Roche, M. (ed.) (1992) *Rethinking Citizenship: Welfare, Ideology and Change in Modern Society*, Cambridge: Polity Press.
Rolando, G. (1991) 'Postmodernism and Human Rights: Some Insidious Questions', *Law and Critique*, 2(2): 149–170.
RothKopf, D. (1997) 'In Praise of Cultural Imperialism?', *Foreign Policy*, 107: 38–53.
Rustin, M. (1988) 'Absolute Voluntarism: Critique of a Post Marxist Concept of Hegemony', *New German Critique*, 43: 147–173.
Salecl, R. (1994) *The Spoils of Freedom: Psychoanalysis and Feminism After the Fall of Socialism*, London: Routledge.
Sandel, M. (1982) *Liberalism and the Limits of Justice*, New York: Cambridge University Press.
—— (1984) 'The Procedural Republic and the Unencumbered Self', *Political Theory*, 12(1): 81–96.
Sarat, A. and Kearns, T. R. (eds) (1997) *Identities, Politics and Rights*, Ann Arbor, Michigan: University of Michigan Press.
Schaap, A. (2006) 'Agonism In Divided Societies', *Philosophy and Social Criticism*, 32(2): 255–277.
—— (2007) 'Political Theory and the Agony of Politics', *Political Studies Review*, 5: 56–74.
Schmitt, C. (1985) *The Crisis of Parliamentary Democracy*, Cambridge, Massachusetts: MIT Press.
—— (1996) *The Concept of the Political*, Chicago, Illinois: University of Chicago Press.
Sellars, K. (2002) *The Rise and Rise of Human Rights*, London: Sutton Publishing.
Shafir, G. (ed.) (1998) *The Citizenship Debates: A Reader*, Minneapolis, Minnesota: University of Minnesota Press.

Shanahan, S. (1997) 'Different Standards and Standard Differences: Contemporary Citizenship and Immigration Debates', *Theory and Society*, 26(4): 421–448.

Shapiro, I. and Hacker-Gordon, C. (1999) *Democracy's Edges*, Cambridge: Cambridge University Press.

Shaw, J. (1997) 'Citizenship of the Union: Towards Postnational Membership?', *Harvard Jean Monnet Working Paper*, No. 6/97, Cambridge, Massachusetts: Harvard Law School.

Shute, S. and Hurley, S. (eds) (1993) *On Human Rights: The Oxford Amnesty Lectures 1993*, New York: Basic Books.

Sim, S. (ed.) (1998) *Post Marxism: A Reader*, Edinburgh: Edinburgh University Press.

Simons, H. W. and Billig, M. (eds) (1994) *After Postmodernism: Reconstructing Ideology Critique*, London: SAGE Publications.

Skinner, Q. (1998) *Liberty Before Liberalism*, Cambridge: Cambridge University Press.

—— and Stråth, B. (eds) (2003) *States and Citizens: History, Theory, Prospects*, Cambridge: Cambridge University Press.

Smith, A. M. (1998) *Laclau and Mouffe: The Radical Democratic Imaginary*, London: Routledge.

Somers, M. (1994) 'Rights, Relationality and Membership: Rethinking the Making and Meaning of Citizenship', *Law and Social Inquiry*, 19: 63–112.

Sousa Santos, B. de (1995) *Towards a New Common Sense: Law, Science and Politics in the Paradigmatic Transition*, New York: Routledge.

—— (2000) 'Toward a Multicultural Conception of Human Rights', Version 30.

Soysal, Y. N. (1994) *Limits of Citizenship: Migrants and Postnational Membership in Europe*, Chicago, Illinois: University of Chicago Press.

—— (1997) 'Changing Parameters of Citizenship and Claims Making: Organised Islam in European Public Spheres', *Theory and Society*, 26(4): 509–527.

Spinner, J. (1994) *The Boundaries of Citizenship: Race, Ethnicity and Nationality in the Liberal State*, Baltimore, Maryland: John Hopkins University Press.

Squires, J. (2000) 'Citizenship: Between Universality and Diversity', Unpublished paper, Exeter Colloquium 24–25 November.

Stavrakakis, Y. (1997) 'Green Fantasy and the Real of Nature: Elements of a Lacanian Critique of Green Ideological Discourse', *Journal for the Psychoanalysis of Culture and Society*, 2(1): 123–132.

—— (1999) *Lacan and the Political*, London: Routledge.

—— (2001) 'Paradoxes of Identification: Reflections on Identity Formation and the Question of European Identity', *Dialogue*, Workshop of the European Commission: 'European Citizenship: Beyond Borders, Across Identities'.

—— (2003) 'Reactivating the Democratic Revolution: The Politics of Transformation Beyond Reoccupation and Conformism', *Parallax*, 9(2): 56–71.

—— (2007) *The Lacanian Left*, Edinburgh: Edinburgh University Press.

Stevenson, N. (1997) 'Globalisation, National Cultures and Cultural Citizenship, *The Sociological Quarterly*, 38(1): 41–66.

Stewart, A. (1995) 'Two Conceptions of Citizenship', *British Journal of Sociology*, 46(1): 63–78.

Storr, A. (2001) *Freud: A Very Short Introduction*, Oxford: Oxford University Press.

Sumic, J. and Nash, K. (1994) 'Postdemocracy, Politics and Philosophy: Interview with Jacques Rancière', *Angelaki*, 1(3): 171–182.

Symonides, J. (2000) *Human Rights: Concepts and Standards*, London: Dartmouth Publishing Company.

Tambakaki, P. (2009a) 'From Citizenship to Human Rights: The Stakes for Democracy', *Citizenship Studies*, 13(1): 3–15.

—— (2009b) 'Cosmopolitanism or Agonism? Alternative Visions of World Order', *Critical Review of International Social and Political Philosophy*, 12(1): 101–116.

Taylor, C. (1989) *Sources of the Self: The Making of Modern Identity*, Cambridge: Cambridge University Press.

—— (1996) 'A World Consensus on Human Rights?', *Dissent*, 43: 15–21.

Tebble, J. (2006) 'Exclusion for Democracy', *Political Theory*, 34(4): 463–487.

Terray, E. (2003) 'Law Versus Politics', *New Left Review*, 22: 71–91.

Thompson, D. (2005) 'Democracy in Time: Popular Sovereignty and Temporal Representation', *Constellations*, 2: 245–260.

Tilly, C. (1995), 'Citizenship, Identity and Social History', *International Review of Social History*, 40(3): 1–17.

—— (1997) 'A Primer on Citizenship', *Theory and Society*, 26(4): 599–603.

Torfing, J. (1999) *New Theories of Discourse: Laclau Mouffe and Žižek*, Oxford: Blackwell.

Touraine, A. (2000) *Can We Live Together? Equality and Difference*, Cambridge: Polity Press.

Trend, D. (ed.) (1996) *Radical Democracy: Identity, Citizenship and the State*, New York: Routledge.

Tully, J. (1999) 'The Agonic Freedom of Citizens', *Economy and Society*, 28(2): 161–182.

Turkle, S. (1992) *Psychoanalytic Politics: Jacques Lacan and Freud's French Revolution*, London: Free Association Books.

Turner, B. S. (1986) 'Personhood and Citizenship', *Theory, Culture and Society*, 3(1): 1–16.

—— (1990) 'Outline of a Theory of Citizenship', *Sociology*, 24(2): 189–217.

—— (1993) *Citizenship and Social Theory*, London: SAGE Publications.

—— (1997) 'Citizenship Studies: A General Theory', *Citizenship Studies*, 1(1): 5–18.

Van Gunsteren, H. (1988) 'Admission to Citizenship', *Ethics*, 98: 731–741.

Van Steenbergen, B. (ed.) (1994) *The Condition of Citizenship*, London: SAGE Publications.

Vandenberg, A. (ed.) (2000) *Citizenship and Democracy in a Global Era*, London: Macmillan.

Vasta, E. (ed.) (2000) *Citizenship, Community and Democracy*, London: Macmillan.

Vogel, U. and Moran, M. (ed.) (1991) *The Frontiers of Citizenship*, London: Macmillan.

Waldron, J. (1999) 'Deliberation, Disagreement, and Voting', in H. Koh and R. Slye (eds), *Deliberative Democracy and Human Rights*, New Haven, Connecticut: Yale University Press.

Walzer, M. (1983) *Spheres of Justice: A Defence of Pluralism and Equality*, Oxford: Blackwell.

—— (1990) 'The Communitarian Critique of Liberalism', *Political Theory*, 18(1): 6–23.

—— (1994) *Thick and Thin: Moral Argument at Home and Abroad*, Notre Dame, Indiana: University of Notre Dame Press.

—— (1997) *On Toleration*, New Haven, Connecticut: Yale University Press.

—— (2002) 'Passion and Politics', *Philosophy and Social Criticism*, 28(6): 617–633.

Warren, M. (1992) 'Democratic Theory and Self Transformation', *American Political Science Review*, 86(1): 8–23.

—— (2002) 'What Can Democratic Participation Mean Today?', *Political Theory*, 30(5): 677–701.

Weber, M. (1993) *Basic Concepts in Sociology*, New York: Carol Publishing.

Wellman, C. (1999) *The Proliferation of Rights: Moral Progress or Empty Rhetoric?*, Boulder, Colorado: Westview Press.

Wenman, M. (2003) 'Agonistic Pluralism and Three Archetypal Forms of Politics', *Contemporary Political Theory*, 2: 165–186.

—— (2008) 'Agonism, Pluralism, and Contemporary Capitalism: An Interview with William E. Connolly', *Contemporary Political Theory*, 7: 200–219.

Weston, B. H. and Marks, P. S. (eds) (1999) *The Future of International Human Rights*, New York: Transnational Publishers Inc.

White, S K. (1988) 'Post Structuralism and Political Reflection', *Political Theory*, 16: 186–208.

—— (2003) 'After Critique: Affirming Subjectivity in Contemporary Political Theory', *European Journal of Political Theory*, 2(2): 209–226.

Wiener, A. (1997) 'Making Sense of the New Geography of Citizenship: Fragmented Citizenship in the European Union', *Theory and Society*, 26(4): 529–560.

Williams, D. E. (1990) 'Crisis and Renewal in the Social Sciences and the Colonies of Ourselves', *International Political Science Review*, 11(1): 59–74.

Williams, G. (1999) *French Discourse Analysis: The Method of Post-Structuralism*, London: Routledge.

Willig, C. (1999) *Applied Discourse Analysis: Social and Psychological Interventions*, Buckingham: Open University Press.

Wilterdink, N. (1993) 'An Examination of European and National Identity', *European Journal of Sociology*, 34: 119–136.

Wittgenstein, L. (1998) *Philosophical Investigations*, Oxford: Blackwell.

Wodak, R. (1996) *Disorders of Discourse*, Harlow: Addison Wesley Longman.

Yash Ghai (1994) 'Human Rights and Governance: The Asia Debate', Occasional Paper No 4, The Asia Foundation's Centre for Asian Pacific Affairs.

Young, I. M. (1989) 'Polity and Group Difference: A Critique of the Ideal of Universal Citizenship', *Ethics*, 99: 250–274.

Zerilli, L. (1998) 'This Universalism Which Is Not One', *Diacritics*, 28(2): 3–20.

Žižek, S. (1999a) *The Ticklish Subject: The Absent Centre of Political Ontology*, London: Verso.

—— (1999b) 'The Seven Veils of Fantasy', in D. Nobus (ed.), *Key Concepts of Lacanian Psychoanalysis*, New York: Other Press.

—— (2001) *On Belief*, London: Routledge.

—— (2005) 'Against Human Rights', *New Left Review*, 34: 115–133.

Zolo, D. (1997) *Cosmopolis: Prospects for World Government*, Cambridge: Polity Press.

—— (2002) *Invoking Humanity: War, Law and Global Order*, London: Continuum.

Župančič, A. (2000) *Ethics of the Real: Kant, Lacan*, London: Verso.

Index